THE
ART
DEALERS

John Russell Taylor *and* Brian Brooke

Charles Scribner's Sons · New York

A-4.69 [H]

Printed in the United States of America
Library of Congress Catalog Card Number 68-17336

CONTENTS

iii

THE ART DEALERS

INTRODUCTION

Why buy art anyway? There is, of course, only one answer which is a hundred per cent sensible: for pleasure. The only man who cannot be cheated is one who buys something just because he likes it, and pays for it only as much as he can afford and as much as it is worth to him for the pleasure it gives him. But then nothing is so simple as that. Pleasure in ownership is as difficult to pin down as love. We know it is naïve and unrealistic to ask "Did he marry her for love or her money?" "Did she marry him for love or his title?": cupidity, snobbery or social aspirations are as likely constituents of "love" as merely physical attraction. He may love her, really love her, because she is rich; she may love him, really love him, because he is a lord. And so it is with art. The inherent attractions of the object are rarely the sole determinant of how much pleasure we take in owning it. Quite apart from any intention they may have of selling it, most people take more pleasure in owning a painting they like if it is by Rembrandt or Watteau or Blake or Giorgione than if it, for all its beauties, is by no one anyone has ever heard of. And this extra amount of pleasure makes it worth paying more for. Equally, if one has paid a Watteau price for a painting which proves not to be a Watteau, the pleasure in owning it is likely to be diminished (sometimes sharply) by this revelation. And even though the painting is inherently the same identical object which one bought in the first place.

In any case, human nature being what it is, there are many other considerations involved besides pleasure, however we define it. Anything which is bought and sold automatically becomes a commodity. And commodities, whether we will or no, obey certain rules which have little to do with enjoyment. A good reproduction, for example, may be undistinguishable from the original except by an expert, but a reproduction is not unique, while the original is; a reproduction can often be repeated ad infinitum. So it loses scarcity value, and therefore costs less than a unique original, even if the difference in effect is minimal for the average art buyer. And then, competitiveness also enters into the game. We have all at some time been so carried away by the urge to beat someone else, to win, that we have lost sight of the real value to us of what is to be won—or rather, one might say, it has been endowed with a quite artificial value. So it is with works of art: our desire to possess them is likely to be heavily influenced, even if not, we hope, totally governed, by how much other people want to possess them. The object becomes a symbol rather than a thing-in-itself. And a real, authenticated Picasso is undeniably a more satisfactory symbol than a fake Picasso painted by an art student in London or a shady dealer in Paris. The fake might well, of course, be a better painting.

But it will certainly not be such a good investment. The exact degree of importance the investment side of art buying has for any individual buyer in any particular deal is almost infinitely variable. But in any transaction which involves the spending of money it is bound to be there somewhere. Even people who will give away a fortune are seldom willing to throw away a penny; the most generous of men does not like to be taken for a sucker. Each object will have its right price for each potential buyer. It may be far above the general market price, for reasons sentimental or personal (this often explains freak prices which are never matched again) : it may be far below, in which case he is unlikely to buy. Mostly, it is somewhere between "I must have it at any price" and "I wouldn't take it as a gift." In any case it is normal and reasonable that no one will want to pay more than he need, and no one will want to sell for less than he can.

Least of all those who make a living from buying and selling art. Almost as long as there has been art to sell and collectors to buy, there have been dealers to bring the two profitably together. It is, at least, a service, and one for which the dealer may properly expect to be paid. More than that, it is often a gamble. A gamble for everyone, from the artist (if he is still alive and hoping to make a living from the exercise of his

5

art) to the final owner. Individual taste, fashion, the state of the market, a correct reading of the personalities involved, all enter into the management of the art market. And there are always imponderables. A crook is an imponderable; an incorruptible idealist is another. Anything can happen and probably will. And the more money there is tied up in it all, the more people will be attracted into this world. Those whom education and the dreadful popularity of culture have not provoked to an interest in art will be driven by the excitement of a flutter and the glamour of big business. And the big business of art is, as never before, news.

THE LIFE AND DEATH
OF FASHION

The state of the art market at any time is governed by three interacting factors: the availability of art to sell, the economic state of the world, and the dictates of fashion. Of these considerations by far the most difficult to pin down is fashion. In trying to explain it we very rapidly find ourselves grappling with the inexplicable. Certain guidelines can be established, admittedly. We know that fashion nearly always moves in pendulum swings. A period of license will be followed by a period of repression which in its turn will lead to another period of license. And so in painting, for instance, one may say that in broad, general terms a period of devotion to paintings of dark tonality will be followed by a period of hunger for brightness and color; a preoccupation with content will give way to a preoccupation with form; a love of "soft" painters inclined to very lazy, fluid handling of paint will be superseded by a desire for "hard" painters much concerned with the precise definition of forms and shapes.

So far, so good. But it is not very far. No one has yet managed to predict with any accuracy how long the pendulum will take to swing, or how possible it is for someone to swing it by conscious effort. And no fashion is ever subscribed to by absolutely everyone. A single collector swimming against the tide may find himself lucky. Two collectors doing so, in competition, can support a market for things which should be right out of fashion. And fashion needs something to feed on. It would mean nothing at all to pontificate now about the relative fashionability of, say, early and late Raphael, since the supply of important Raphaels of any period to the market has completely dried up.

And even in eras when major paintings by major old masters were much more common on the market than they are now, there was still no reliable way of assessing beforehand the relative popularities of different painters or periods within a general movement of taste. Rarity might have something to do with it, but there must be many painters comparable to Giorgione and Vermeer—to take two of the rarest great masters— whose work is rarer still than theirs but is not worth anywhere near as much. Romantic incidentals may play some part—a picturesque history attached to a picture or an objet d'art can even today up its value considerably. The preferences of an influential critic can color the views of a whole generation. But the heart of the mystery remains, after all analysis, mysterious.

To see how all this works out in practice it may be useful if we take a brief look at the way fashion has swung this way and that in the last 150 years or so, since the end of the Napoleonic Wars. Let us take Britain as our yardstick, since Britain was entering its period of maximum power and prosperity, and the British were the best able to buy major works of art, anywhere in the world, at the prices they wanted to. At the very outset of the period old masters—the works of dead painters of the past—were, oddly enough, very much under a cloud compared with the works of new British painters. What was admired most in both was just what had been admired throughout the latter half of the eighteenth century: sobriety and dark colors. Collectors liked their old masters to look like old masters, and new paintings to approach as nearly as possible to that condition. In any case, it was a time of stagnation in the art market: too much wild speculation during the Napoleonic Wars had gone wrong, and led to distrust. Too many copies and studio works had been taken for originals, too many people had been too vague about what exactly lay underneath the dark, smoky surface required of the old master. John Smith's *Catalogue Raisonné of the works of the Most Eminent Dutch, Flemish and French Painters* (1829-1842) began, for all its errors and omissions, to throw a little light into dark places, and put buyers on their guard. At least if you bought a painting straight from the man who painted it, you knew pretty well what you were getting.

But already signs of change were visible. Darkness had been in vogue for about half a century, and now it was the turn of color. Around the end of the 1820s fashionable painters like Wilkie found that they had to change style in order to stay fashionable. Suddenly a wave of new romanticism, inspired largely by the author of *Waverley,* dictated brighter colors, stronger passions and a good deal of the exotic, either in time or in place, or in both. The old master market was still in the doldrums, and seemed likely to remain so, if only because old masters, whatever the intentions of their makers, had nearly all been reduced by time to a now unfashionable state of dinginess. The obvious exceptions were the primitives, but taste was not yet quite ready—they were still considered as, well, primitive, since they had not yet mastered the technical complexities of perspective and could not therefore be admitted to have more than historical interest. Raphael remained the one unshakable old master, revered and sought after by everybody. Rubens was still high during the Regency, but his inclination toward pagan and fleshly subject matter was soon to tell against him. Titian was down, for various reasons, including the most practical: that so many important alleged Titians had proved when seriously scrutinized to be nothing of the sort that no one felt confident enough to stake much money on the vexed question of what was and what was not a Titian. Rembrandt and the Dutch school generally, being dark and/or unromantic, were down. The highest prices went to Wilkie for his later, more dashingly romantic works, to Turner, for his earlier, less difficult paintings, and to perhaps three or four other living painters who knew what the public wanted, and supplied it directly.

But changes were on the way. By the 1840s "Victorianism" was firmly established, and if the new Puritanism was neither so instantaneous nor so complete as we tend to suppose, a wave of determined respectability flowed like a tide across Europe. Rubens was out unless his subjects were religious or at any rate thoroughly clothed. The too lush effect was frowned on, though a certain amount of sentiment, even sentimentality, was not amiss—hence the enormous popularity of Murillo's more sugary religious works. The rise in prices of early Raphaels during the 1840s was a straw in the wind, and an exhibition of primitives at the British Institution in 1848 had a marked success: the literally Pre-Raphaelite painters had the advantage, not only of the enthusiastic if not always very well informed support of the Victorian Pre-Raphaelites and their German kin the Nazarenes, but of their undeniable purity, propriety and religious subject matter allied with the bright clear colors now so much prized. Some salesroom enthusiasm for Italian primitives in general around 1850 proved little more than a flurry, but at least it ensured that almost any large, important-looking primitive would fetch a good price in the second half of the nineteenth century. A fading of the first flush of romanticism and a general straitening of laces was also likely to bring back a taste for the Dutch realists of the seventeenth century, and from the early 1860s it did, first in Paris and then in Britain and Germany. Rembrandt stayed relatively unpopular, except in Germany, whither many of the best examples on the market gravitated.

During the middle years of the Victorian era what has been called "the golden age of the living painter" continued. The painters of the moment painted for and sold to the newly prosperous middle classes, the industrialists who were making good and the financiers who were making better. The great collectors were no longer kings and nobles, but private individuals with new fortunes to spend. Most of the old masters to come on to the market came from the collections of scholars (who had bought them cheaply when they were unfashionable) or speculators, and went, as their prices increased, to Rothschilds or well-endowed European museums and galleries, particularly the Kaiser Friedrich Museum in Berlin. But if the nobles were not generally buying, they were not selling either. Any faint feeling that more forward-looking Continental collectors might be stripping Britain of her treasures could be countered at once by the cheering thought that the great aristocratic collections were inviolable. But events in the 1880s were to prove that this was by no means so. The profits from agriculture were going down and down, and land becoming far more of a liability than an asset. An increasing number of noble families needed to liquidate their heirlooms, and in 1882 the Settled Lands Act made it easier for them to do so.

Oddly enough, the release of old masters on to the market that this precipitated did not lead to a new liveliness in the London art market, as might have been expected, if only because of an influx of foreign buyers eager to bear off British treasures. In fact, the market in Britain stayed fairly stagnant until the 1900s, when Duveen and the advent of the big American buyers brought about a major revival. Meanwhile, though, the swing of fashion followed its inexorable course. The romantics of the early nineteenth century, so highly prized in their own day, fell from favour as the primitives and the Dutch consolidated their position. And what the romantics had been principally reacting against in eighteenth-century art also rose in popular favor as their stock fell. The movement was again closely connected with changing literary tastes; what Scott had been to English taste in the 1820s Thackeray was in the 1870s. (He even built himself, in the interval between writing *Henry Esmond* and *Pendennis,* one of the earliest neo-Georgian houses at No. 2 Kensington Palace Green—and a very good, accurate one too.) At first the taste for French eighteenth-century art was an eccentric English taste—which explains why the Marquis of Hertford was able to collect so many Watteaus, Bouchers, etc., with hardly any competition in the 1850s. But by the late 1860s and 1870s the eighteenth-century mania was really on, embracing not only the French but also the English painters, and pushing up the prices of Gainsborough and Reynolds, who had always had their admirers, as well as those of Romney, Hoppner and many lesser portraitists. Nostalgia and snobbish associations played a large part in the build-up of this latter market; mid-Victorian earnestness was fading fast.

Even more radical changes were soon to come. The activities and influence of Joseph Duveen (1869-1939) belong more to the history of merchandising than to that of fashion proper. And yet fashion was influenced, spectacularly. For it may be said, broadly but not too inaccurately, that Duveen created the fashion for old masters—any old masters—at the expense of the moderns. Duveen's heyday, 1900-1928, was a time of boom in the sale of old masters without parallel before or since: at no other time have there been so many people ready and eager to buy at the highest prices, and so much available for them to buy. The boom was no respecter of persons or periods. Almost anything, provided it was at least a hundred years old and respectably warranted to be what it appeared to be, was salable and was sold. To such an extent that it becomes almost meaningless to talk about fashion except in respect of relatively new pictures, where taste was beginning, inevitably, to turn against those contemporary and near-contemporary painters whom the previous generation had most respected.

Of course even at a time when everything sells, some things sell at higher prices than others. In 1906 Van Dyck became, rather surprisingly, the most expensive painter in the world, when one of his paintings, the "Marchesa Grimaldi Cattaneo", was sold for £103,-300—£3,300 more than the previous all-time high, paid for a Raphael in 1900. Also passionately favored were the English eighteenth-century portraitists, whose prices continued to advance right up to the Wall Street crash. If Duveen helped to create these extraordinary prices—and to maintain them, or make sure the question never arose, by persuading most of his clients to set up foundations or leave their collections to public museums beyond the reach of further resale—his associate and adviser Bernard Berenson had an almost equally marked influence on the restoration of the great Italian painters to saleroom favor. His pioneering works, whatever their shortcomings, put some scholarly order at last into the jumble of misattributions which had gone on unchecked for generations. At last a painter like Titian could come back on to the market with every expectation of a high price (though not so high as an eighteenth-century English portraitist) if Berenson vouched for his authenticity. Dutch painters reached in the 1920s a pitch of popularity they have never since equaled, except for the obviously exceptional Rembrandt and Vermeer. The popularity of primitives was also advancing, under Berenson's guidance, though not so rapidly, and remarkable bargains were still to be found even in the 1900s. The market for decorative pictures by French eighteenth-century artists also held steady or advanced, though the greats of the previous century, Poussin and Claude, were left conspicuously out in the cold.

In fact it was a period of extravagant eclecticism in art buying, ended only by the 1929 crash and the subsequent depression, and by the world picture famine. The second, oddly enough, had more noticeable effects than the first: by the time the slump came most of the big prices for old masters had been paid, and most of the major old masters had been earmarked for public ownership, one way or another. Thus the slump did not mean, as it might have done, the sudden release of vast numbers of notable paintings on to the market, and a consequent rapid sorting of sheep from goats. Naturally what did turn up in the salerooms fetched much less than it would have two or three years earlier; but this meant first and foremost that far less turned up in the salerooms anyway, even of what little there was left to turn up. However, when things began to get better, around 1934-35, some of the falls in price proved to be more lasting than others. The English eighteenth-century portraitists, for example (of whom there were anyway far many more examples around than there were of the major Italian masters or of Rembrandt or El Greco) took a tumble from which even today they have not recovered, and relatively speaking probably never will. Van Dyck was another victim, and the expected slump in mid-Victorian English painters, the Barbizon School and such, already initiated before the Depression, continued to its logical conclusion.

Revival of the market was not too long in coming, but revival for what? Andrew Mellon's spectacular purchase of twenty-one treasures from the Hermitage Museum, Leningrad, in 1930-31 for £1,400,000 was virtually the last chance anyone would have to buy a first rate, authentic Botticelli or Titian, or Perugino or Raphael. What then would take their place? Rubens was now doing well again, and there was enough of him in all conscience. Rembrandt and the Dutch were improving more slowly and tentatively. There were faint signs that even Poussin and Claude might at last be returning to favor. But clearly the art market needed something new to bite on. Two possibilities presented themselves: the old master drawing (as opposed to painting) and the Impressionists and Post-Impressionists. The old master drawing had the advantage that there were still plenty around, even by painters whose

major paintings were quite unobtainable. Hence the
prices of drawings, especially those which had a finished
effect as of a work of art in their own right, progressed
by leaps and bounds in the later 1930s. The Impressionists and Post-Impressionists were more of an unknown
quantity. It might seem that the 1930s were precisely
the time that they should have been going out of fashion, as Sargent and other of their contemporaries were.
But then they had the advantage of never having been
noticeably in fashion, even though representative examples of the major Impressionists had begun to command four figures in the salerooms as long before as the
1900s. Moreover, they were generally regarded as very
pleasant to look at, and became more so each year, as
even the most conservative and insular were won over.

All definite formulations of the changes taste had
undergone had to be put off, however, since hardly had
the market begun to recover from the Depression when
another World War came along to throw things off balance. Within a year or two of its end prices were up to
pre-war standards, and for very much the same things.
Old masters still cost more than Impressionists—if you
could find old masters. In the absence of old great
masters, old little masters began to be priced up, in
response to the understandable desire of the private collector to own something. Claudes and Poussins moved a
little further towards their threatened revival. Blake
and especially Palmer (*de sa meilleure période*) were
radically revalued, and Stubbs came into his own as a
far more desirable painter than most of his once so
highly prized contemporaries who concentrated on

humans instead of animals. And the Impressionists sim-mered quietly until around 1952, when their prices suddenly leaped up in Paris and began to creep up re-sponsively everywhere else.

They filled a felt want. By the early 1950s there was again a lot of money around for art, in search of something for it to be spent on. Especially in the United States, where new tax regulations (until 1966) permitted the donor of a work of art to a public collec-tion to deduct its assessed value from his taxable income in the year of donation up to a total of 30 per cent of the income—even if the donor retained custody and private enjoyment of the painting for the rest of his natural life. With such a regulation in force it would be merely wasteful for a millionaire not to make use of it to reduce his tax burden. And if he could enjoy doing so by acquiring in the process something that looked nice, so much the better. And what better than the Im-pressionists, who were both easy on the eye and quite readily available, unlike earlier masters? Paintings which even just after the war could easily be bought for under £500 jumped to £20,000 or £30,000 by the early 1950s, and ten years later had disappeared into the stra-tosphere of over £100,000 or even £200,000 each. Un-doubtedly, in the virtual absence from the market of really first-rate old masters, the most expensive picture likely to be sold today would be a Renoir or a Cézanne or a Van Gogh. It will look more expensive than any picture has ever been before, though in real terms it is probably no more expensive than some of the higher-priced paintings in the great boom of the 1890s and

1900s. Of course, some of those would probably command even higher prices today than the major Impressionists if they were to come on the market, but since works like Rembrandt's "Aristotle" are so seldom in the saleroom, there is no way to be sure. Is a Raphael worth more than a Renoir? It is a question which can no longer be answered, (though when the Liechtenstein Leonardo "Ginevra dei Benci" was acquired by the Washington National Gallery of Art in 1967 the price was claimed to be between $5 and 6 million, which may be some guide), but we can be pretty sure a Renoir is worth more nowadays than a Van Dyck. Fashions, we say, will always change, but so much fine art these days has moved altogether beyond the reach of fashion. Fashion of course will dictate how much a Sargent or a Burne-Jones will cost today; their reputations, while clearly on the up-grade, are still unsettled. But everyone is now so canny that such a thing as a really cheap picture by any notable or once notable painter hardly exists. If a painter is really unfashionable (say, the British neo-Romantics of the 1940s) his pictures will not be cheap, they will just be unobtainable, because someone, somewhere, is hoarding them in the confident expectation that with the art market as it is now things can only get better. After all, when most of the Renoirs, Cézannes and even Picassos have found their way after the Raphaels and Watteaus and Vermeers into public collections, the collector will still have the urge to collect something. And what is there which, once fashionable, has sunk so low that no one will ever now raise it again to respectability, if not quite to the heights?

ART ON THE MARKET

In this recital we have tended to write as though fashion were something that just happened by itself, like some intellectual lemming migration in one direction or another. But not so, or only partially so. Already the name of at least one dealer, Joseph Duveen, has occurred prominently. A few collectors really enjoy paintings and know what they like. Most ask no better than to be told what to like, to be directed, and fed practical reasons (investment prospects, for instance) why they should like a particular painting, or at least buy it, whether they like it or not. And these directions they get, as likely as not, from a dealer.

There is a whole history of picture-dealing to be written, but this is not the place to write it. Probably there have been people to sell or procure works of art as long as there have been people eager to buy them. Or nearly as long; since, at any rate, the purchase of a work of art ceased to be a simple, direct transaction between a patron and an artist working directly on the patron's commission. And even then the humbler patron no doubt received advice from someone, while the less humble rapidly became too lofty and remote from the marketplace to negotiate such matters themselves. Soon the job of commissioning a portrait, an altarpiece for a favorite chapel or decorations for a new banqueting hall would be delegated; an entrepreneur would be needed, and a courtier perhaps would take this role. And no doubt would be paid for it, in all likelihood by both sides in the deal. Sometimes the agent-adviser would be an artist himself, in the patron's permanent employ, and when the taste for the antique and the exotic arose, particularly at the time of the Renaissance, advice would even more be required. For it is one thing to have a work of art made, as it were, to measure, and quite another to choose among works already in existence, and to decide what is the right price to pay for them.

Hence gradually a whole string of middlemen grew up. As soon as the direct link between artist and buyer was severed, a work of art might go through any number of hands before it reached an owner who wanted to keep it for himself. An antique statue, for example, would first of all have to be found somewhere, unearthed by chance or by design. It would have to come into the hands of someone who recognized that it might be valuable, pass most probably into the hands of someone who, being more expert, knew more exactly what it was worth, and from there, directly or indirectly, to an agent of some rich collector on the lookout for something suited to his employer's taste and pocket. Already by the end of the sixteenth century a rudimentary art trade was in existence.

The thing which conduced more than anything else to the development of the art trade as we know it today was the rise of the middle classes as an important factor in an artist's livelihood. Already in the seventeenth century the prosperous burgher class in Holland was making itself felt in the art world. Still the directly commissioned work, especially the portrait, counted for something. But the sensible middle-class Dutch liked, when it came to choosing decoration for their homes, to have their pick of works already in existence which they could see displayed and evaluate for themselves, rather than take the risk of commissioning a landscape, a genre painting or a flower piece which they might not like when they got it. The aristocratic patron could always reject a commissioned work for no other reason than that he did not like it; the middle-class patron, dealing with a middle-class painter, was in no position to be quite so lofty. And if there was to be any risk in the venture of art buying, naturally he preferred it to be on the artist's side rather than his own. So, the painter began to paint as a venture, and the prospective buyer to size up what he had to sell in the studio or, more conveniently, in shops set up for that purpose. There was already a sort of machinery for this, in the shape of the Guild of St. Luke (traditional patron of painters), set up in the fifteenth century to organize painters as a trade and thereby, incidentally, to regulate the sale of works of art.

These guild shops were the immediate ancestors of the art dealer as we know him today. They brought together a selection of paintings and displayed them for the benefit of prospective customers; their stocks were dependent on what was selling at the time, and they were an immediate and efficient way of channeling back to the artists some idea of how the market stood. They were at the outset cooperative ventures set up by the artists themselves, but the step from them to shops independently run by merchants who bought paintings from artists and sold them (hopefully) at a profit, or sold paintings for the artists on commission, was a short one, quickly taken. Already in the early seventeenth century dealers like Hermann Becker were buying the output of artists like Rembrandt in return for a regular income. Of course the older system of direct patronage persisted side by side with the newer painting-shops; it was some time before the aristocratic art lover would be willing to deal with living artists as independent tradesmen rather than as dependents, or for that matter go out himself in search of middlemen with desirable older works of art to sell. He had his agents to do that for him; or at least he might expect to be approached personally by an agent of another collector who wanted or needed to sell something.

But one way and another something recognizably like the art world of today was developing. And a great aid in this was the auction sale. The sale, and then the saleroom, proved an excellent way of gathering together, offering for sale and dispersing collections of works of art. The auction began in classical antiquity, and up to the eighteenth century may be presumed, though the records are scant, to have been in one form or another the normal way of disposing of miscellaneous possessions on the death or bankruptcy of the owner. In connection with the art market its most important aspect is its function as a meeting ground between the aristocracy and the bourgeoisie. The usual place for an auction to take place was on the property of the former owner of the goods to be auctioned—an excellent opportunity for the interested and curious to see for themselves how the other half lived or had lived. The possessions of the great could be viewed by all sorts of people, and broken up into the smallest possible units to facilitate sale. Hence there was every inducement for the rising bourgeoisie all over Western Europe to emulate their richer and more powerful brothers: seeing how the rich lived, how the rich collected works of art, they were moved to collect in a small way themselves, and would generally find something in a sale within the reach of their own purses. The auction sales of the eighteenth century, therefore, served both as powerful popularizers of art collecting, and as the means by which the mania could spread in the most practical and immediate way.

And in ways less immediate. The advantage of the auction sale, then as so often since, was that it favored the quick-witted, that the advantage tended to be with the knowledgeable rather than with the merely rich. An acknowledged masterpiece would probably change hands only from one rich collector to another with a minimum of intervention by agents and middlemen. But at a less elevated level the intelligent layman or the enlightened if not over-wealthy artist could often pick up bargains and hand them on at a profit to wealthier collectors who were willing to pay him for, if nothing else, his time and trouble, and maybe for his expertise. In this way a whole new breed of more or less speculative buyers and sellers of art sprang up, aided by the growing passion for the old master. If as yet old furniture, tapestry, etc., was just old, and therefore to succeeding generations old-fashioned and undesirable, old paintings were already, in the right circumstances, coming to be valued for themselves. By the mid-eighteenth century the passion for the old had grown to such a degree that a writer in the *St. James's Chronicle* on April 25, 1761, wrote (with noticeable but pardonable exaggeration) :

> It is a well-known melancholy truth that the tribe of auctioneers, connoisseurs, picture-dealers, brokers, menders, etc., etc., have monopolised the trade of pictures, and by their authority, interest, and artifices with the great, have made it a matter of ridicule to purchase any modern production, or encourage an English artist. By this craft the leaders of taste of these kingdoms acquire fortunes and credit, whilst many of our painters, men of genius and industry, are absolutely starving.

A complaint which has been heard, in one form or another, all too many times since!

If all this was indeed the case, or anything like it, it was to be expected that two things would happen: that the art market, in which allegedly so many glittering prices were to be obtained, would organize itself more coherently, and that these same starving artists should try to organize themselves into some sort of commercially effective opposition. In the event, both these things happened. The first regular auction room was founded in London in 1690, in Covent Garden, by Edward Millington, and he was rapidly joined by others. In 1766 one of the world's most famous and important auction rooms was established in Pall Mall: that run by James Christie, which bears his name to this day. (Sotheby's, the other great modern auctioneers in London, was founded in 1733 but dealt mainly in books until the early 1950s.) In Paris the first great dealers were already established by the mid-eighteenth century: Gersaint, Lebrun, and Lazare-Duvaux. These catered mainly, as might be expected, to a small number of very rich collectors (prominent among them Madame de Pompadour), and they dealt more in objets d'art than in paintings and sculpture. Sales in Paris at this time were still somewhat haphazard, taking place as a rule in the homes of the former owners; it was not in fact until 1854 that the official center for art sales, the Hôtel Drouot, was organized, and even then the sales did not become the fashionable events they had long been in London. In Paris sales remained the rough-and-ready hunting ground of the bourgeoisie and of middlemen, dealers and dealers' runners; it was only through dealers themselves or through private agents that the nicer class of art collector would dream of buying.

On the other side, the artists too were organizing themselves. In France, as in Holland, there had been a guild of painters going back to the Middle Ages, and indeed first officially constituted in 1391. It was a straightforward professional association, with its rules of apprenticeship and qualifications for full membership; it guaranteed for its members exclusive rights to set up as sellers of their own pictures and practice professionally. At the Renaissance this system fell apart, owing to the increasing cosmopolitanism of artistic milieus and to the spread of the new lofty concept of the painter as an inspired and ungovernable artist rather than a solid tradesman. In 1648 the guild system, moribund, was virtually replaced by the Académie Royale de Peinture et de Sculpture, a body made up of painters and artists outside the old guild. The Académie was suppressed in 1793, during the Revolution, but reconstituted in a different form in 1795 as the Institut National de France, reorganized in 1803 and again at the restoration of the monarchy in 1816. The Académie and its successors were both the instructors and the arbiters: painters were instructed in its schools, judged by its standards (and it rapidly became the dictator of rights and wrongs in artistic taste, of what was and was not stylistically acceptable), and found their buying public by way of the Académie's Salons. Painters did not have to be members of the Académie, but if they did not find favor with the Académie's jury and so achieve a reasonable showing at the Salons they were, until the 1860s at least, very much out in the cold. In 1863 Napoleon III set up the Salon des Refusés, which at least gave those who did not conform to the standards of the Académie a chance to be seen. But already by then we are into the age of the Impressionists and therefore of the first important picture dealers in the modern sense of the term.

In Britain things took a similar if, characteristically, a more casual course. In 1745 Hogarth had the idea of rivaling the popular sales of old masters, real or faked, by staging a sale of his own works, including such famous series as "The Rake's Progress" and "The Harlot's Progress"; the total proceeds came out at £427.7s. In 1761 Hogarth supported a group of artists who decided to hire a room in Spring Gardens and show their own paintings there. He suggested they should call themselves "The Free Society of Professors of Painting." Despite all their efforts, the exhibition was a failure, and so was the auction with which they followed it up. But a start had been made, and in 1765, after a petition, the "Spring Garden" group of painters was granted a royal charter of incorporation as "The Society of Artists of Great Britain." Among them were Gainsborough, Reynolds and Richard Wilson. The next stage was the setting up of a Royal Academy to guard their interests, and this was achieved three years later, in 1768. From then on the British Academy came to hold much the same sort of position in the artistic life of the country as the French, though even at its worst it was seldom so doctrinaire about style as the French Académie under the rule of Ingres, in the 1840s and 1850s. In 1805 a group of leading British water-colorists set up their own professional body, later to become the Royal Society of Painters in Water Colours, and in 1852 another group was organized, later to be called the Royal Institute of Painters in Water Colours.

The Academies, organizations of painters with the

express purpose that these should band together to sell their own works and preserve their own professional standards, would seem at first glance to be inimical to the development of the art trade through independent professional dealers. And so for a while they were. But they were limited in one obvious direction: that they offered for sale in their official exhibitions only new paintings by living painters; the whole limitless field of old masters and antique or exotic objets d'art was untouched. And here the auctioneer and the private dealer remained supreme. Also, in another way, the Academies prepared the way for the dealer by establishing the exhibition as the normal way of marketing art: they presupposed that painters would paint what they wanted to, or thought might sell, or preferably both, and then offer the results to a critical public which would inspect the current product and make comparisons before finally deciding what to buy. In other words, the Academies' exhibitions were ideal for the small-scale, middle-class collector; they broke down still further the convention that the normal, proper relationship between artist and buyer was that of client and patron. The painting was regarded, in fact, as something ready-made, take it or leave it, rather than as something essentially made to measure for a particular patron and a particular purpose.

This was all very well; it was indeed only a just recognition of the changing state of things, the changing status of the art buyer. And the Academies might have held on to their virtual monopoly had they not been foolish enough to set themselves up not only as guardians of basic professional standards—the successors in this of the medieval guilds—but as the final judges of what should be the acceptable style and content for paintings. Of course, the standards they applied were, for obvious reasons, bound to be the most conservative, and by the middle of the nineteenth century they had fallen far behind the work of the newest, youngest painters. Their determination to exclude everything except the most retrograde art of the time from their exhibitions and so from public recognition was bound to provoke a reaction. The Salon des Refusés was only the most spectacular recognition that the Academies failed to do their job, or at least took an unrealistically limited view of what that job was. And the existence of a large number of talented and ambitious young artists to whom the doors of the Academies were closed automatically meant that they must have somewhere to show their work, some way of access to the art-buying public. It was even possible that there might be some money in presenting them to the public. Obviously, the answer was the private gallery, the art dealer with his premises for showing works of art and his regular clientele to whom he could show them.

This change was facilitated by the nineteenth century's blurring of what in the eighteenth century was still a clear distinction, that between the collector and the patron. The collector bought the art of the past, and needed some sort of middleman, dealer or agent, to help him. The patron patronized the artists of the present. And it happened relatively seldom that the two enthusiasms resided in the same man. But as we have noted, by the middle of the nineteenth century the patron in the traditional sense had become far less important, if not largely extinct. He was replaced by the collector of contemporary painting. And since the collector mentality had spread to the acquisition of works by contemporaries, aided by the establishment of official exhibitions which enabled one to select modern paintings in the same spirit that one selected objets d'art of the past, it was natural that the two enthusiasms should more and more often be found in the same man. The collector, especially the smaller, bourgeois type of collector, trade with whom, *en masse,* was becoming a more and more important part of the art trade's total turn-over, was bound to have contacts with dealers. So what more natural, when the close bonds of the Academy system began to be loosened and a number of important painters found themselves functioning by choice or compulsion entirely outside that system, than that the dealer should step in as the obvious go-between linking the artist and his potential public?

Of course this sort of commerce in art involved a degree of speculation. The dealer was going, one way or another, to risk money on the artist and his work. It had therefore to be a good risk. He had to judge the potential public, the selling possibilities of his artists, and the likely profit margin from dealing in them. The dealer's public was made up of all sorts of people, but with the smaller bourgeois buyer predominant. It would seem, therefore, that the natural tendency of a dealer catering to such buyers would be to take up the most conservative of artists. Here, however, the continuing power of the Academy system intervened. The Académie was still the high road to success for a French painter, and if he was conservative enough to achieve a broad-based popular acceptance in a world where Meissonier, a facile and prolific painter of military and historical genre scenes, reigned supreme, he would almost certainly find a ready enough outlet in the Académie's Salons. So there was a built-in inducement for the dealer to be a little ahead of the public taste and the Académie's standards. That way was his best bet if he was to find and keep artists who would sooner or later turn out to be major acquisitions. But having taken this step, it was necessary that the artists he had taken on (contracted is often too formal a term for the relationship) should be presented and sold to the public; it was only by "selling" the artist that the dealer could hope to sell his works. Obviously, the Salon was still the best place for presenting a new artist's works, and its safeness and respectability guaranteed a certain sale and conventional reputation. But there were other ways, ways around the Salon's apparent monopoly of serious attention. And the most effective ally the new dealer in contemporary art had in France in the mid-nineteenth century was another new phenomenon: the independent art critic.

The art critic, writing professionally—if seldom as a whole-time job—on current art was an increasingly familiar figure in the nineteenth century. The great explosion of the literate middle classes had meant a corresponding increase in the number of magazines and journals to cater to them. And part of the way of life of this new readership was bound up with the rapid acquisition of culture. Self-education (though only the humbler members of the new public would have called it that) was the big new thing, and to be educated in this way it was necessary to be interested in all the right things, especially literature and the arts. Nor, of course, was this entirely a façade, acquired in the cause of snobbery. The possibilities for the wide popular diffusion of culture which the Industrial Revolution and its by-products offered brought millions into direct contact with the best in the arts for the first time, and the result was just as likely to be genuine enthusiasm as dutiful assumption of the "right" attitudes. Anyway, for whatever reasons, there were numerous openings for journalists ready and eager to write about the arts, scholars ready to play their role in educating the public, and many others of indeterminate abilities and qualifications. These writers, or the best of them, had their following, and were increasingly looked to for guidance in sifting out the important from the unimportant in the ever more crowded and unwieldy Salons.

Dealers were quick to see the possibilities of this new situation. Critics could publicize their artists and their works; critics, particularly, could act as mediators between the new and perhaps difficult artist and his potential public. Where it came to explaining and putting over the unexpected and original the better critics and the better dealers could happily join hands, and the lesser breeds were likely to follow suit at the first palpable signs of success. The pattern was formed above all by the Durand-Ruels, father and, especially, son, who can claim to be the first art dealers in the full modern sense of the term, and the models for all who have come after.

The business was founded as a stationers in 1803. In the 1820s, Jean-Marie Fortuné Durand-Ruel extended it to include artists' materials, then works of art. His taste and business instinct led him to specialize in the most advanced painting of the time: Delacroix, Constable, and later the Barbizon school of landscapists. It was Durand-Ruel père who first saw the possibilities of the new bourgeois buying public in relation to new art. They were, knowing less initially, less wrapped up in academic prejudice. They were willing to be led, instructed by critics and dealers. And, having made their money in business, they were ready to see even their art buying at least partly in terms of speculation: they were open to the argument that while the most favored academic painters were already expensive and the possible return on an investment in them at resale would be small, a new painter just making his way in the world might well be a good investment, as it was unlikely that his paintings would long remain cheap. The combination of acute artistic judgment and acute business sense had already brought the art side of the Durand-Ruel business a gratifying degree of success— branches in London, Germany and the Low Countries, a large and prosperous clientele—when Durand-Ruel père died in 1865 and was succeeded by his son Paul.

It was Paul Durand-Ruel (1831-1922) who brought the business of art-dealing to a fine art in its own right. He was a clear-headed and ingenious dealer in old masters, with a remarkable knack of picking up important Rembrandts, Velázquezes, Goyas and others at low prices and choosing exactly the right moment to sell. But his abiding fame is as "the Impressionists' dealer." And in selling these, the most important painters on his books, he missed not a trick—he even went so far as to set up in 1869 an apparently independent magazine, the *Revue Internationale de l'Art et de la Curiosité,* to keep modern artists, particularly those he was dealing in, before the public and to explain their work. He was indefatigable in jollying clients along into buying at advantageous prices the paintings he thought they ought to buy, and at presenting the works he had to offer in the most favorable possible way: exhibitions to drum up public interest and critical attention, private presentations of carefully selected individual paintings to follow up the publicity with actual sales.

And meanwhile, behaving in a very proper and decent way toward his painters. The major Impressionists—Manet, Degas and Pissarro, Monet, Renoir, Sisley and Cézanne—were not entirely unaccepted when Durand-Ruel got to know them. They had, in fact, had a quite respectable showing at the Académie's Salons, and drew the line at exhibiting in the Salons des Refusés of 1863, 1864 and 1873, having no desire, or indeed pressing need, to be labelled as "refused." On the other hand, despite the successes of the Barbizon School a generation earlier, landscape was still considered in Academic circles a very humble, unimportant sort of painting: indeed, the devotion of most of the Impressionists to landscape probably explains why they did not encounter more Academic opposition early on. It also explains why they did not achieve particular fame and notice until Durand-Ruel took them up and put the publicity machine in motion in the early 1870s. He met Monet and Pissarro in London in 1870; he had fled there with his stock from the invading Prussian army; they too were in temporary exile. Returning to Paris the next year, after the Commune had run its course, he met Renoir and Sisley and began buying the works of the older and more established Manet and Degas.

At this crucial time he proceeded to become virtually the patron of the younger Impressionists. The word "patron" is not used at random. When the private patron of the arts had virtually vanished, and state patronage was irregular and uncertain, the dealer was to take the patron's place. Of course it helped that the Impressionists were all, apart from Renoir, of bourgeois background themselves, and longed for the sort of financial security which the rough-and-tumble, the fight for a place in the sun enforced by the overcrowded Salons, had failed to give them. For a while at least, before the depression of the mid-1870s hit his own finances, Durand-Ruel could and did provide them with just this. He took all his painters' output, or as much of it as he could; he paid them a rough standard amount per picture (generous compared with the prices they were achieving elsewhere at the time); and he was willing to make sizable advances which the artists could pay off in paintings over a period. And he would do all this as a speculation, acquiring, frequently, paintings which he had no immediate or definite prospect of selling. If they could be sold, it was on the cards he would know how to sell them; but sometimes, when money was short, they just would not sell—and that was his risk. As Maurice Rheims remarks in his book *La Vie Étrange des Objets,* no one had behaved with such munificence towards artists since the Renaissance.

And, of course, he had his troubles. The depression of the mid-1870s was one: it meant that he could not always support the Impressionists as he had done, and that sometimes they had to go elsewhere for advances (much to his hurt and irritation). The notice into which he had helped to bring the Impressionists, as a group and individually, did not always work in their favor: it certainly helped to solidify and intensify opposition, both to them and to him. By 1884, with a number of his regular customers made too poor to think of picture buying in a succession of financial setbacks, Durand-Ruel owed more than a million francs, and found the other dealers ganging up on him in a conspiracy to dispose of all the available Impressionists on the market so cheaply that the value of his stock would plummet. He fought back by expanding his activities: in Paris a series of one-man shows for his principal painters; abroad important group shows in London, Rotterdam and Boston. In 1886 he went further, and founded a gallery in New York, a gamble which proved more than justified when the United States became in the space of a decade or so one of the most important markets, if not the most important, for Impressionist painting. By 1897, and the Victor Chocquet sale in Paris, where major Impressionists sold for previously unheard-of prices, the money value of the Impressionists was assured, and what has happened since is common knowledge.

Even so, Paul Durand-Ruel had no money when he died in 1922. But he had 1500 paintings, including many masterpieces by Impressionist and Post-Impressionist painters. And he had, meanwhile, done more than any other single man to create the ideal image of the modern art dealer: expert in art as well as in business; a connoisseur in his own right, with a deep knowledge of his own specialties; a patron to artists; a counselor and guide to art buyers; a shrewd assessor of the possibilities of speculation for those who wanted to speculate; his name alone a guarantee of quality for those whose ambitions were quieter. As an ideal it is admirable. How far it is normally put into practice by others, of course, is quite another matter.

THE WHEELER-DEALERS

Granting, for the sake of argument, that Durand-Ruel represents a sort of ideal and model for the art dealer of today, we may also grant that it is far more difficult now for a dealer to live up to that ideal than it was in his day. Particularly has this been so since the end of World War II. The reasons are not far to seek: with the spectacular escalation of modern art into big business, it becomes increasingly difficult for the impractical idealist to exist at all among dealers, while the practical idealist needs to start out with at least a long-established art-dealing business on which he can build or a large private fortune to support his ideals until they can be prevailed upon to support him.

And this is true whichever of the two main traditions of dealing he wishes to follow, or whether he wants to have a part in both. Durand-Ruel, the great supporter and promotor of living artists, and originally of artists just starting to make a place for themselves in the art world, represents one side of it. But there is, of course, another tradition, represented most famously by Joseph Duveen: that of the dealer who deals only in the works of the past, and has no truck whatever with living artists. This tradition too is eminently respectable, if not perhaps so highly thought of today as the Durand-Ruel tradition. Dealers are seldom happy, for all sorts of reasons, to be regarded as just dealers and no more. Partly it is the lofty reputation of the commodity in which they deal: few are ready to be taken merely for money-changers in the temple of the Muses. So there is nearly always another, more or less fictional image toward which each dealer strives, or which at least he hopes to imprint on the minds of those he comes into contact with. For the Durand-Ruel type of dealer this image is obviously that of the patron, the knowledgeable, independent-minded, munificent person whose dedication to art is expressed primarily through dedication to artists and their interests (his own interest and profit being, of course, largely incidental). For the Duveen type of dealer the image is that of the expert, the scholar whose knowledge of and feeling for the art of the past is entirely reliable, even infallible. His dedication to art expresses itself in a single-minded care for the conservation of works, their proper recognition and display. If the first type of dealer equates himself, by implication, with the enlightened collector of contemporary art, the second equates himself with a museum.

In practice the two functions of the dealer, in themselves quite distinct, tend to become confounded. Each type can be found existing somewhere in a "pure" state, but more often every dealer does a bit of everything, willingly or from necessity. There are few dealers, even among the most fanatical supporters of the most advanced modern art, who do not have a few select minor Impressionists or something more traditional and approachable hidden away among their stock to tide them over. Similarly, as the Impressionists and Post-Impressionists retreat further and further into the past, to become themselves by the inexorable processes of time "old masters", it becomes increasingly difficult for the dealers in old masters to make any hard and fast rule about where old masters leave off and "modern art" begins—though they can, and most of them do, steer clear of first-hand contact with living artists, buying probably only their "classic" works (blue period Picassos, say) at second- or third- or fiftieth-hand.

But whichever way the dealer's interests go, he will nowadays find greater and greater difficulty in exercising them to any important extent without a background either of valuable stock already in hand or of money. For he is caught between two fires. The supply of old masters on the market or likely to come on the market is ever diminishing. And the demands of living artists in the shape of immediate return on their time and talent are constantly increasing. Both these situations are vicious circles set up largely by dealers themselves. We are so used to the idea that the proper place for any major work of art from the past is in some sort of public collection that we forget how recently established the notion is. It was created, in so far as such an idea can be created by one man, by Duveen. And created for the most practical of reasons. Duveen wanted rich men to buy his pictures. Many rich men were not interested in pictures as such, but they could be provided with reasons why they should buy them. They could become public benefactors; they could set up galleries, institutes and foundations which would bear their names forever. They could even gain financially from it (and here a number of states obligingly played ball with Duveen by allowing all sorts of tax advantages to those who would give or leave works of art to public bodies).

All this had an incidental but by no means negligible advantage for Duveen. Dealing with businessmen, he had to show them evidence that their money was being wisely invested in art, that the paintings they bought were constantly increasing in value. The most reliable way of doing this was to make sure it never came to the test; that collections assembled at the top of the market were not dispersed at a time when money might be less readily available and prices consequently lower. How better to do this than by seeing to it that most of the paintings he sold never came on the market again? Safely deposited in a museum, they were no longer evidently subject to fluctuations in value resulting from fluctuations in taste or in world economics. And the more old masters to be taken permanently off the market, the fewer would be left; their rarity value would increase, and when they did come on the market their prices would naturally continue to rise.

Anyhow, the general result of this regular and inexorable reduction in the number of old masters on the market, with the consequent forcing up of prices for those there are, has been to make the acquisition of any sort of reasonable stock of old masters almost impossible for a new dealer. The older established dealers are likely, for the moment, to be better off. For example, in 1959, according to Jean Clay ("L'Epopée des Wildenstein", *Réalités,* March 1959) the New York storerooms of Wildenstein contained over 2000 paintings, including 400 primitives, a Fra Angelico, two Botticellis, eight Rembrandts, eight Rubenses, three Velázquezes, nine El Grecos, ten Goyas, five Tintorettos, four Titians, a dozen Poussins, seven Watteaus, seventy-nine(!) Fragonards, and always, on principle, at least twenty Renoirs, fifteen Pissarros, ten Cézannes, ten Van Goghs, ten Corots, ten Gauguins, twenty-five Courbets. There were ten of the 300 Seurats in existence, and at one time Wildenstein had 250 Picassos, until he decided to sell them all up as he did not care for them. No doubt even this treasure house has been somewhat reduced now, but it is a striking example of how stock provides the securest possible background for those able to wait: among the painters who have been fashionable for fifty years or more will be noticed at least one, Poussin, who has been long out of fashion with collectors. Acquiring Poussins was therefore one of the apparent follies of Wildenstein, and yet the recent upward movement in the price of Poussins at auction suggests that his confidence in and patience with this particular painter will at last be rewarded.

But any business set up much more recently than Wildenstein will find very little margin for this sort of retrospective enterprise. The dealer will not be able to wait, unless he has vast resources. And even if he has, waiting is unlikely to do so much good. The prices a dealer would have to pay now for any major painting by any important old master are such that very few dealers can afford to make the huge initial outlay, and then maybe sit on the painting for years until the right buyer comes along. As often as not, therefore, where such transactions are concerned the dealer is likely to find himself acting mainly as an agent for a particular buyer, working on a set commission. It is impossible to imagine that a firm such as Wildenstein could arise now, because the number of paintings important enough and now available on the market just is not sufficient to permit it. Instead, the dealer in old masters is driven increasingly to deal in lesser figures at lower prices, or in obviously slighter works by the great— sketches, drawings, etchings.

And even here the prices escalate, sometimes alarmingly. Admittedly the famous Leonardo da Vinci cartoon "The Virgin and Child with St. Anne and St. John the Baptist," sold to the National Gallery in London for £800,000 (it might have brought £1 million at auction) in 1962 is an extreme case, but the lesson is clear enough: when it seems unlikely that any important painting by one of the greatest old masters will ever come on to the market again, attention turns to cartoons, drawings and whatever may be available, and the prices of these in their turn become astronomical. Hardly a month goes by now without another record amount paid for a drawing or an etching by Rembrandt, or something of the sort. And even falling back on minor artists does not help for long. Either they rapidly become revalued into major artists, as it seems the long-lived British artist Marcellus Laroon (1679-1772) will do, with a major exhibition and a vast and exhaustive work of scholarship already devoted to him in 1967. Or while remaining in everybody's opinion minor artists their prices rapidly double, triple or quadruple: another eighteenth-century British instance is the marine artist Charles Brooking (1723-1759), whose works were not especially sought after until 1963, when suddenly one of them was sold for the record price of £5,460 at Christie's. Within a few months two more of his paintings, one almost identical with the first, fetched £14,500 and £15,500. And Brooking was another artist to move from the small collectors' class into big business.

But if the new dealer finds things difficult with old masters, he is not likely to find them in the long run much easier with new painters. Here, even more than with old masters, the pace has quickened alarmingly in the last twenty-five years. The great advantage for the patron-dealers of Durand-Ruel's generation and those who came after, such as Ambroise Vollard (1865-1939), dealer of the Post-Impressionists, and Daniel-Henry Kahnweiler (b. 1884), dealer of the Cubists, was that, like the Wildensteins, they could wait. They were able most satisfactorily to combine ideals with business. They felt a genuine enthusiasm for the work of some still relatively unknown painter; they got to know him, subsidized him, gave him perhaps a regular income in return for some of his paintings or acquired (Kahn-weiler seems to have been the first to do this) a monop-oly in his work. The investment might not be large, or it might be very considerable; often there seemed no immediate chance of its maturing, if indeed it matured at all. No doubt you could not go wrong if you found a major artist early enough and began buying when his work was cheap; but first you had to pick your major artist of the future, and here all sorts of mistakes were possible. Vollard and Kahnweiler gambled on the right artists, having the confidence to back their own good taste, and so they succeeded and we have heard of them. But there were others who, setting out with equally good intentions, picked wrong and vanished into limbo along with their unfortunate protégés.

And if, eventually, those who picked right became rich and famous, who could grudge it them? For the most part they kept their artists on a loose rein, a gentleman's agreement of some sort. If they did not always treat their artists well—there are enough horror stories about Modigliani starving while his dealer sat tight waiting for him to die and his prices to go up—the artists did not always treat them well, leaving it to the first dealer to give the first show of confidence, to do all the work of promotion, and then, once they had ar-rived, moving away to someone more immediately pros-perous and prestigious. Relations between dealers and artists are seldom completely serene anyway: it is all part of the game that each is ready at the slightest prov-ocation to accuse the other of greed, unreasonableness and general turpitude. But at least at that time the system worked fairly well. Since the war, though, it has sometimes seemed in danger of falling apart altogether.

The main reason for this is the time factor. The 1950s and 1960s have been a time of boom in the sale of new paintings almost as much as in the sale of old. Paradoxically, this has in many ways made things more difficult for the dealers. It has made young painters at the outset of their careers demand more, more quickly. Accusations tend to fly to and fro. The dealers are mean and rapacious, say the painters; they want to buy cheap and sell dear. The painters are greedy and unreasonable, say the dealers; they don't appreciate the initial investment necessary, the overheads, the expenses involved in launching a new painter, the element of risk. . . . As usual, there is some reason on both sides. Apart from the fact that greedy painters and rapacious dealers are by no means unknown, the problem arises even with the most normal, well-meaning and reasonable. Of course the painter, like anyone else, wants as much as possible as soon as possible. If reputations are made overnight, he wants his to be. If paintings in a first show are being sold at high prices, he wants his to be. He cannot remain unaware of the present state of the art market, since after all it represents an important part, maybe all, of his livelihood. Natural enough. But this virtually rules out the sort of dealer who can afford to finance young artists on a very modest scale, build them up gradually in the minds of picture buyers, and be prepared to wait for years before his investment begins to justify itself. For this is possible only when the investment is relatively small—in relation, that is, to the total funds the dealer has available. As soon as we reach the stage at which the new painter expects high prices immediately, the situation is radically changed.

For one thing, it means that the dealer has to make a much larger investment directly in the painter: he has to pay him a lot more from the start. This means that not only does he have to have a lot more money (or get backing from somewhere), but that the element of risk is greatly increased and so is the need to see a more rapid return on the money. In any case, this is what the artist wants. There are few if any who are entirely untempted by the idea of fame and fortune, and the sooner the better. The whole machinery of the art world today is geared to instant success: few exhibitions of a new painter or a new group just go on and are left to fend for themselves. The dealer has to have a publicity machine to work for him: critics, columnists and potential buyers have to be made aware of the novelty, the right people have to be invited to see it at the right time and in the right place. All of this takes time, money and a number of talents which have, or till recently had, nothing essentially to do with the dealer's business at all. Of course, if he can afford all this, and if it works according to plan, he will share in the benefits which accrue. But if his finances are shaky and if the response to the new artist is discouraging—even with all the advantages of modern publicity it is impossible to ensure that it will not be—then he is likely to be in real difficulties.

There are ways out, of course, Even today there are artists who are reasonably content to sell cheap, bearing in mind, perhaps, Picasso's precept that only those who have sold at low prices to begin with can hope to sell at high later on. If they do not depend for a living solely on their sales of pictures—if they teach, for instance—it is that much easier. And there are still small dealers working on a small scale: galleries started, perhaps, by one or two enthusiasts with very little capital but the good will of a group of painters for whose work they provide a platform. Such galleries rarely last for long, but there is a fairly constant supply of new ones to take the place of the old, particularly in Paris, where rents on the Left Bank are still a fraction of what they would be in any comparable area of London or New York. More reliable, and generally more long-lasting, are the smaller dealers who do a bit of everything: sell old as well as new paintings, and also not so-old but not-quite-new paintings. We are now reaching the stage where, the prices of new paintings being often artificially, optimistically high, the value of a lot of them drops appreciably as soon as they are bought and leave the gallery, much as a new car loses value as soon as it leaves the garage. Therefore the dealer who wants to function on a fairly modest scale will often find that it involves less outlay and is in general less risky to buy "slightly used" paintings by newish painters rather than set up a stable of completely new painters under his direct patronage. Naturally, this way he will not be in on the ground floor with some painter whose works may become very expensive in a few years' time, but he will, too, avoid making any sizable investment which does not pay off.

Other dealers find other ways. There are those, for instance, who sell on commission, which obviously reduces the risk, or at least spreads it more equitably between artist and dealer. In such arrangements the dealer exercises choice to the extent, evidently, of choosing to sell the works of painters he admires and/or thinks will sell, and probably pays for the publicity, etc., but at least he is not paying first and selling after, which is something. There are also dealers, or people who look like dealers, who are actually merely landlords, letting out their gallery premises to anyone who will pay the price and undertaking to organize the exhibition, have catalogues printed, and so on, strictly at the hirer's expense. In Paris it is surprising how often this is done, surprising, particularly, how many artists there seem to be willing and able to gamble for a place in the sun—maybe as much as 5000NF (£400 or $1000) all told for a fortnight on the Left Bank, and 8000 NF or so on the Right. And at the other end of the scale it is of course still always possible for a dealer ambitious enough, and daring enough, to jump in at the deep end, taking on and financing a string of painters in the Durand-Ruel tradition. Provided he has enough money of his own to do it, or can find a backer.

But most dealers nowadays, naturally enough, attempt to follow some sort of middle course. Frequently a smallish dealer will settle for one major acquisition among painters, to whom he can devote a lot of time and energy, and whose work he can exhibit fairly regularly—once every year or eighteen months, maybe—as well as making it known that he has always some of the artist's work available to buyers. In London, for example, there are a number of obvious instances. The two Waddington Galleries, run by a father and son, each have a specialty: Waddington senior has Jack Yeats (W.B.'s brother) and Waddington junior has the American painter Milton Avery. In each case there is, if not a watertight contract, at least a clear understanding between dealer and artist or artist's estate and in each case both stand to gain. The artist's work has a proper showcase and the services of a dealer's know-how devoted largely to it. Both galleries, of course, show other things as well, but the name Waddington immediately suggests to the average interested person Yeats and Avery, and that is something worth having to the artist, especially when, as is certainly the case with Yeats, there lies behind it years of devoted nursing along of a reputation which, though solid, was never fashionable until recently he became the first twentieth-century British artist to be included in an international, large-circulation series of popular art monographs originating in Italy, and this, seemingly, in reply to a felt demand abroad as well as at home. Equally, of course, all this reflects back on the dealer, and is to his advantage, since the more famous and sought-after his artist is, the better his business is likely to be.

Instances of this sort of dealer specialization are innumerable. To look no further than London, one could mention the Lords' Gallery and Kurt Schwitters, whose total artistic legacy they seem to have divided with Marlborough Fine Arts, and whose own personal brand of Dada is always on offer there along with Art

Nouveau posters and such. Or the Maas Gallery and the Pre-Raphaelites, especially drawings and watercolors, which they have exhibited regularly each year since the early 1960s, with ever-increasing publicity and public interest and, of course, ever-rising prices. There is the Lefevre Gallery and James Taylor, an elegantly atmospheric landscapist tending towards abstraction, whose Paris-based work has provided some memorable interludes in the gallery's more usual preoccupation with dead Impressionists. The Grosvenor Gallery, taking over the premises of the late Arthur Jeffress, whose interests as a dealer were mainly with the precious and bijou, has continued this tradition with a number of exhibitions given over to Art Nouveau (Mucha) and Arts-Déco (Erté), but has also established an alternative line in Russian experimental art of the 1900s and early 1920s—presumably reflecting the interests of its director Eric Estorick, a man of Russian origin whose acquaintance evidently includes a number of viable pipelines to stores of works by such mysterious, now officially frowned-on and otherwise largely unobtainable artists as Malevich, Tatlin and Lissitzky.

This sort of thing—a personal connection, a specialization in a particular school, genre or period—is of course the norm for art dealers: it results naturally from a combination of personal preference and business acumen, which rapidly demonstrates that the specialist nearly always has the advantage over the general dealer, unless the general dealer can operate on what is nowadays an almost unthinkably large scale. Some still continue to do it, though fewer and fewer. Wildenstein is an obvious and well-known example, backed as it is by years in the business and an enormous storehouse of material for gradual release on the market. But even they are finding it progressively more difficult to maintain their position. Recently a director of Wildenstein in Bond Street remarked that if they were to buy no more and rely simply on selling what they had for the next five years they would still be happy. "But what then?" the questioner inquired. "Then we would not be so happy." The problem is not any more to sell paintings, but to find a continuing supply of paintings of the right stature and quality at the right price, or indeed at any price. Agnew's still manages better than most, mainly because of its large financial resources, which permit it to persevere in its traditional practice of buying works of art outright whenever possible, rather than dealing in them on commission as most American and European dealers prefer to or are forced to by lack of the necessary cash to lay out. This means that Agnew's has an immediate advantage over most of its likely competitors when it comes to dealing directly with a private owner: it can make a firm offer, to be accepted, negotiated or rejected, and the owner it is dealing with knows that the offer will be safely backed up by cash on the line.

But the problem still remains: where are the necessary works of art to be found? It is not only the established dealers in major works of art who are hit by this. Colnaghi's, for example, the oldest established art dealer in Britain, has specialized in Old Master prints and drawings for two centuries, including long periods when the drawings in particular were considered very small beer beside the eminently desirable finished works of the same artists. Now, of course, things have changed radically. As major paintings become scarcer drawings and sketches come increasingly into prominence, and indeed are often found more congenial (as well as more physically manageable and cheaper) to modern taste than the paintings—Ingres is an obvious example. This situation does not, naturally, make things any easier for a firm like Colnaghi's, and James Byam Shaw, for many years director of the firm and an eminent scholar in his own right, was often heard to grumble that as the materials available to them dwindled, he found himself spending more and more time advising, attributing, authenticating, valuing, and doing everything except actually buying and selling drawings and prints. And even on the sales side, the investment angle bulks increasingly large: as prices go up, purchasers want more and more assurance that their purchase is a wise move financially. Many dealers disclaim, like Mr. Byam Shaw, all qualifications as stockbrokers or investment advisers. But a buyer is a buyer, whatever his motives, and it is unrealistic not to take this into account.

To complicate the situation of the dealer in this sphere of art, there is the continuing rise in importance of the auction house as direct intermediary between sellers and buyers of art works. The days when the auction rooms were almost exclusively the preserve of the dealer, and the layman ventured in at his peril, are long gone. Especially since 1945, the amount of publicity the newspapers have given to art and art sales has been almost entirely to the advantage of the auction rooms. Hardly a week goes by without news from somewhere of some new record figure paid at an auction for something—a painting, a drawing, a piece of furniture or china, a rare book, even a vintage automobile.

Obviously all this has two results. First of all, it makes the would-be owner of a work of art—anything from the most obviously valuable to the probably valueless—hope against hope that he may strike lucky, that a new record may be set up with his possession, and that an auction house may do the trick for him. As the constant stream of people with parcels under their arms and hopeful expressions on their faces lining up to have some possession appraised at Sotheby's, Christie's, the Hôtel Drouot or Parke-Bernet attests, it is now the auction house rather than the dealer that potential sellers turn to. In the upper reaches, very few major works these days are sold straight to dealers or are even left to be auctioned in situ at the breaking-up of a home or collection. They make their way inexorably to the major auctions in London, Paris or New York, where dealers wishing to buy them for stock have to compete. with well-endowed museums, private buyers or their agents, or for that matter with other dealers acting merely as agents. For the second result of the publicity given to art auctions today is that private buyers know about them, are emboldened to try for themselves, and embark on bidding with the basic assumption that within reason they cannot go too far wrong, since clearly whatever they pay for the object of their desire it is bound to be appreciably less than what they would pay if a dealer had bought it instead at the auction and then had his own profit to make on the resale.

This is not, as a matter of fact, inevitably true, though long-term no doubt it must be, in that any upping of prices brought about by auctions will eventually be handed on to the buyer through dealers. But in any given instance a number of imponderables are likely to come into play in the saleroom, not all of them working in the private buyer's favor. To begin with, there are the special excitements of competitive bidding in the saleroom, which often develops into a sort of collective hysteria and drives the price above what any of the participants might consider paying in cold blood. Equally, the more laymen there are around, the less reasonable and reasoned on the whole the bidding is likely to be—a gathering made up exclusively of dealers and experts would often stop bidding at a much lower level, so that the price subsequently paid to a dealer for the object he had bought at auction might be less even after allowing him a fair profit. And then again, estimates based on saleroom records are always to some extent thrown off by the activities of the buyer with special reasons for wanting something, so that he is willing to pay two or three times the normal price in order to secure it. There is the famous story of a British biscuit-king with a passion for toby jugs who heard that a particularly desirable example absolutely vital to his collection was coming up. He bought it, through an agent, and was shattered to find that he had paid for it some twenty times the largest sum ever paid for a comparable piece before. It was only later that he discovered that in

his eagerness to get the prize he had inadvertently commissioned two agents, unknown to each other, to bid for
it, and instructed each to bid without limit and pay
whatever was needful to get it! That is obviously an
exceptional case, but it may frequently happen that a
record price at an auction comes as a result of just one
person's willingness to pay far over the odds for, say, a
family portrait, a piece of silver or china needed to
complete a set, the last remaining first edition of a favorite author which has consistently eluded him, or a
painting by an artist he has long sought an example of
in vain. At a dealer these, if they were available, would
be priced according to the seller's assessment of the
average desire of the normal buyer to possess such a
piece—and the price would necessarily therefore be considerably lower.

All this, anyway, is to some extent beside the point.
Auction houses have taken over their position in the sun
with the utmost confidence in the last twenty-five years,
and seem unlikely now to be displaced from it. In the
process, they have taken over many of the functions
which before were the exclusive preserve of dealers.
There is little the dealers can do to reverse the trend.
All they can do is to go along with it, and make of it the
best they can. Prices go up and up, supplies dwindle,
and they are likely to be caught between the devil and
the deep blue sea. How, then, do they keep going, and
what new means are open to them? The problem resolves itself into two parts: where do they get their stock-
in-trade from, and how are they to sell it so as to put the
auction houses in some ways at a disadvantage? The an-

swers to the second question are in many ways contingent on the answers to the first, and so it is advisable to start with some more detailed consideration of exactly where the works of art on sale at any given time come from, and how the dealer's (or for that matter the auctioneer's) stock-in-trade is built up.

TOP DOLLAR

Dealers, as we have said, fall roughly but recognizably into two groups: the Durand-Ruel type, whose interests are almost entirely contemporary and who deal in the work of living painters with whom they have some sort of personal relationship; and the Duveen type, who deal exclusively in the more predictable work of dead artists as it passes from collection to collection. Auctioneers, naturally, are confined for the most part to deals of the second kind: all their stock is, almost by definition, secondhand. This may not necessarily be so: you may remember that in 1745 Hogarth, annoyed by the popularity of "old master" sales at the time, decided to stage an auction of his own works, and did so with reasonably satisfactory results. What has been done before could be done again, and indeed it is not quite unknown (or so rumor has it) for modern painters of some note, in need of a little quick money and perhaps restive under the restrictions of a tightly drawn contract with a dealer, to slip some of their earlier works discreetly into an auction as "the property of a gentleman." But there has not in recent times been any important auction by an artist of his own works, and so that particular area of the art market remains at present the preserve of the dealer.

Hence, one way out of the impasse that a Duveen-type dealer probably finds himself in when it comes to replenishing his stock may well be a partial move into the other category, even if it is only making a couple of small wagers on the side about the future potential of some living painter, who need not necessarily be either young or aesthetically "advanced." Others, with more daring or more money to invest, will go into this market in a big way—the most spectacular example in the world being, no doubt, the meteoric rise of London's Marlborough Fine Arts during a mere twenty years. But this sort of dealing, with its particular sorts of promotion techniques and its special problems in dealer-artist relations, calls for separate consideration. For the moment, therefore, let us concentrate on the market in the old, the dead, and anyway the establishedly respectable.

Clearly, this market is a continuing one. Indeed, if prices and sheer volume of business are anything to go by, it has seldom been healthier than in the last five years. And this despite complaints of a falling off in the supply of materials for the market and a lowering in the quality of what there is—not to mention the perennial cry of the pessimist that what goes up must come down, that every boom is followed by a slump. Maybe, but for the time being the demand seems to be limitless, and demand must at all costs be supplied. Where from? That, of course, is for dealers and auctioneers alike the $64,000 question. The answer depends to a large extent on the level at which they function or desire to function. Let us consider the top level first.

The top level is not easy to define exactly, but it is easy to recognize. In painting, for example, we might draw an arbitrary line at the sum of £20,000 or $60,000. Certainly any painter, a major, well-authenticated work by whom did not fetch more than that, could not be considered in the top class commercially, whatever one's judgment of his artistic value. But even today, when many paintings on the market bring five or ten times that sum, the amount is still a very fair lump of money to have tied up in a single piece of merchandise, especially something so relatively fragile and so difficult to value except by quite subjective standards as a painting. So we may reasonably regard dealers who regularly handle paintings in this price range as functioning on the top level of their calling. Of course, no dealer can deal exclusively in works of this caliber, and even the grandest dealers have many cheaper works available— Agnew's, for example, by no means disdains the humble "Christmas present" sale of small framed drawings and watercolors by small masters at no more than £5 or £10 each. But a major dealer's reputation and clientele are somehow set by the upper ranges of his stock, and prestige is very important. A good Rubens or Italian primitive or Cézanne sold is a relief in some ways, but it at once poses the problem of how to replace the work in stock with something of comparable quality.

The first answer is the private collector who is, or

may, or might be, or will one day be, willing to sell his collection, or some painting from it, to a dealer with cash in hand and an acceptable reputation for fair dealing. This was once the easiest, most natural way in the world for the dealer. Collections were nearly always the pet hobby of one man. Even if he hoped and believed that he was creating something which would be handed on and treasured by his descendants, in the nature of things this very frequently proved not to be the case. His legatees preferred the money to the goods, felt little or no interest in their elderly relative's artistic eccentricities, or purely and simply needed to sell up in order to put the estate to rights. Agnew's, still a family firm after a hundred and fifty years, with its five present directors all related by blood or marriage to the founder, has existed mainly throughout its history on "selling pictures to one generation and buying them back from the next."

But not any more. Such a pattern depended on the continuance of a traditional kind of art buying and selling, one dictated largely by personal interest and enthusiasm and backed up by a large number of sizable private fortunes. This sort of buying continued, with various ups and downs, until 1939, but now some new factors have come on to the scene to disrupt the pattern completely. They may be capsulated roughly as follows: (1) the decay of riches; (2) taxation and philanthropy (intimately linked); (3) the rise of the auction-houses; and (4) increasing restrictions on the export of art. All these factors have helped to change radically the old art-market set-up. Let us try to take them in order, though it is difficult, since they are all to some extent interdependent.

The decay of riches is not a new thing since the Second World War, but it has accelerated since then and its direst effects on the art market have been making themselves felt. It is not true, of course, that no one has money to spend on art any more—hardly, or how would the record prices arise? But it is true that the economic position of many of the traditional classes of art buyer has become more and more precarious, and personal fortunes have become far less durable than they once were. Taxation and other sorts of governmental interference have played a large part in this process. They began to do so in Britain back in 1882, when the Settled Lands Act made it relatively easy to break up settlements in trust, both of land and of chattels. This allowed many time-hallowed collections to be sold off for the first time, and the result was a dealers' field day, even if many of the finest pickings went straight into the booming collections of new American millionaires. That, anyway, did not make much odds as far as the dealers were concerned: they would sell to anyone who could buy, and the fortune of the British-based Duveen, and of many others, was after all largely founded on sales to the wide-open American market. Moreover, no one (except perhaps Duveen himself) believed that the collections thus built would not in the fullness of time come under the hammer in their turn and the works they contained come back into the market again as they had done so often before.

Thus when the government went further, not only

facilitating the breaking up of the old estates and collections, but virtually enforcing it by the introduction of
ever more stringent death duties and estate taxes, there
was no widespread feeling in the art world that this
would prove a serious threat. What did it matter why
collections came on the market, provided they kept on
coming? It was not until too late that dealers began to
realize that the process was not self-perpetuating. The
works of art came on the market, true, and were bought
up with greater or lesser enthusiasm depending on the
general economic conditions then prevailing. But while
the great old private collections dispersed, no new ones
came to take their place. Those which did arise were
already semi-public, in that their proud possessors were
coming to see themselves (and were receiving every
governmental encouragement to see themselves) as
trustees only, assembling their collections not so much
for their own private pleasure, but as a sort of duty to
society and the public institutions which would ultimately be their heirs and the final resting place of their
possessions. In any case, fewer and fewer private individuals could afford to collect grandly on any other
terms. In France collecting had been mainly a bourgeois preoccupation ever since the Revolution, and remained so. In Britain the holders of hereditary fortunes
were being constantly weeded out and deprived of the
means to collect on a large scale even if they would,
while the newer middle-class buyers were more and
more finding that crippling taxation prevented them
from indulging their tastes except very modestly: the
prosperous professional man who was the steady back-

bone of the art-buying classes in the late nineteenth and early twentieth centuries is liable to find now that if he is earning £40,000 a year, he is paying close on £30,000 of it in taxes. With few exceptions, it was the age of the small buyer and therefore, in time, the small seller. No more the earl whose mansion walls housed a hundred or so miscellaneous half-forgotten old masters, but the penthouse dwellers with perhaps half a dozen important paintings, well kept, well documented, and offering no dramatic surprises when and if they came on the market again.

In the circumstances, not surprisingly, it has become a matter of urgent importance to the art market, dealers and auctioneers alike, to flush the last few forgotten masterpieces out of whatever unlikely coverts they may be lurking in. Wildenstein are known to have vast card indexes in which the present whereabouts of every painting conceivably of interest to them still in private hands is scrupulously noted and documented. One of the greatest gifts attributed even by his bitterest rivals to Peter Wilson, prime architect of Sotheby's spectacular rise in the art market during the last two decades, is an encyclopedic knowledge of where anything possibly salable may be and a unique gift for charming it out of its present owner's hands and on to the block in Bond Street. Dealers scan the "Deaths" columns of newspapers anxiously, and keep an ear glued to the ground for news of the imminent demise of any stubborn and secretive collectors whose possessions may at last be about to become the world's property.

And even today, just occasionally, that favorite fantasy of the popular newspaper, the big art find by a complete amateur, does actually come true. Not often —the days when one might hope to pick up a Rembrandt in the Puces, or even a Tiffany lamp in a downtown junkshop, are long gone. But sometimes something does turn up. Early in 1966, for instance, the eighty-two-year-old widow of a picture framer brought into Christie's thirty-five apparently unremarkable paintings amassed by her late husband through the years. One of them, an elaborate treatment of the "Judgment of Paris" theme thrown in with a 10s. deal for old picture frames in 1933, was catalogued as a Lankrink, with an appraisal of £100 ($280). But then it was recognized as a possible Rubens by Oliver Millar, deputy surveyor of the Queen's pictures, properly examined and withdrawn from sale, to come up later as a Rubens, well authenticated by several experts. The sequel is a little sad, however: by a curious coincidence another long lost Rubens, a sketch for "Samson and Delilah", turned up meanwhile, and was put into the same sale. Result: the second brought a relatively modest figure, 24,000 guineas, and the first was withdrawn after failing to reach its reserve price. Later it was sold to the National Gallery for an undisclosed sum, but still presumably less than the first optimistic estimate. The lesson would not have been lost on Bergson: that one discovery is news, but two comes dangerously close to the ridiculous.

Other famous finds have had happier outcomes. Sometimes it is a museum or gallery which makes the find for itself. Early in 1967 the Prado announced its acquisition of a panel painting by the very rare fifteenth-century Italian master Antonello da Messina, only twenty-two to twenty-five of whose works are known to exist now, all of them in museums. This one was just brought in by an inquirer, a private individual interested to know whether the picture was of any value. In 1961 the London National Gallery bought one of the very few reasonably authenticated Giorgiones still in private hands, "Sunset Landscape with St. George and St. Anthony", which though not entirely unknown was certainly very obscure before the purchase. Here controversy ensued, not so much on the genuineness of the gallery's discovery, as on the vexed question of why the gallery had apparently refused to buy the picture at a much lower price a few years before, when it had a hole in the middle, but had now snapped it up in its "restored" condition. The gallery's critics obviously had a point, but controversy died down somewhat when cleaning revealed the painting to be, repair apart, in remarkably good condition and even more unquestionably from Giorgione's own hand.

The catalogue of discoveries could be considerably extended. In 1954 an architect fogbound in north London lunched in a Hendon hotel and was struck by the likeness of the ceiling-painting there to a Tiepolo he knew. Expert examination confirmed his hunch and came up with an explanation of how it could have got there, as a souvenir of David Garrick's foreign travels still decorating a house he once owned. More surprising, though, it turned out that a guidebook to Hendon published in 1890 drew particular attention to the quality of the ceiling painting as an important local sight, though subsequently it had passed completely from recollection. On a less spectacular level, something very similar happened to the famous English viola player Lionel Tertis when some statuary in the garden of a house he had bought in Wimbledon proved to be early work of Henry Moore and was sold at auction in 1964 for £5,200, a sizable proportion of what he had paid for the whole property. Here again, investigation showed that the house had once been advertised (though not when Mr. Tertis bought it) as "complete with garden sculptures by Henry Moore."

In 1961 a French nun sent in to Sotheby's a small wooden sculpture, previously unknown to experts, which she said was by Gauguin. It was, and it sold for £11,500 ($32,200). In 1964 a dealer sold at Sotheby's for £110,000 a Rembrandt still life he had bought at a Midland sale for under £100. Some mysterious paint-covered sculptured decorations in the tuck shop of Canford School turned out to be Assyrian reliefs worth £14,250 ($32,200) to the British Museum. In 1933 the London art critic Pierre Jeannerat bought at Christie's a job lot of four small sculptures for £11 ($31). One of them was a bronze statuette of a rearing horse, which in 1961 appeared in an exhibition at the Victoria and Albert Museum authoritatively identified as one of the three sculptures by Leonardo known to exist, probably cast in bronze in Florence around 1508 from Leonardo's wax original. Its value today could hardly be less than £100,000 and possibly a great deal more. Early in 1968 a bronze statuette of Juno from a Swiss collection was identified by Sotheby's as a hitherto unknown work of Benvenuto Cellini and sold for £32,200.

But even continued indefinitely, this list of discoveries is only a drop in the ocean of the whole art market, and though amateurs will always go on hoping for such a bit of luck to come their way, the professionals, the dealers and auctioneers, will build little or nothing on the possibility, and tend to regard exaggerated claims with great reserve until they prove themselves to be justified. The main body of the pre-twentieth century art works on the market at any time must always come from the private collector, and so the likely collector must be sought out and cherished: he is getting to be a rarer bird every day.

And yet so much is sold, every day of every week of every year. Where does it go? A little of it goes to the well-publicized private collections of well-publicized public figures. A handful of cosy Impressionists is a status symbol for any important screen star, but it is rarely indeed that a star's collection is chosen with acumen and personal flair, as was Edward G. Robinson's collection (sold, perforce, when divorce entailed a fifty-fifty division of property), and as is Vincent Price's (but then Price cheats by having been a trained art historian first, and become an actor only as an afterthought). For the most part art bought as so many status symbols by instant celebrities can be relied upon to come back on the market in due time, when its owner gets bored with it or finds his or her career drooping. But few other large-scale modern collectors can reconcile themselves to a collection which will only last out their lifetime. And here the unbeatable combine of taxation and philanthropy comes into operation.

It has been brought to its finest pitch of perfection in the United States. How it operates is something like this: since 1917 American law has permitted charitable donations of various sorts to be tax-deductible. There was always argument over the precise interpretation of the act, and gifts of works of art to public institutions were not generally recognized as charitable donations within its terms. This state of affairs was rectified in 1954, by provisions of the Revenue Code then introduced, which has been the envy of public-spirited art lovers (and others) elsewhere in the world ever since and the despair of long-sighted art dealers even as they profited spectacularly from the shorter-term effects. What the regulations allow is for art donations to properly constituted and recognized galleries, educational institutions and various other nonprofitmaking foundations to be deductible; they may be set against the donor's taxes up to 30 per cent of his total liability. "The amount of the deduction is determined by the fair market value at the time of the contribution". Moreover, it also permitted for some years that, provided a change of ownership legally took place, the donor might continue to enjoy his former possessions in his own home for the term of his natural life, and that they need revert to their designated recipient only on his death. This, of course, was a superlative way of having one's cake and eating it: to spend money on a luxury item, nominally give it away while retaining the private enjoyment of it as long as one wishes, and actually save money in the process by having the cost of the donation (or maybe even more than the cost) set against one's current tax bill. In 1966 the regulation was modified in response to much criticism of its laxness; the tax deduction is still permitted on gifts to recognized institutions, but they must be executed immediately.

The purpose of the legislation, clearly, was to encourage rich collectors to make over their possessions to museums and galleries which were finding it more and more difficult to supplement their collections as they might wish through normal art-market channels. And in this it has been eminently successful. Nowadays a big collector just cannot afford to sell his collection—the tax bill on the capital gains which accrued, or the inheritance tax on his estate at his death, would be crippling. Donation or legacy to a public institution is the only way out, and is certainly giving the fun way. Obviously the law has certain loopholes, and lends itself to some abuses: in particular the phrase "fair market value" lends itself to a number of eccentric interpretations, since obviously an assessment of fair market value depends very much on who is doing the assessing and why. It is not unknown for museums to put an optimistically high valuation on a painting offered them, knowing that to them the matter is academic anyway, while their chances of getting it may depend on their suggesting a more favorable estimate for tax purposes than some rival institution.

Still, by and large the system operates to the advantage of public art collections and to that of the people who donate to them. It is also advantageous, short-term, to the dealers and others who sell the works of art. It provides a tremendous stimulus to art buying, and not only among the rich who love art anyway. Even the complete philistine, if offered the choice of handing his money straight to the tax collector or buying with it instead a work of art which, once handed over to a museum, will gain him not only repute as a public benefactor but further advantages in dealing with his overall tax bill, is bound to see the wisdom of the latter course. Moreover, if within reason the more he spends on the works of art in question, the more good their giving away does him financially (the one test of "fair market value" no one can cavil at is a clear bill of sale in open market), then he will probably be less inclined to be overcautious about the price he pays. So, at one level, the dealer stands to gain more customers and higher prices than he could otherwise expect. But he must face the fact that each sale achieved is almost certain to be final, locking up yet another unique and irreplaceable work of art somewhere it is destined to remain as long as paint and canvas hold together.

So each state-inspired donation to an American institution reduces still further the amount of first-rate marketable art in circulation, and the dealer finds himself in a still more difficult position when it comes to restocking. Admittedly not quite every donation to a museum need be final—it all depends on the conditions under which a gift is made or accepted, and the museum's constitution. Though this is not widely realized,

some museums are permitted to sell off surplus or unwanted possessions, and many would refuse a gift if the
conditions attached were too restricting. Even a body as
august as the New York Metropolitan Museum of Art
may do so, and from time to time does. And even the
Metropolitan makes mistakes: a little-prized "school of
Titian" portrait sold off in 1930 for $400 was snapped
up by the Detroit Institute of Art and proved in cleaning to be an excellent Tintoretto, estimated contemporary value around $150,000. In the 1950s they did it
again with a *Madonna and Child,* "school of Cima,"
which cleaning showed to be a genuine Cima salable at
four times its purchase price of $500. But errors of this
sort seldom occur, and anyway many museums are not
permitted by their constitution to sell or otherwise dispose of anything, even those recognized fakes which are
hiding somewhere in every museum's chamber of hor-
rors.

British law does not offer much consolation to the
art-hungry dealer. True, it offers no such spectacular
advantages as American law to the art owner, but since
the 1950s it at least makes the concession of allowing
works of art to be accepted by the State in lieu of death
duty. Naturally the estate may prefer to take its chances
on the market and pay the duty instead from the proceeds, but this is seldom done except in some sort of
revenge against the State, since any unexpected bonus
above the official valuation may only serve to up the
sum on which duty is payable, while auctioneers' commissions, etc., also have to be taken into account.

So, whichever way you look at it, the dealer has

every reason to work hard at extending his field of activities, being first in to get hold of any important works of art which are going and looking much farther afield than he would have done in the past to find them. In both these aims he is likely to find himself frustrated in two ways: by the auctioneer and by the laws of virtually every country in the world where something to his purpose might be lurking. In the last chapter we touched on the reasons for the advance of the saleroom and the relative decline in the fortunes of the dealer. Publicity obviously counts for a lot here: it is record-breaking prices at auctions which make the headlines, and it is not hard to persuade the prospective seller that he has the best chance of the best prices in a saleroom rather than a dealer's gallery.

Certainly, there is always an element of the gamble in a sale, and the dealer may have the ideal buyer at a nearly ideal price safely lined up. But then a little flutter appeals to almost everyone. It is easy for the auctioneer to persuade an owner that anyway he has nothing to lose if he puts a large enough reserve on his possessions, so that they cannot be sold for less than what he considers an acceptable figure. Moreover, the auctioneer can hold forth the prospect of quick cash for anything he sells, while a dealer's ways quite possibly have to be more devious and slow-moving. Agnew's has the advantage of always offering cash on the line whenever this can be arranged with a would-be seller. Many other dealers just do not have the resources to buy a major work outright, and if they cannot put together enough money in shaky combine will have to offer to sell it on commission. In other words, they function very much as an auction house does, but with less splash, less publicity, and usually less chance of obtaining a sensationally high price for their client. It is understandable, then, that Sotheby's or Parke-Bernet (now anyway a branch of Sotheby's) generally win out over the dealers. Understandable, but still a cause of great bitterness among dealers, who often unreasonably regard the salerooms as upstarts catering to amateurs and taking the bread out of dedicated professionals' mouths.

And what the auction houses do not snap up—to pass on to dealers only at inflated prices, if at all—is as likely as not caught in one official net or another while the dealer impotently looks on. Up to the beginning of this century art was a commodity which could be imported and exported more or less without restrictions. The art market was truly international, because art was regarded as the prerogative of the rich individual rather than part of any one nation's patrimony. But soon all that was to change. As so often during this century, it was the intervention of the United States which set the changes in motion. Already in 1884 a director of the Victoria and Albert Museum was complaining in *The Times* that too many of the best pictures in Britain were likely to "go to the Rothschilds or to Vanderbilt" (he might have added the Kaiser Friedrich Museum in Berlin, at that time one of the best advised and best endowed art institutions in Europe). Little official notice was taken, and by the 1900s the trickle abroad, especially westward across the Atlantic, had become a flood.

In 1909 Congress helped things along by repealing all duties chargeable on works of art over a hundred years old brought into the country (which up to then had stood at a flat 20 percent). In 1911 the law was further emended to remove the duty also from works by living artists. The immediate aim of this legislation was to lure J. Pierpont Morgan's fabulous collection, at that time mainly divided between his London and Paris homes, over to the United States where it was felt by rights to belong and which, Morgan had said, should have it all once the law was changed. The immediate aim was achieved, and in 1912-13 the collection arrived in New York, most of it destined for the Metropolitan Museum of Art. But Morgan was not the only American collector induced to bring his loot from Europe back to his native land, and the lifting of tariffs also encouraged the leading European dealers to extend their transatlantic activities.

Especially, of course, Duveen. Duveen was by no means the first on the scene. Durand-Ruel, you will remember, had opened a New York branch back in 1886, and even in Duveen's own special field, the selling of eighteenth-century English portraits to newly rich Americans in search of ancestor-surrogates, he was anticipated by Samson Westheimer, who was already buying up Raeburns and Romneys at fancy prices in the 1890s, a decade before Duveen embarked on his wild career. However that may be, it is with Duveen's name above all that the greatest migration westward of European art treasures is associated, and it was his labors in the field which excited the most publicity, and consequently the most alarm. Despite this, and frequent

appeals by museum directors, nothing was done officially to limit the export of works of art from Britain
until 1946, though the government might intervene to
buy "national treasures" which looked as if they might
be going abroad, and later on a short-list of "paramount" art treasures was compiled which might be pur-
chased through a special parliamentary grant of funds if
export seemed to threaten.

Even in 1946 the instructions were not specifically
designed to protect works of art in Britain, but were
merely part of the general controls then instituted on
all imports and exports. The position was rationalized,
after a fashion, in accordance with the findings of the
Waverley Commission, published in 1952. The main
result of this was the setting up of a Reviewing Committee on the Export of Works of Art, which examines
all applications for export licenses, and may refuse them
if it thinks fit, conditionally on some British institution's
as being able (sometimes with State aid, though that is
by no means guaranteed) to put up an equivalent sum
to the purchase price already agreed upon. It is open to
any public institution to appeal against the granting of
an export license for a work in which it is particularly
interested, and it is allowed a period of grace in which
it can find the necessary money, though this period may
not be sufficient if there is a lot of money to be found,
like the £105,000 the Victoria and Albert would have
had to find in three months to prevent the fifteenth-
century Louvain brass lectern owned by Oscott College
from going to the New York Metropolitan Museum in
1968 for $250,000.

The system is somewhat ramshackle, but it seems

on the whole to work reasonably well. As a rule it is only called upon where some very important work of art is in question, such as the Leonardo Cartoon which the Royal Academy announced its intention of selling in 1962. Here the issue was simple. The Academy, to put it crudely but not unfairly, wanted government money without the government's having any say in how it should be spent. Not very reasonable, perhaps, but then people's wants rarely are. And they had a weapon, in the shape of two very important works of art they owned, the Leonardo Cartoon and Michelangelo's sculptured Tondo. Pleading poverty, they announced their intention to sell the Leonardo in open auction, expecting it to bring £1 million or more. There was consternation, a demand that if it were bought by an American collector or institution an export licence should be refused, and a further alarm over whether, if this happened, any British institution could afford to match the fixed price. The Academy emphasized its desire to be reasonable and safeguard this treasure for Britain: they would settle for £800,000. The National Gallery launched an appeal which came nowhere near the target, the National Art Collections Fund offered a grant which was also insufficient, and finally at the eleventh hour the government stepped in with a special grant to make up the difference. The Royal Academy had got its government money without strings, and the nation had got a Leonardo which in free market conditions would almost certainly have gone to the United States never to return.

Despite this, the British government shows every sign of wishing to be reasonable about the export of works of art, as well it might, considering the importance of the London art market in Britain's balance of payments. This keeps the dealers fairly happy, and the auctioneers even happier, since their sales become more and more international, both in where the things sold come from and in where they go to. But other countries are not always so easygoing as Britain in such matters, and their restrictions give dealers less reason for satisfaction. The United States, needless to say, has little call to establish restrictions on the export of works of art, since virtually all the traffic is anyway going the other way; and so no such restrictions seem to exist.

But France has quite strict rules and regulations. The present set dates from a 1941 law governing the export of art (modified in 1958) and a 1944 law concerned with the general regulation of import and export. Briefly, the combination of these laws permits a specified variety of public authorities and bodies to pre-empt a work of art destined for export and secure it at a figure matching that already set by the would-be exporter. The main thing to be determined in the customs governing export of works of art is the relevance of any given work, whatever its value (above 500 NF), to the "patrimoine national." This determined, an export license may be refused, but this does not involve any necessary engagement of the State to buy the work instead. This situation may well be iniquitous for the owner and would-be seller of a work of art, which he may be rendered unable to sell at a fair price either abroad or at home if the necessary funds are not forthcoming. Clearly some reform is needed, both to rationalise the system (and aid the French art market, which chafes under these restrictions) and to bring it up to date, seeing that at present it protects only works of art dating from before 1900. Plans for reform are now under way: the main points proposed are to make it obligatory for the State to buy any works it will not allow to be exported, and to set up a duty of perhaps 15 percent on works which are exported, the money to go into a special fund for buying those which may not be.

Other nations have simpler but sometimes tougher regulations. In Italy some sort of control has existed since 1802 (when, incidentally, it did little to prevent wholesale art plundering by Napoleon). Today practically everything has to be classified and permission to export granted, subject to the payment of export taxes. Anything may be preempted, and an increasing number of art objects are. West Germany has had since 1956 a national register for cultural treasures, which may be exported only under strict control, with an export license; exporting without a license is a criminal offense. In Greece, by a law enacted in 1932, the State monopolizes excavations and the preservation of archaeological finds; all art exports down to the least important icon must be specifically authorized after examination and classification. Spain placed all artistic and cultural objects under state protection in 1931; they must all be classified and licensed for export; the State has the right to preempt any intended export, and levies duty on those the export of which is permitted. Russia controls the export of art works at source, since all officially countenanced sales are nationalized and nothing the government did not want exported would be sold to a foreigner in the first place; as an additional precaution against the export of illicitly acquired works of art a written authorization to export must be shown to customs on leaving the country. Egypt, Turkey, and Iran have state control of all exports, and close official supervision of any archaeological work carried out, with the right to preempt any important finds.

And so on. Few are the countries which now have no controls at all to ensure that at least the most important works of art at present within their boundaries stay there, whatever their origin and, for that matter, whatever the nationality of their owner. (There were, for instance, endless legal disputes about the proposed removal of Calouste Gulbenkian's art collection after his death in 1956 from his home in Paris to the Foundation he had set up in Lisbon to receive it. The collection had been acquired all over the world, and Gulbenkian was a British subject of Turkish origin permanently domiciled in Portugal.) The virtues and faults of any system which tries, in the interests of some sort of chauvinism, to limit the free movement of art from country to country can be endlessly argued, like the meaning of such terms as "national treasures," "patrimoine national" and such. But to do so would be beside our point. Whatever the rights or wrongs of such restrictions, the more of them there are, the more the art dealer's field of activity is limited. Especially if he hopes to continue functioning on the top level of buying and selling, where suitable pieces for sale are ever fewer and farther between.

It all adds up to a pretty gloomy picture of the

prospects of any new Duveen who might hope to break on to the artistic scene, and suggests a hardly less gloomy outlook for the old-style superdealers whose names and reputations have dominated the international art market since the turn of the century. But modify or die is the rule of survival, and a number of possibilities for modification still present themselves.

MODEST MEANS

The most immediate and popular way of meeting and beating the increasing shortage of major works by major masters on the open market is obvious: a scaling down of operations so that the main weight of the business is carried by many small transactions instead of a few very big ones. This modification is all the easier in that it can be done gradually and almost unnoticeably, without any radical change or rethinking at all. After all, even the grandest dealers have never existed exclusively on the heights—Duveen himself dealt in minor works by minor masters, and in fine furniture, tapestries and any other objets d'art his rich customers might desire. Even if his chosen field is the loftier old masters, no sensible dealer would disdain a good drawing or sketch, an acceptable studio or school work, or an attractive unattributed painting in a style and of a period which he knows will sell. This has always been true, even in the spacious Edwardian days when there were many more first-rate works of first-rate masters for sale than there are now.

Thus for all sorts of reasons—the purchase of a whole collection, a known demand for a particular kind of minor master, even personal vagaries of taste and buying—practically any dealer is bound at any time to have stored away somewhere a number of paintings far less notable, and far less expensive than the cream of his stock. Once the cream is skimmed, and proves impossible to replace, all he needs to do is to concentrate more and more on the lesser works, hoping to make up in volume of trade what he loses in high-priced exclusiveness. The case of Agnew's is an instructive example. Agnew's, one of the oldest and most respected of London dealers, is still among the readiest to buy the big, important pictures when they come up for sale. But the days when one might hope to find a spectacular bargain among their lesser works, their sketches and drawings, are long gone. Once these were likely to be dismissed as beneath serious notice, and sold casually, almost shamefacedly. Now, though, the bulk of their business is accounted for by smaller sales, of pictures costing under £5000 and often under £500. The process of popularization has been gradual and almost accidental. Agnew's showrooms still have a slightly forbidding air of red plush and dark oak, a little like a grand London club. But a succession of memorable loan exhibitions devoted to such reliably popular subjects as Cotman and Crome, Victorian painting, and Turner, have brought all sorts of new people interested in art into the gallery. A number of Christmas exhibitions of drawings under £15 and old masters under £300, plus a tactful display in their arcade-like Bond Street entrance windows of reasonably priced English watercolors and drawings, have served to confirm the initial impression that there is nothing to be frightened of and one really does not need to have £10,000 at the ready in order to cross the sacred portals and contemplate a purchase.

The result of this has been a large increase in the number of regular clients on Agnew's books—three times as many as in 1939—and an enormous increase in the sheer number of sales. The directors estimate that a good half of their sales now are to foreign buyers— among whom are probably most of those making large individual purchases—and they hope and expect to expand still further as more and more people are bitten, if only in a small way, by the art-collecting bug. And here is the key to the new art trade. The "average" art collector these days is not Paul Getty; he is not even remotely like him. As likely as not he is a middle-class, professional man of some sort who lives in an apartment or a modest house, does not have the room to hang a large Rubens even if he had the taste for it and the money to afford it. £1000 or $2500 is probably his normal limit, and small oils, watercolors and drawings generally suit his pocket and his taste best. If Poussin and Claude, darlings of the eighteenth-century connoisseur, are now the least fashionable of the great masters, it is no doubt principally because their best works can be adequately displayed only in a palace, and hardly anyone these days, even the very richest, lives in a palace. A Claude would be quite difficult to dispose of profitably today unless one happened to have the right museum all lined up. A nice, approachable, reasonably sized Canaletto, on the other hand . . . Or a Stubbs, or a Palmer drawing, or a Fragonard, or an Impressionist pastel, or a good early impression of a Rembrandt etching . . .

Thus the whole market is scaled down, but vastly widened. And if the dealer accepts this situation, and rearranges his pattern of dealing to fit in with it, then his task is much eased. To begin with, obviously the supply of suitable material is not so drastically restricted. When every undoubted major Leonardo or Michelangelo is tucked away in some museum, it is safe to assume that drawings and sketches will still be around. At a price, of course. Tiny but unarguably genuine scribbles have in the last five years been fetching as much as £19,000 (a Leonardo drawing at Sotheby's 1963) and £12,500 (a Michelangelo sketch at Sotheby's, 1964). But expensive or not, they are there, still in private hands, and what is true of the most sought-after great masters is even more abundantly true of many lesser. Equally, with the lesser masters it becomes correspondingly easier to find major works, while when they in their turn become scarce there are always others, forgotten or little valued, who can be rediscovered and revalued to fill the gap.

But these paintings, etc., must come from somewhere. Where? Almost anywhere is the answer to that question. The unrecorded and recorded major old master paintings in private hands dwindle down to a precious few, even in Britain, which a director of Sotheby's described recently as still having "the greatest reservoir of fine art of any country in the world." But anyone, anywhere, may have a couple of acceptable works by an important English watercolorist or a seventeenth-century Dutch oil which, even if not attributable to any significant painter, is nevertheless perfectly salable to many collectors or merely apartment decorators who like that sort of thing. Like string too short to be saved, works of art too insignificant to be recorded and kept track of somehow never seem to disappear forever, and keep turning up in the most improbable places. Over the years, a whole ad hoc system has grown up to channel them ever nearer the center of things, and particularly since the mid-1950s, which saw a vast extension in the whole market for antiques, junk, anything old, anything "amusing," it has become possible to track the course of individual pieces with surprising ease.

To illustrate, let us take two small cases in our own knowledge of very minor art works indeed. One was a small but characteristic and, no doubt for those with a taste for it, charming tinted drawing of a child's head by Sir Thomas Lawrence. We found it first in a very reasonable suburban antique shop in London. It looked right, and it had a respectable history, coming from a sale at a country house then occupied by a descendant of the young sitter, whose identity was noted on the back. As a matter of interest we checked this out and were able to date it and place it exactly in Lawrence's career. It was well framed, and only £8, which seemed very cheap. The only thing that prevented us from buying it was that neither of us actually liked it very much.

It stayed where it was for some months, then finally was sold. The next time we saw it it had moved up slightly in the world—to an "antique arcade" nearer the center of town, priced at £26. A further gap of a month or two saw it in a grander antique arcade, priced at £60. The last we saw of it was in a London saleroom, where it was knocked down to a distinguished West End dealer for £130. An enquiry a fortnight later elicited the information that he had already sold it to an interested collector. We would dearly like to know for how much, and how much the drawing will fetch when it next comes on the market.

The other instance is more dubious. One of us, browsing in the Portobello Road, London's fleamarket, came across a pen drawing, ostensibly by Phil May, which at once rang a bell. Recalling it from May's illustrations to *A Zig Zag Guide to the Kentish Coast,* he hurried home (which was just around the corner), and returned with a copy of the book. On comparison, it was evident that the drawing was copied from the book, being fairly convincing at first glance but feeble in detail. This was pointed out to the stall-holder, who took it in fairly good part, said that anyways ours was just one opinion, and as he wanted only £4 for it and made no explicit claims he saw no harm. Fair enough. A month or so later, though, the same drawing turned up, now for £12, in a West End print-seller's which claims that all its goods are authenticated by experts and guaranteed; it was offered without equivocation as a Phil May original. We went through the history again with the man in charge, and were virtually shown the door for casting doubt on his merchandise and making "damaging allegations."

The next time we saw the drawing it was part of an exhibition of English drawings and watercolors in a very respectable Bond Street gallery. It was equipped with a fictional provenance and priced at £45. Girding ourselves we tried again. The gallery's director, whom we knew personally, was very distressed. He had accepted the information provided by the man he had bought it from. Unfortunately the drawing had already been sold, to an enthusiatic but not very expert collector, but he would get in touch with him at once and explain the position. The aftermath was odd. The collector brushed the gallery's embarrassed explanations aside. He had bought it as a Phil May, he believed it was a Phil May, and any other view was after all only one man's opinion. He carried off his purchase. So the next time this drawing comes on the market it will be well authenticated, with a provenance which by then it will be impossible to prove fictional, exhibition as a Phil May in a reputable West End gallery (with catalogue entry to attest it), and some years spent in another collection which certainly contains many fine and genuine drawings. How much will it then be worth?

These stories are somewhat by the way, except that they do give some idea of just how the minor works we see in the major galleries of London, Paris or New York may reach them. Sometimes the route will be more direct. A hopeful bringing a dark and grimy old painting for evaluation at a metropolitan dealer or auctioneer is highly unlikely to have under his arm a Rembrandt or a Leonardo (though such things have happened). On the other hand he may well have something which a dealer would happily buy for £100 and sell after cleaning, restoration and authentication for £1000. There is hardly any town, however small, which does not have some place willing to buy up the miscellaneous contents of houses. From these, pictures and objets d'art (straining that obliging term to its uttermost) may move on to the local antique shop, and there be found by higher-powered dealers or their agents. Few provincial sales, however unpromising, go entirely unremarked by the trade, and quite often the layman is surprised to find quite lively and obviously professional bidding going on for just one or two items in an otherwise quite routine and uneventful list. Old scrapbooks, so beloved of our great grandparents, sometimes yield small treasures along with a lot of rubbish (the "Phil May" drawing was no doubt not originally a deliberate forgery, but a careful amateur copy later cut loose from its scrapbook context and given quite unintended airs). And there is always too the whole indeterminate areas of the "unfashionable," which may at any time return to fashion, sometimes just by the natural uncharted shifts of public taste, sometimes with more than a little aid from those who have most to gain.

In many respects this last area is the most interesting of those covered by the middle-range dealers with middle-range buyers in mind. It is a phenomenon which has often been observed that when a style or an artist some years out of fashion returns with a bang, as if from nowhere an amazing volume of relevant material seems to flood into the market. There need not necessarily be any sinister explanation for this. One of us, for example, was studying Art Nouveau at a university some eight years before the Art Nouveau craze hit and one could scarcely open a glossy magazine anywhere in Europe or America without being brusquely told that to be in the swim you had to go Art Nouveau. During that time his consistent and exhaustive search for objects to satisfy his craving turned up extraordinarily little; by 1965 every other stall in the Puces or the Portobello Road, every other Second Avenue antique dealer, seemed to be stocked to overflowing with Art Nouveau of some sort, if rarely of any high quality. The obvious conclusion is not that wise people somewhere were hoarding it all until a swing in fashion should make their fortune, but that an almost total lack of demand stimulated no serious attempts to supply, and it was only when the style came back into the news that anyone was inspired to begin a systematic turning out of attics and cellars in the hope of coming up with something salable. As the dealer Jacques Seligmann once remarked, "Nothing is more abundant than the rare"—it is just waiting for the profitable moment to appear.

On the other hand, there is no doubt that the absolutely reliable, predictable swing of fashion over a fifty-to-sixty year span has become so well understood now that at certain levels art has become either fashionable or unobtainable. All the manuals for collectors a few years back used to advise that one should start in a small way, and seek out works by artists fashionable some years ago but now in the doldrums. A great example was made of the Victoriana craze launched for good and all in the mid-1940s. Even a very cursory inspection of auction records showed that the Pre-Raphaelites had toppled from such dizzy heights as £11,000 for a Holman Hunt in 1874, nearly £4000 for a Rossetti in 1903 and £5250 each for three Millais around 1900 to respectively under £300, just over £100 and around £50 for comparable works in the 1930s. Then came the great revival, prices were back into the four-figure category again by the later 1950s and still rising. How wise, the corollary ran, were those who had ignored fashion and bought Victorian in the 1930s. Clearly what the budding collector should now do, with major Pre-Raphaelites already beyond his pocket, was to look for the presently most unfashionable and snap them up for a few pounds each. The men of the 1890s, perhaps—Brangwyn, Condor, Clausen, Nicholson, Rothenstein, to mention only a few, or in an American context Robinson, Twachtman, Brush or Metcalf.

Wise counsel, economically speaking, but easier said than done. A couple of happy chances brought one of us, already independently tuned into the Nineties, a first-rate Clausen landscape of his best period for £8 and, even luckier, a good unfinished Steer oil for £25, both with complete pedigrees. But in the main, search as one might through piles of unwanted paintings, drawings and watercolors, works of this vintage were just not to be found. Where were they? For the most part being hoarded by dealers who, determined not to be caught twice the same way, were indulging in the same sort of foresight as the more instructionally minded of them were urging on amateurs. And needless to say, during the late 1950s and 1960s there has been in England a constant succession of "rediscovery" exhibitions devoted to the Camden Town Group, the Art Nouveau and Decadent artists, the artists of the Nineties poster, the New English Art Club, and to such individuals as happened to have some convenient anniversary, such as Robert Bevan and Frank Brangwyn (centenary 1967). And on each such occasion additional allied works slipped on to the market from wherever they had been hidden meanwhile.

Equally true of more recent painting. It is one thing to remark that, say, the American surrealists of the 1930s, the English Neoromantics of the 1940s, such postwar continental crazes as Buffet and Marini, are now out of fashion. But it is quite another to find examples of their art to be bought at a reasonable price anywhere, however eager one may be to do so, and sometimes odd pieces which come on the market fetch unexpectedly high prices, fashion or no. One day they will come out of hiding, the Baziotes and Bermans, the Craxtons and Mintons, and all the rest. But only when they have proved the old art market adage that what goes down must come up.

Meanwhile, the dealers keep their own counsel, and sell what their new public wants, or can be persuaded it wants. Oddly enough, the very opening-out and diversification of the market has led to a new sort of specialization among dealers. Duveen could afford to specialize simply in the best. Even today, any major gallery anywhere in the world would know exactly how and when to sell any first-rate old master it was clever or lucky enough to get its hands on. But at a lower level hopeless confusion sets in, or will unless some sane pattern of specialization is established. The reasons are not far to seek. With the select band of universally accepted, universally desirable old masters (up to and including the Impressionists) there is a world market, a body of international scholarship, and a vast amount of documentation. Even so, terrible disagreement may arise and terrible mistakes sometimes be made, but at least in general you know where you are with a Raphael or a Monet.

Not so with the lesser masters. To begin with, the markets for them are likely to be limited, at least geographically. To some extent the market has even to be created, certainly to be encouraged. Everybody in the world knows that a Rembrandt is theoretically desirable; a certain number of people, people likely to buy, may need persuading that the same is true of a Laroon or a Julius Caesar Ibbetson. Barbizon painters may be coming back, but how about their Dutch contemporaries? And so on. How exactly dealers may set about encouraging, cajoling, blackmailing, or otherwise maneuvering buyers into the desired position is something we shall go into more fully when considering the techniques of promotion. But for the moment let us concentrate on what such a selling policy does to the dealer's buying habits.

First of all, the dealer must catch his hare. He must pick an artist or school or genre, examine its purely commercial possibilities, both in buying and in selling, and go on from there. Obviously there is little business advantage in his deciding in the abstract that it would be a good thing for some particular artist to be restored to public favor and working enthusiastically toward that end if he does not have and is not able to acquire more than one or two examples of the artist's work. He may, of course, very well be right and be performing a public service by bringing the artist back into the limelight, but he is doing a critic's rather than a dealer's job if there is really nothing in it for him. So, having settled shall we say on Angelica Kauffmann, an easy, approachable painter of pretty, manageable-sized paintings, or Atkinson Grimshaw, a minor but individual Victorian landscapist, he will set about buying their paintings whenever they come up at a conceivable price. He will even pay what has hitherto been considered quite inconceivable prices for them, knowing that anyway a good reputation in the saleroom as a painter whose prices are constantly advancing will certainly not hurt his protégé. He will also not turn his back on the possibility of discoveries. A small eighteenth-century house due for demolition may yield several decorative panels by Kauffmann, or at least very respectable school-of. A country sale or a junk shop might easily be harboring a Grimshaw long after any half-forgotten Millais or Watts has been snapped up.

In the process of buying the dealer may well have to become his own expert. There is no book on Grimshaw at all, and no very helpful study of Angelica Kauffmann for a hundred years or more. There is no internationally respected body of scholarship to turn to in difficulties. In sheer self-defense, the dealer has to learn as he goes. If he becomes an authority, even *the* authority, on his subject, so much the better, though undeniably this is a situation which has occasionally lent itself to abuse, as in the case of the world authority on Sargent back to whom, on investigation, at least thirty-five forged Sargents on the market were traced in 1967. But such lapses happily seem to be quite rare. Few dealer-authorities seek to push their authority further than it reasonably may be pushed, and those who choose to go their own way—such as Jacques Matthey, the Parisian who has carried out a one-man campaign over the years for the acceptance of some one hundred paintings hardly anyone but he believes are by Manet—are generally eccentric idealists who lose more than they gain by their intransigence.

So, let us suppose that the new dealer has equipped himself with a speciality of some sort, and the necessary expertise—or that the established dealer has found himself, by choice, luck or force of circumstance, tending in this direction. Thus placed, he must continue to develop or his business will stagnate. He must constantly replenish his stock, and acquire as far as possible all examples of his specialty that come on to the market, since the uniqueness of the service he is offering is an important part of his business equipment; if he cannot buy them himself he must at least contrive as far as possible to act as agent for others in their purchase. Sometimes a special opportunity may come his way—and many successful specializations have been founded on such a chance. A collector may die, and a cache of

works by some minor figure come on to the market.
When Mrs. A.M.W. Sterling died in 1965 at the age of
ninety-nine, by a happy dispensation her home, Old
Battersea House, and its contents had been safeguarded
as a museum. But had this not been so, what a field-day
a dispersal of her possessions would have made for just
such dealers as we now have in mind! She was sister-in-
law to the great potter William De Morgan, sister of his
painter wife Evelyn De Morgan, and niece of the minor
Pre-Raphaelite Spencer-Stanhope. Her house was (and
is) a perfect reflection of high artistic taste in the
1890s, filled with an unparalleled range of De Morgan
ceramics and innumerable paintings by Evelyn De
Morgan, Spencer-Stanhope, and some more notable
contemporaries, such as Burne-Jones.

This collection is remarkable for its size, but it is
by no means unique; there must be hundreds of smaller
reflections of it up and down the country, if the dealer
knows where to look. Such a cache might set up a specialist in stock for many years to come. So might a fruit-
ful contact with the family of a deceased artist. There
are always artists to be found, such as Robert Bevan, by
general consent the most striking and individual of the
Camden Town Group, who had some private means
and did not need to sell their paintings or were too shy,
retiring, advanced or unworldly to do so. In Bevan's
case this has meant that most of his works, and nearly
all of his major paintings, remain in the possession of
his family. If they showed less knowledgeable family
pride or a more mercenary spirit, some dealer or they
themselves might now be handsomely cashing in, after

two well-publicized retrospective exhibitions and the appearance of a lavishly illustrated book devoted to the artist. They have not done so, but others are less scrupulous—or more practical, depending upon which way you look at it.

Once supplied, and his specialty launched, the dealer must safeguard his image. Even if the artists he sponsors appreciate vastly in value and prestige—as, say, Stubbs did at the end of the 1940s—it is highly unlikely that he can live on them alone. Apart from anything else, a market can easily be swamped, and while he cannot afford to have too few examples to sell, he cannot either afford to appear to have too many. But in extending beyond his major specialization, it is good if he does not diversify too far. It is one of the most important assets a dealer can have—especially at this middle level where many of his customers are not experts, do not have unlimited money to spend, and are likely to be nervous or cautious—to be known as just the place where a particular taste in art is fairly sure to be satisfied. If his pet artist is an eighteenth-century landscapist, an eighteenth-century constellation would seem a good idea. A sporting artist or two, a constant supply of topographical watercolors and drawings, lesser works by the more famous masters, and an occasional major work when and if he can get it. This way he will acquire regular clients, put them at their ease, persuade them to rely on him, and to some extent take color from their taste. If a client had an insatiable desire for the crags and cattle of James Ward, for example, what better provocation could there be for an intensive search for them and the deliberate building up of a reputation as the man most likely in all London to find them?

It is by such means that most of the middle-range dealers build and maintain their clientele. Not necessarily only dealers in the fine arts. Even more, perhaps, does it help to specialize intensively in eighteenth-century cottage furniture, Meissen china, antique glass, Art Nouveau silver, inlaid armor or any of the thousand-and-one things people decide at some time they are going to collect. This sort of dealing is a way of escape for the lofty general dealer from the present impasse brought about by the sheer famine in great pieces to sell, because there is no limit to the possibilities of specialization, even within one business (a dealer may have at least as many specialties as he has clients), and it is to some extent within the dealer's power to create and foster new specialties whenever he chooses. How he may go about this is a subject we shall return to. But before we do we must look at the lower reaches of the art market, the role of the middlemen, and the various underworlds which lie hidden beneath the respectable upper crust.

INTO THE FLEA MARKET

There was a time, and not so long ago either, when dealers were paid above all for the inconvenience and discomfort, even at times the danger to life and limb, they saved the collector. Up to the end of the nineteenth-century, changes of fashion were more extreme and complete than ever they are now. The average cultivated man was sublimely confident that by the mere passage of time, the ineluctible march of progress, he was bound to be that much wiser, more enlightened, more *right,* than his father or his grandfather. Therefore he naturally did not hesitate to throw out and destroy anything that his grandfather had liked and he did not. A partial exception might be made for the truly ancient, because that was history, and then there were a few great, unassailable masters from the past whom everyone recognized, like Raphael. But in general museums were useful mainly so that we might learn from the mistakes of the past, unravel again the few lost secrets of things which earlier men had known how to do better than we did (how *did* they produce that wonderful intense blue in medieval stained glass?), and observe with charitable gratification the slow stumbling steps by which the past had contrived to make its uncertain way into the present.

In the circumstances, it was only to be expected that however high a work of art had once stood in the favor of connoisseurs, once it fell out of favor it would drop to the lowest and most despised condition. To pick it up again and replace it on its pedestal was a job to try the resources of the most intrepid. One can only wonder at the daring, recorded in her voluminous diary, of that remarkable personage Lady Charlotte Schreiber as she roamed Europe, often disguised in old clothes, hesitating to plunge into no slum, however unappetizing, in search of her beloved antique porcelain. The early exploits of the notorious Thomas J. Wise and his friends, picking over shady and possibly verminous barrows of old paper, sometimes mixed with rags and bones, in search of unrecorded Defoe pamphlets or Elizabethan play quartos which to others were still so much waste, are hardly less impressive. But in the main collectors preferred to pay others to do the dirty work for them. The dealer and his agents had to search, sift, find, clean and present. The collector could then select in comfort, and pay for the privilege.

But things could not long continue so. The unhalting rise of the middle classes, with, as the century ended, the working classes hot on their tail, the spread of education toward universal literacy, and the vast amount of popular-educational propaganda in favor of culture and the arts for all were putting the idea of collecting, if only on the most modest scale, into the minds of thousands who a generation or two before would have had hardly a nonutilitarian possession to their name, except, perhaps, a family Bible. These newly interested classes did not have unlimited money. Nor did they have the tradition of the self-consciously civilized client-dealer relationship, let alone the notion of aristocratic patronage which lay still deeper in the established collector's psyche. For them art was a commodity. It was also something you went out and bought for yourself, if only on the sound principle that you got it cheaper if you cut out the middleman.

These are wild overgeneralizations, needless to say. But they contain enough truth to explain some of the shifts in the dealer-client relationship during the twentieth century, especially where it concerns the average small collector rather than the millionaire exception. In particular, the effect of this shift in buying habits has resulted in the laying open to the public at large of what was once almost exclusively the preserve of the trade: the whole system of narrow and sometimes unsavory channels by which one man's junk gradually ascends to the position of another man's dearly paid-for art. The acquaintance of the layman with all this may be said to have started, to all intents and purposes, in the 1890s, when stolidly respectable poets felt it their duty to wait at stage doors, frequent music halls and even drink absinthe because that was the proper decadent thing to do and *nostalgie de la boue* was *de rigueur*. The fleamarkets of the time feature, somewhat luridly, in literature of the day, generally in the guise of mysterious dens in Chinatown where the philosopher's stone might turn up among the leavings of the ages in a dusty shop window while unnamable delights were offered in some sinister recess behind beaded curtains.

Colorful, but not very likely, and certainly not very tempting for the timid. But with the advance of the twentieth century, slums got less slummy and better lit, the cloak of mystery in which the other half lived was gradually lifted, and by the 1920s it was already smart, if still a trifle daring, to venture out slumming in lively parties and pick up some amusing junk at the Puces or in "Petticoat Lane" (which the natives always stubbornly persisted in calling Middlesex Street). But the amusing excursion into Bohemia was one thing, and regular combing of the street markets and junkstalls for treasures quite another. Out of town the enthusiast would probably "do the antique shops" if he found himself somewhere suitably equipped for his attentions. But this, after all, was just the humbler provincial equivalent of a visit to a metropolitan dealer's; it was still, as a spare-time occupation, eminently nice.

It was World War II and its aftermath which really changed all that. Not at once. In France the top and the bottom of the market have always been closer together— even physically at the Hôtel Drouot, where the top floor is reserved for the more important works (not on the whole the most important, which go instead to the Palais Galliera), while down below all sorts of rubbish which no other international saleroom would let through its doors is piled in miscellaneous heaps to be combed through. The hardships of the Occupation made many

Parisians who had previously not been conscious of the advantages of a flea market painfully aware of them, and from this grim introduction the Puces itself, on the margins of Paris in "the zone" just near the Porte de Clignancourt, and some more refined and accessible relatives such as the Village Suisse, have gone from strength to strength. In London the process was more gradual. No one seems quite sure when the agglomeration of small, unimpressive antique shops and stalls began in the Portobello Road, near Notting Hill Gate. Even in the mid-1950s it was still in reasonable bounds, the vendors as a rule old and practical, some of them full-time dealers dealing mainly with the trade, others weekend semiprofessionals who found a little spare-time antique dealing a healthy open-air hobby. Bargains were still to be found, provided you did not expect anything too spectacular—you were simply going to a trade clearing-house to get at trade price what otherwise you might later buy, in better shape and better guaranteed to be sure, at an appreciably higher price in the West End. The really adventurous might venture even further afield, to Bermondsey market on a Friday; this was a stage farther down the line, and the place where many of the things sold in the Portobello Road on Saturday were bought more cheaply the day before. Most of the merchandise at Bermondsey was straight junk, off the junk merchant's cart, and beyond that one could hardly go, unless to provincial junk merchants where if you found anything desirable—if—the price might possibly be lower still.

But antique dealing at this humble level was not to

remain for long undisturbed. Already a certain ineffec-
tual knowingness was creeping in. Ignorance is not always productive of bliss for the knowledgeable buyer:
the ignorant stall-holder is as likely to be asking you £5
for something you know is worth 50s. as he is for something you know is worth £50. More likely, since his stock
contains far more in the 50s. than the £50 class. But
once this starts, the trade becomes less interested and
the field is left open for the suckers. That is precisely
what began to happen in the late 1950s, and the whole
thing mushroomed fantastically in the 1960s.

To bring about any such change in the business
world two things are necessary: a body of sellers and a
body of buyers. It is seldom difficult to work out why
the sellers want to sell, but to work out why the buyers
want to buy is much more problematical. Why did all
these small-time collectors—for this area of the art market is essentially small-time—take it into their heads to
start buying what they did at the particular moment
they did? One answer is that during the post war
austerity period it became smart and amusing—as well
as necessary—to make do, to improvise from the previous generation's throw-outs. True, but why then the
time lag? Again, the affluent society of the 1960s has
been seen as a reason, people had money to spend,
money to burn just for fun, and chose to spend it this
way; or alternatively, people wanted to feel as though
they had money to burn without actually having
enough to do the job properly, so they devised this way
of spending with seeming extravagance and at the same
time surrounding themselves with nostalgic objects

which recalled a misty but settled and safe-seeming past.

The latter variation at least brings us nearer a sort of explanation if we want to know why this way rather than any other. But it is not enough by itself. It has been noted that, on the very top level of art dealing and collecting, the trend since the war has been constantly upward, whatever the setbacks in the rest of the international economy. This is principally because investors have finally tumbled to the fact that, despite all the changes in fashion, there are some works of art which never lose their value, or not permanently. A really good Old Master or Impressionist is as near a foolproof investment as you can get, and may offer fantastic percentage returns: Richard H. Rush, an American collector, investment banker and author of the book *Art as an Investment,* has obligingly worked out for us that if we take prices in 1930 as a base (a good low year to start, at the worst of the American Depression) and examine the sale records of Van Gogh, Gauguin and Cézanne in the next thirty years we shall find that they appreciated overall 177 percent by 1950, 566 percent by 1955 and, staggeringly, by 4,833 percent in 1960. Of course there are all sorts of arguments against the meaningfulness of such figures, qualifications to be introduced (it still depends which Van Gogh, Gauguin or Cézanne you are concerned with), and doubts to be raised on the reliability of any possible prognosis derived from them. But even given all that, the rise thus charted is pretty impressive, and many people in many places have got the message.

But not only—and here is the point—the big boys

who are actually in the possible running for Van Goghs, Gauguins and Cézannes. There is a sort of jungle drum which operates, muffled but persistent, through the pages of the popular press, and thousands who have never heard of Mr. Rush and his statistics have somehow got hold of the idea that art is not only a good, respectable, even prestigious thing to buy and have around them, but also that it is almost certain to be a good investment, holding or increasing its value while everything else one has is worth less and less every day. Optimistic and unrealistic certainly, especially if applied to the sort of thing the flea markets normally purvey, where any picture "signed," no matter by whom, is likely to cost more than any which is not. But the tangle of motives, good, bad and indifferent, which sends the new collector out rummaging, driven by who knows what combination of magpie acquisitiveness, avarice, snobbism, the desire for self-expression, love of bargaining, even love of art, has helped to create a bonanza for the smaller dealer who was once little more than the anonymous supplier of the big.

Once something like this has started, everything conspires to build it up. The same period has seen a sudden flowering of color supplements to formerly staid and monochromatic newspapers, of new glossy magazines for young men and women defiantly flaunting their neck-or-nothing with-itness. Instant fashion is their business; it is a basic necessity for them to keep their readers ever ready to follow something new, ever insecure lest an even newer fad sneak in and catch them unprepared. It may be Art Nouveau or jazz-modern, old clothes for smart wearing or enamel tableware (genuine Edwardian workmen's or something obligingly manufactured new to fill the want), cottage furniture painted with Union Jacks or Battle of Britain pinups. The turnover is too rapid for the grander dealers to supply those requirements even if they felt it would pay them to do so. But for the small easily maneuverable dealer, with perhaps no more overhead than the hire of a stall in an "antique arcade" for one day a week (at a pound or two upwards), this constant flurry of excitement is ideal.

Even so, success cannot be absolutely guaranteed. Some are really expert, and prosper from selling Art Nouveau costume jewelry, Nazi regalia, Victorian plate or whatever. Some are just lucky, for a while at least. Some just enjoy the day out, the bustle, the new faces, the tinsel glamor, and are content if the day's business covers their costs. Many, drawn by the supposed Bohemian smartness of the business, lose money, get bored or disillusioned, and vanish as suddenly as they came. But for the moment there is always someone else to take over the empty stall at number 13 with a brave display of silver-headed canes or slightly used Victorian tea cosies.

For the time being the expansion of this sub-trade in "antiques" (including what our parents would have called curios or just plain junk) seems limitless. In the West End itself as well as in arty suburbs like Chelsea, Kensington and Islington the rundown shop of today may always turn out to be the "antique arcade" or—lovely term—the "antique supermarket" of tomorrow.

Hope springs eternal, and their landlords and tenants are nothing if not hopeful. But one wonders. Rising prices, the sheer physical expansion of the market and the consequent spreading of the really good stuff thinner and thinner over a wider and wider area has tended to frighten off the big dealers who were originally these little dealers' main *raison d'être*. By hitching himself instead directly to the fantasies of the private buyer the small dealer may have done better for himself today, but he has deprived himself of something which could provide an invaluable buffer in times of misfortune. And those hard times, in Britain at any rate, may be just around the corner.

For the preponderance of what the stall-holders and other semiprofessionals have to offer is not really easy to mistake for art by even the simplest visitor. A lot of it may be fun, but people are prepared at the best of times to pay only a limited amount for fun which is clearly nothing more. Art may be an investment, but fun of this sort is a dispensable luxury. Interestingly enough, the recent economic recession in Britain has not affected the sales of real art at all—indeed the rising curve in sales and prices has been consistently maintained. But go out into the suburbs or the provincial towns and see which shops have closed in the last year or so. Nearly always it is the small dealer in what are hopefully if not very accurately described as antiques. The arcades still spread, the markets become supermarkets. But if anywhere the days of the art boom are numbered, they surely will be the first to feel the blow.

MIDDLEMAN TAKES ALL

In the last three chapters we have been concerned specifically with dealers. But a shadow has fallen from time to time across the pages: that of the auctioneer. And now it is time to look in more detail at the substance beyond the shadow. For if there is one thing which is quite unarguable about the art business—in Britain and America at least—in the last twenty-five years or so, it is the quite remarkable extent to which the major auction houses have taken over the work formerly performed by dealers. In the past it was normally supposed by dealers, and by most of their clientele, that the auction houses were merely intermediaries, convenient channels through which works of art might be brought up from whatever depths they were hiding in and handed on to dealers, ready for classification and proper, gentlemanly sale. You would hardly more dream of going to an auction room to buy for yourself than you would spy out what small East End workshop actually made the suits for your smart West End tailor and then order them directly from there instead. Of course the cleverer (or meaner) collectors were too astute to fall for this line of reasoning, but in general even they were decent enough to use a dealer as agent to secure what they wanted in the saleroom. And either way the auctioneers occupied a position in the trade which was, by implication at least, only a step or two above the junk man.

Not any more. Somehow the tables have been turned so that instead of the auctioneer being regarded as the menial but convenient middleman between the root source of any marketable work of art and the one fitted by nature and training to market it, he has become in the eyes of the world the true marketer and the dealer often no more than a sometimes convenient, often unnecessary middleman between him and the art buyer. More and more sales are made directly to private buyers in the salerooms of Sotheby's, Christie's, Parke-Bernet, the Hôtel Drouot or the Palais Galliera, without any intervention by dealers at all. And when a public institution does buy from a dealer, the cry is nearly always raised of why, if they knew they wanted the piece in question, did they not have the prescience to bid for it instead of giving the dealer his profit on a platter?

There are some good answers to this sort of question, but seldom quite good enough. There can be little doubt that, except in the special field of contemporary art by living artists, the auction rooms have taken over permanently from the dealers when it comes to the really big stuff. Their strength has certain limitations attached, and those we shall come to shortly. But first let us examine the whole phenomenon of the auction house, its organization, its means of functioning, and the very valuable things it can do for both those who sell and those who buy.

First, some basic distinctions. Broadly, a dealer is someone who sells his own property at a price he fixes. True, the price may be negotiable, within limits, but finally he determines what these limits are. Equally, he may sometimes sell on commission for someone else, but this is not usually his central concern. In either case, it is his judgment of what someone, somewhere, may be willing to pay for any specific work, and his estimate of how long he may have to wait to find the buyer who will pay the price, how long he can afford to wait, pitted against the realities of the market situation and the individual determination of the individual buyer. The auctioneer has the advantages, and sometimes the disadvantages, of a far freer, more fluid set-up. He does not as a rule own what he sells, but merely sells it on commission. He does not fix a price, though he may advise the owner in setting a reserve, the minimum price under which an article may not be sold. Beyond that, the potential buyers fix the price themselves, by competing with each other. All sorts of imponderables enter into this, not least the immediacy of the operation. Nobody waits, nobody thinks over, there is little room for baiting, tempting, selling as the dealer understands it. Sometimes the price which results is far higher than any dealer would dare ask; often it is appreciably lower than what a dealer might eventually hope to get. That is a chance the seller takes, and it is a gamble which seems at least to guarantee some sort of "fair" price, openly arrived at, while, he may reflect, selling to a dealer, however reputable, is a gamble of another sort, in which he, as the nonexpert, is quite likely to come off a trifle the worse.

Moreover, an auctioneer has the advantage over a dealer in flexibility as to the scale of his operations. A dealer can handle a single work or a small group, provided they fit in with his preoccupations and possible clientele. But a large collection is a problem for him, and even among single works of undisputed quality he is likely to pick and choose. The auctioneer, on the other hand, will take on anything, from the largest collection to the single work, and will impose few conditions except perhaps to eliminate things he considers unsalable at any price.

For their services auctioneers charge a percentage of the total price reached. What this percentage is varies from place to place. In France the rate is fixed on a sliding scale, ranging from 16 percent on sales up to 6000 NF in value, through 11.5 percent for sales of from 6000 to 20,000 NF down to 10 percent on sales above 20,000 NF. These charges, which include various registration fees, taxes, fees to the commissaire-priseur (the ministerial official in charge of the whole transaction) and various other expenses, are borne by the *purchaser,* not the seller, who is responsible only for the appraising expert's expenses (more of him in a moment), 5 percent for the sales expenses, 5 percent for the "droit de suite" (a special charge which reverts, when applicable, to the original artist of the work in question) and the cost of catalogues, publicity, etc. In the sale of modern paintings the costs are higher: ranging from 21 to 27 percent of the price divided between seller and buyer. All this tends to make the business of buying, if not of selling, considerably more expensive in France than elsewhere, though the French claim that their system has unique advantages to offer in exchange, particularly in the guarantees provided for the buyer as to the exact nature of what he is buying.

These are provided by a special panel of experts employed directly by the commissaire-priseur, who as a ministerial official has no ax to grind, to examine and authenticate any work of art which comes up for auction and frame accordingly the terms in which it shall be catalogued. The roster of experts is drawn up by the governing body of the Hôtel Drouot, and admits of no variation by the commissaire-priseur: it is not published, though it is possible to know who authenticated any given article. The expert is consulted by the commissaire-priseur at the charge and on the written instructions of the seller; a piece may be offered for sale without authentication, but few of any importance are, since the absence of official authentication is drawn to the notice of the possible purchaser and the implication is obvious. Legal responsibility for the terms of the catalogue entries and their accuracy rests jointly with the commissaire-priseur and the expert.

The major British and American salerooms are less complicated in their procedure. At Sotheby's the buyer pays nothing more than the price he has bid; the seller pays a 12.5 percent commission on sales of pictures at less than £100 and 10 percent on sales above, plus insurance costs and, where applicable, the cost of reproduction in the catalogue. In principal there has traditionally been nothing to prevent a seller from putting up anything for sale and calling it just what he likes; caveat emptor (let the buyer beware) has been the rule. But in practice Sotheby's catalogues have been full of scholarship and sound sense for many years, provided the buyer has been sufficiently informed to learn the "code" in which the catalogues are written.

This "code", which has applied at Christie's also, may be briefly summed up thus: the more detail and elaboration is given to the name of the artist, the more faith the auctioneers have in the genuineness of the work. "Sir Peter Lely" would imply that the work was as certainly as possible his own work. "P. Lely" would suggest a studio work or at least some serious doubt about how much of it was from his hand. "Lely" would imply no more than "school of" or "copy of"; it could conceivably mean "pretty certainly a forgery of". This code, which properly mastered amounts to a free expert's opinion on the work offered, has been the subject of lively debate in the art world of late. Dealers on the whole have been for it, since it all adds to the mystery of the saleroom and helps keep the layman out. Their attitude is usually that a private buyer who gets his fingers burned because he does not understand the conventions has only himself to blame—though unless he is clearly given to understand that there are conventions to be learned in the first place it is hard to see how.

On the other hand Sotheby's and Christie's have

come to see that it is in their own interest to make themselves as readily approachable for the man in the street as possible. Rows like that which blew up early in 1967 when an American businessman tried to file charges against Christie's for selling him three years previously a fake Renoir pastel catalogued as "Pierre August Renoir" (he knew of the code, but did not know it applied only to Old Masters) help nobody, and do a lot of harm. Sotheby's has for some years made the concession of allowing return within twenty-one days of purchase in cases where the authenticity of a work is seriously challenged, and the Misrepresentation Act which came into effect in April 1967, governing all sales descriptions, further strengthens the buyer's position by depriving of all legal force the auctioneer's disclaimer of responsibility for the accuracy of his catalogue descriptions and making him personally liable to repay and pay damages when the sale has been made on behalf of an anonymous client. As a result of this legislation both Sotheby's and Christie's now print a "key" to their description-code in the front of all catalogues.

Christie's charges and conditions of sale are much the same as Sotheby's. Both have been accused from time to time by jealous rivals of making special arrangments to lower or waive altogether their commission in order to entice a particularly desirable collection their way. This would no doubt be worthwhile occasionally, if only because the enormous publicity which any major sale producing record prices receives in the world's press is money in the bank as far as the auctioneer is concerned—success breeds success, and where one owner has made a lot of money in a blaze of publicity others will be tempted to follow suit. Whether it has happened is another matter. Maybe, particularly in the 1950s, when the London houses were throwing a lot of energy into fighting off the challenge of Parke-Bernet, but if so they are not saying and since Sotheby's took over Parke-Bernet in 1963 it would seem to have become quite unnecessary. Until the Hôtel Drouot changes its regulations considerably, London does not have any too serious competition to fear from that quarter.

Parke-Bernet is the latest on the scene of the major auction houses, though not the most recent to embark on general art-selling; incredible as it seems, considering its fantastic rise in the world, Sotheby's did not branch out seriously from book sales until 1957, with the record-breaking Weinberg sale of Impressionists and Post-Impressionists. For much of its checkered career, Parke-Bernet prided itself on being rather different in its mode of operation from its European rivals. No standard rate was ever advertised for Parke-Bernet's services, since the percentage was regarded as widely variable and subject to negotiation. It might, they volunteered, be as low as 12 percent on some really large and important collection, the collective price of which could run into seven figures. It could, their rivals replied, be as high as 23½ percent. Parke-Bernet shrugged these suggestions aside—what did it matter how high the percentage was (within reason) if the prices they were able to get were sufficiently far above anyone else's? There, indeed, was the rub. The gallery might well have got some of the highest prices in the world, such as the

$2,300,000 it got from the Metropolitan for Rembrandt's "Aristotle" in 1962. But in all probability such a picture would bring a similar amount whoever sold it, and it did not follow that in general Parke-Bernet had any sufficient advantage over its competitors to justify such a high-handed approach.

In any case, all this changed with the takeover of the galleries by Sotheby's. The full story of how this surprising rapprochement of deadly rivals came about has not been told, and probably will not be told for many years. But its effects, even in the brief time since it happened, are evident. The curious ramshackledom, even amateurishness, which obtained at Parke-Bernet before has been eliminated. Leslie Hyams, former president of the galleries, might have originated, as he claimed, the elaborately detailed catalogues which soon became standard in London and Paris, but they often contained more to impress the layman than to inform the expert, and their standard of scholarship was decidedly variable. Sotheby's has changed all that, and brought modern business order into the picturesque confusion the galleries had developed. It also stopped all the nonsense about no standard charges: Parke-Bernet now states flatly that its charges to the seller are between 10 and 20 percent, depending on the selling price of the object and the incidental expenses of publicity etc., while the buyer must pay a 5 percent local sales tax unless he is a dealer buying only to resell.

The real battle of the three giants, Sotheby's, Christie's and Parke-Bernet, for supremacy (the Hôtel Drouot has long been safely in fourth place) was engaged in earnest only from the middle 1950s. Before that, Christie's held virtually unchallenged the first place among international salerooms, both in the volume of important art merchandise to pass through and in the amount of money realized. Its progression had been steady and continuous from the first small beginning in 1766. The first great advantage to come its way was the French Revolution, which brought about a speedy transfer of the major art sales from France to London, along with fleeing aristocrats and what possessions they could snatch from the holocaust. Unfortunately the European upheaval that followed shortly afterward, with the rise of Napoleon, played havoc with the art market everywhere, and picture prices remained low until a gradual recovery started in the 1850s. At this time important pictures came on the market fairly infrequently and were hard to sell at any reasonable price. The complex and gloomy history of the famous Orleans collection and all the ill-fated attempts to sell its treasures, singly or *en bloc,* between 1792 and 1800, shows how things stood at the beginning of the period, while the wonders of the Wallace Collection, and the comparative ease with which Lord Hertford acquired them, often at surprisingly low prices, shows how little things had revived even toward the end. The real money which was being spent on art went mainly on contemporary art bought or commissioned from living painters, and of course almost none of that passed through the auctioneer's hands. So Christie's sold jewelry, furniture and other objets d'art, and waited for the tide to turn in favor of the fine arts. By the 1870s it had decisively done so. The international banking families like the Rothschilds were in a buying mood, the vast expanding American market was on the horizon, and a golden age had set in for Christie's which lasted until the First World War.

In the interwar years Christie's began noticeably to lose ground. Partly it was the result of an understandable degree of complacency born of nearly fifty years at the head of the trade. Partly it was a result of the very efficiency with which the house had come to manage its affairs, which once established resisted any marked change or modification in its clockwork functioning. And partly it came from an aging management with aging, conservative tastes. There were still big sales to be negotiated, of reliable old masters, but the Impressionists and Post-Impressionists were frowned on (the first Picasso was sold at Christie's in 1937, when it brought £157. 10s.) and any new departure in what was sold or how it should be sold was deeply distrusted. Christie's was set in its ways, and the Depression in 1929, which instantly cut off from them most of their most reliable market was a crushing blow. Again, as in the early nineteenth century, the main weight of the firm's business shifted from painting to objets d'art, jewelry and such. That, of course, is not nothing. Some lively newcomers to the management have introduced new notions, with-it sales devoted to Art Nouveau or whatever happens to be the fad of the moment, and the agglomeration of sales of smaller items can be astonishing: in 1965, for instance, Christie's established a European record for take in a single day's sales with no less than £1,186,279. But even so, the leadership has appreciably passed elsewhere. In the 1965-66 season Parke-Bernet for the first time passed Christie's in turnover, taking £8,400,000 as against Christie's £7,241,636 and Sotheby's £13,026,720. Christie's surged forward to regain second place in 1966-7, but barring any sudden and unforeseeable changes, it seems likely now to have a constant struggle on its hands to avoid frequent relegation to third position beneath Parke-Bernet.

Christie's decline has been partly a matter of circumstance, partly one of miscalculation. Supremacy in the auction field is a battle it lost some time before anyone else decisively won it. Certainly it was not Parke-Bernet alone which wrested the crown from them. It would be remarkable if it had, considering the vicissitudes that the institution has gone through since its foundation (as the American Art Association) in 1885. Its originator was one Thomas E. Kirby, no art expert but by general consent a great auctioneer. For most of the expertise he depended on his staff, which acquired through the years the auctioneer appraiser Hiram H. Parke, the auctioneer/businessman Otto Bernet, the authority on rare books Arthur Swann, and an enthusiastic and studious cataloguer, Leslie Hyams. In the 1920s the galleries were bought from Kirby by a businessman/collector, Cortland Field Bishop; the staff went with the deal. Bishop wanted his firm to rival Christie's, and with that end in view bought out and incorporated its chief New York rivals, the Anderson Galleries, to form the American Art Association-Anderson Galleries, the undoubted leader among American salerooms.

Then in 1935 Bishop died. What happened afterwards is half farce, half cheap gangster movie. The firm,
which was at that time handling about $10,000,000
worth of business a year, passed into the hands of Bishop's widow and her adviser-confidante, Edith Nixon,
who had formerly been Bishop's private secretary. Both
women seemed strangely under the influence of a protégé
of Bishop's, an ex-janitor and self-made businessman
called Milton Logan. Logan already had some say in the
business organization of the firm, and wanted more. In
1937 he joined forces with an insurance salesman, John
T. Geery, who had framed all the galleries' policies, and
offered the widow $175,000 for the business, lock, stock
and barrel. She accepted without question or consulta-
tion. The figure was ludicrously low, but even so Geery
did not have the money: he agreed to put up $75,000 in
cash and $100,000 in promisory notes; of the $75,000 he
in fact raised $10,000 on his own and "borrowed" the
other $65,000 from the business. Before the deal was
concluded the sorely tried staff, headed by Parke,
Bernet, Swann and Hyams, walked out en masse, and
set up their own rival firm on credit and their own
talents.

Left without expert guidance and run by men determined to get every penny out of the business while
they could, even by downright fraud, the American Art
Association-Anderson Galleries went from bad to worse,
until in eighteen months they were bankrupt and the
records and goodwill could be picked up by the former
employees for $12,500. Meanwhile, however, Geery,
pushed to desperate measures, had the idea of insuring

his partner's life and then murdering him to recoup. He bungled the job completely, and when he heard that his intended victim was still alive and had reported the crime, went quietly off and shot himself. As the survivor, Logan, came up on trial for fraud, the new company, Parke-Bernet Inc., moved back into its old home and set about rebuilding the business.

In this new phase of its career, Leslie Hyams was the guiding light. His great contribution was the lavish and detailed catalogues prepared for every sale, one of a number of moves intended to bring in and reassure the moderate-income public, the private buyer as well as the high-powered dealer. In this Parke-Bernet was setting a trend which Sotheby's was to seize on and develop in the 1950s; the success of Parke-Bernet in its new incarnation was more than anything a triumph of public relations, and here again Sotheby's was not slow to learn. Parke-Bernet gradually built up a large clientèle in America, including a remarkable number who bought from long distances mainly on the strength of the catalogues, and also attracted an increasing number of buyers from Europe, who often found the average level of prices lower in New York than at home (despite Parke-Bernet's seller-orientated claims to the contrary). Britain at first seemed fated to be left out of this particular reversal of the east-west flow of art works, since the postwar controls of dollar spending were stringent, but in 1954 the Chancellor obligingly relaxed them where works of art were concerned, and since then until the latest series of currency restrictions British dealers have been able to compete freely even in the United

States, though by that time the bargain days at Parke-Bernet were numbered.

As a result of all this activity, Parke-Bernet began at last to do what Bishop had hoped for its forerunner: become a serious threat to the status quo by winning a significant proportion of the big sales, and many not so big, from Paris and London. Christie's should have been worried, and no doubt it would have been if meanwhile a much graver threat had not arisen on its own doorstep. This was Sotheby's of Bond Street. Of course, Sotheby's had been around a long time, nobody was quite sure how long. It is perhaps significant of one of the reasons for Sotheby's tremendous success as a modern business that nobody there seems to know or care very much about ancient history—it has no archives and few formal records beyond the files of catalogues. The traditional date for the founding of the firm as auctioneers by the Covent Garden bookseller Samuel Brown was 1744, but recent research has pushed it back at least as far as 1733. But true to its origin it dealt almost entirely in books and related materials (maps, some prints, literary relics) for the first two centuries of its existence. A few miscellaneous sales, including fine art, began to appear around 1914, but they were generally fairly modest, and the chief glory and fame of Sotheby's remained its book sales, the greatest in the world.

Until, that is, Peter Wilson took over. Wilson joined the firm in the 1930s, after a sketchy preparation at Eton, Oxford, and on the staff of *Connoisseur* magazine; he began as an auctioneer in 1938, after buying into the partnership, and has been the firm's chief

auctioneer of paintings ever since. In 1958 he was
elected chairman of the company, which today has
twenty partners, each of whom has bought his way in
and runs a particular department—jewelry, rare books,
china and such new additions as veteran cars, ballet
relics, Art Nouveau and musical instruments.

The turnover in paintings, though healthy, was
still comparatively modest in 1938, and remained so for
some years. But changes were coming. The turning point
was signaled, oddly enough, not in London or New York
but in Paris, with the sale of Gabriel Cognacq's collection
of Impressionists and Post-Impressionists at the Galerie
Charpentier (predecessor of the Palais Galliera as the
venue for the most important Paris sales) in May 1952.
The prices there achieved by Cézanne in particular, and to
a lesser extent by Renoir, Van Gogh, Manet and Degas,
created a new standard and marked the beginning of a tremendous boom in the saleroom reputation of the Impressionists and Post-Impressionists, with the whole flock of
originators of modern art in their train. Two years later
the sale of the Rees-Jeffreys collection at Sotheby's
showed the same movement beginning in London, with
high prices for a Matisse, a Soutine, and a minor Picasso. In New York the same year the Bradley-Campbell
sale carried the glad tidings to America, and further
stages in the moderns' triumphant progress were marked
by the sales of William Weinberg's collection (record-
breaking prices for works by Van Gogh, Renoir, Monet
and Seurat) at Sotheby's in 1957, Georges Lurcy's collection (ditto for Renoir, Gauguin, Toulouse-Lautrec,
Pissarro and others) at Parke-Bernet in 1957, and

Jakob Goldschmidt's collection at Sotheby's in 1958, which brought in £220,000 for a Cézanne, £132,000 for a Van Gogh, £113,000 for a Manet, and so on, a total of £781,000 for seven Impressionist and Post-Impressionist paintings sold in a bare twenty minutes.

None of these sales, you note, took place at Christie's. Incredible as it seems that selling Impressionists, and at high prices too, could have seemed daring and advanced in the late 1950s, that was still the case. Sotheby's jumped in then where Christie's hesitated, and took over the lead in the world art market that it has maintained to this day. And seem likely to maintain for some time to come, on present showing. Every year something new to sell, and every year some new way of selling it. Veteran cars, perhaps, with a stand at the Earl's Court Motor Show. Or ballet costumes and relics, with a theatrical gala preview. A famous author's picture collection, with a glossy book from his pen to accompany it. The old dealer's jibe that the auctioneer may raise money on goods, in a workmanlike sort of way, but he cannot present his merchandise, he does not know truly how to *sell,* has long become archaic. In this high-powered modern world it is the auctioneers who have entirely mastered the art of selling, the knowing management of publicity, the cunning creation of precisely the right context in which any particular piece will appear to best effect. And none manage it all so well as Sotheby's. The absorption of Parke-Bernet is only the latest in a series of coups which, in hardly more than a decade, have built the firm into the most fabulously prosperous enterprise in the whole art world. No doubt the inevitable cycle of stagnation and decay will affect it, as it does any business sooner or later. But as yet there seems to be not even the tiniest cloud on its glowing horizon.

THE UNDERWORLD
OF ART

Our principal concern in the last few chapters has
been with the supply of "secondhand" art, that is, art
which has already, in some cases hundreds or thousands
of years ago, passed out of the hands of its first maker
and its first owner, and has become instead an item in a
collection. This is not the only sort of art dealing, of
course. We have been looking just at those who buy and
sell under the prickly patronage of St. Joseph Duveen,
and have left out of our calculations those whose dealings are, we may hope, watched over by the more indul-
gent eye of St. Paul Durand-Ruel. These latter, with
their own particular advantages and problems, we must
turn to soon, but before we do there is one aspect of the
first type of dealing which calls imperatively for treatment. And that, needless to say, is the shady side.

The very size and scope of the market at present,

its almost limitless ability to absorb desirable new material, inevitably leads to the development of a thriving underworld. It takes all sorts to make an underworld, the hard-headed and the neurotic, the practical and the wildly impractical, big crooks and small crooks, businessmen and nuts with a chip on their shoulder. And even the shady side is not uniformly dark, there are infinite gradations from the very palest shade of gray to unrelieved black. And hardly anyone is entirely in the shade or entirely out of it. It is all a matter of interpretation and degree. Take the little matter of authentication. When there is no absolutely reliable external documentary proof, the only thing to do is to call in the expert. Experts may differ—they usually do—and it is only human nature to incline, ever so slightly, toward the verdict one would most like to be true. Is that dishonesty? Well, if it is, there can be few of the most eminent, reputable dealers in the world who have not at some time slipped into it.

It is perhaps only a tiny dishonesty, nothing more than a failure in self-criticism; not to be worried about if the dealer (or owner), while naturally preferring his own opinion, plays quite fair with other, less convenient views. If he suppresses them to suit his own ends, either of pride or of monetary advantage, he is being less honest. If he turns down opinion after opinion, shopping around until at last he finds an expert ready to back him up, he is perhaps being less honest still. And what if he tries to influence the expert, persuade or overpersuade him? What if he employs the expert? (Even the great scholar Berenson, after all, during the many years he was retained by Duveen as an expert with a 10 percent commission for all sales resulting from his authentication, sometimes showed a convenient gift for coming up with the answer which happened best to suit Duveen's book.) Sometimes he need not bring any pressure to bear at all—he can rely on the expert's desire or need to please him. But failing that, there are always bribes, direct or indirect. It is even possible, in extremis, to forge authentications or corroborating documents. And by now the slide into clear dishonesty is complete. But where along the slippery slope can anybody be quite sure of drawing the line?

Equally, when we casually speak of forgery we tend to forget that the same term can cover all sorts of phenomena, from the most innocent to the most guilty. Everything called a Vermeer is not a Vermeer; but neither, necessarily, is every non-Vermeer a van Meegeren. It may not be forgery at all, but a mistake of attribution, in itself honest or not so honest. It may be something else perfectly genuine, merely equipped with a forged signature or a dubious provenance. It may be a studio work which the master himself sold as his own work—when is a Rubens not a Rubens? It may be a copy or an imitation, an exercise in the style of, undertaken with no original intent to deceive. If it is used to deceive, then the deception may be accidental or deliberate. Or it may after all be a real forgery produced with every intent to deceive. But even here there are degrees. To deceive whom, and for what purpose? The experts for a wager, or a potential buyer for money? Is it a deception meant to be uncovered, by its perpetrator if no one else, or one which is entered into with every hope of permanence? Anyway, once the thing is in existence, it is liable at any moment to break free of its originator's intentions—one man's joke may turn into deadly earnest for another, a professional challenge to a third, a money maker for a fourth. So much, after all, is in the eye of the beholder.

Including, as often as not, the monetary value of a work of art. Most of the trouble with forgeries, jokes, misleading or questionable attributions, etc., boils down eventually to the whole thorny matter of authentication. Authentication, so important in the modern art market, brings us back to the key question of aesthetic value vis-à-vis monetary value, the difficulties of correlating artistic judgment (which is bound to be opinion) with value in cash (which can be established objectively, after a fashion, by simply testing on the open market exactly how much any given work will fetch). Before we look in more detail at forgery and allied techniques, it is worth returning to first base and considering exactly what decides the price of a work of art anyway.

The first answer, as we know without being told, is fashion. If we take any particular work of art, we can chart its ascent and descent in value fairly reliably through the years entirely in terms of fashion and irrespective of the specific unique qualities of the piece itself. Consider, say, a Gainsborough portrait, any Gainsborough portrait. Its first price was dictated by fashion: how many other people at the same time thought it was a good idea to have their portrait painted by Gains-

borough, rather than Reynolds or Romney or the little
man around the corner who could produce a good
workmanlike likeness? Thus, if you had wanted Gainsborough to paint a full-length portrait of you around
1748 it would have cost you perhaps 8 gns. By 1758
the cost of a half-length was 15 gns and a whole
length perhaps twice that. In the 1760s a whole length
would have cost you about 80 gns, and in the 1770s
nearer 160 gns. Just after his death the value of Gainsborough's landscapes and subject paintings went up,
but few of the portraits came on the market, and those
that did, being after all merely pictures of someone
else's relations, did not do terribly well: in 1797 "The
Blue Boy" brought £36.15s.; in the 1800s and 1820s a
portrait might bring anything from 30s. to £6. By the
1860s the climb has begun again: Gainsborough is returning to fashion (more than Reynolds, because more
romantic) and the National Gallery in London buys
two portraits at £1000 each. The arrival of American
millionaires in the market, and of Duveen to provide
them respectably with other people's ancestors sends the
market in Gainsborough portraits sky-high during the
1900s; already in 1901 "The Duchess of Devonshire"
brings between £30,000 and £35,000 from Pierpont
Morgan, and the climax is reached in 1921 with £148,000
given for "The Blue Boy". The Depression hits all picture prices, but none more than those of eighteenth-
century English portraits—a single Duveen-Mellon
price of £50,000 in 1935 does not alter the general picture of relative unenthusiasm, and major portraits by
Gainsborough are selling for little more than £1000,

And the taste for Gainsborough, when it does revive in the late 1950s, is mainly for another sort of Gainsborough—not so much the famous portraits of his maturity, but for such earlier portraits-in-a-landscape as the National Gallery's "Mr. and Mrs. Andrews in a Park", bought for £130,000 in 1960.

Of course, there are variations at all stages, in that a good Gainsborough would always fetch more than a nondescript one. But even there fashion enters into it, for fashion dictates what shall be considered a "good" Gainsborough at any time—early or late, portrait or landscape, sketchy or highly finished. Other circumstances are also relevant. The state of the market in general at the time, for instance: the greatest slumps in Gainsborough's prices coincide with the greatest slumps in all picture prices, during and after the Napoleonic wars and during the inter-war Depression. But fashion decides that portraits by Gainsborough and his contemporaries shall slump more than most other things at these times. And through all these ups and downs the pictures themselves remain much the same, better or less well cared for, darker or less dark with brown varnish according to the taste of the day, but fundamentally unchanged. The value is in the eye of the beholder, or at least is reached by a rough correlation of how a variety of beholders who are possible buyers see the object on offer.

All this applies, naturally, to an unquestionably genuine Gainsborough. But it applies equally to paintings not by Gainsborough but masquerading as his work. Clearly it would have been to no one's advantage around 1820 to forge a Gainsborough portrait, or even to pass off as Gainsborough a perfectly genuine portrait by some lesser contemporary: it might even just have been worth trying to pretend that a Gainsborough was in fact a Reynolds, since Reynolds at that time still usually brought higher prices. On the other hand, Gainsborough still had reputation enough for tyro artists, wanting to learn by copying, to copy a Gainsborough in all innocence and with no intent to deceive; copies might even be commissioned by owners whose interest was a familial one in the subject of the portrait rather than any particular artistic interest in the man who had painted it. Once the prices of Gainsborough began to climb the situation changed; the essential financial consideration in forgery is whether a painting will (a) fetch more than it cost to produce; (b) fetch more as whatever it is pretending to be than it would as an original work by an unknown artist. No doubt in the 1860s a Gainsborough forgery would have brought more than it cost to produce, but the return on forgeries of other painters would have been considerably greater; moreover, in this, the "golden age of the living painter," it was at least arguable that any painter with sufficient ability to produce a really convincing forgery of a Gainsborough would probably be able to do as well for himself if he set up as a professional painter under his own name. Things had changed again by the mid-1870s, and that was when the mysterious and dubious "Duchess of Devonshire" already referred to began her notorious career.

This painting was and remains a mystery. It was

134

beyond doubt cut down and heavily repainted. Many capable judges doubted Gainsborough's hand in it at all (Millais, for instance, opined "I don't believe Gainsborough ever saw it"), at least one critic alleged that he knew the man who had painted it, and there was another version for comparison, undoubtedly genuine, which made the picture up for sale look very decidedly like an amateurishly altered copy. Whatever the picture's origin—copy, work by a follower, deliberate forgery—it sold in 1876 for £10,605. It was promptly stolen from the purchaser, Agnew's, and did not reappear until 1901, when Pierpont Morgan bought it for somewhere between £30,000 and £35,000. When it next appeared on public show in 1913 at the Metropolitan, doubts about its genuineness were even more strongly expressed, and since then the mattter has been left hanging. No doubt a number of other forgeries or possible forgeries or misrepresented pictures appeared on the market during the next forty years as Gainsboroughs, until the fall in the market after 1929 again made the game, as far as Gainsborough was concerned, hardly worth the candle. Perhaps things have changed again now, but there are fashions in forgeries as well as in genuine paintings, and for reasons mainly ambiguous and quite subjective it is hardly likely that anyone setting out to forge for profit nowadays would choose Gainsborough as the object of his attentions. Gauguin or Van Gogh, maybe, but that is another story. . . .

All this, though, raises another question. In what way, if at all, is a forgery, or need it be, artistically inferior to the genuine article, and exactly why should its worth be a fraction of that of the genuine article? There are cynically realistic answers to both questions. Many forgeries are not, or not at any rate at the time they are produced, at all inferior to the genuine article. They may well be superior to poor examples, and in the case of nearly every well-known forgery some expert, perhaps even the majority of experts, can be found to have come forward with the honest, considered opinion that the work concerned stood high in its alleged creator's oeuvre. Financially too the forgery, so long as it is undetected as such, is in no way inferior to the genuine article. "The Duchess of Devonshire", whether Gainsborough ever laid eyes on her or not, remains one of the most expensive "Gainsboroughs" ever sold, and indeed one of the most expensive British paintings ever in terms of real money value. There are even more striking instances. If the famous "Sleeping Cupid" carved by Michelangelo in his youth and treated by him to pass for a Roman antique were now to come to light, it would undoubtedly be worth more as a Michaelangelo than it would if accepted as what it originally purported to be. These observations, whether palatable or not, are undeniably true. Perhaps they ought not to be, but the arguments introduced to explain why not often savor more of mysticism and justification by faith than of reason. Can it really be true that there is some charisma which invests a works genuinely touched by the hand of the master and nothing else? Would, say, the "Mona Lisa", if it were established beyond doubt tomorrow to be a forgery, a copy, or the work of someone other than Leonardo, at once be drained of virtue, and stand revealed in the cold light of common day as an inferior, unmagical piece of painting?

It is certainly unreasonable that it should, but as all aesthetic judgment is by its very nature unreasonable, the answer is probably yes. Let us take a concrete example. If you had been in London in 1820, and had wished to see a Rembrandt masterpiece you would probably have been advised to go to the recently opened Dulwich Art Gallery and look at "Jacob's Dream", by general consent of the day's critics one of his supreme creations. And indeed, it is a beautiful picture—it is still at Dulwich, only now it is labeled Aert de Gelder. It is not a forgery, and was not, or only to the limited extent that de Gelder's signature had been overpainted at some date, in the hope no doubt that the painting would then pass for the handiwork of his more illustrious teacher. But de Gelder is not Rembrandt, and no one now would point out the painting as one of London's supreme art treasures. And yet the painting itself is still the same.

Or is it? Physically, yes, but the eye of the beholder has changed. Partly, no doubt, it is snobbery. We know Rembrandt's name, and we know that all the books agree that he is one of the greatest painters, so we find ourselves in front of anything authoritatively labelled "Rembrandt" already in the frame of mind to receive a great artistic experience. It would be childish to suggest therefore that all artistic experience is no more than so many conditioned reflexes, but undoubtedly they do help: they give an aura which it is impossible for any of us to guarantee seeing through every time. De Gelder does not have that aura, and we are more likely now to walk past his painting without a second glance than we were when it benefited from all the associations and expectations produced by the label Rembrandt.

But beyond this—call it what you will, snobbery, conventionality, gullibility—there is something else. And that something is the time element, the one factor to which all art, genuine and forged, is subject, and the one thing which sooner or later, but almost infallibly, separates the real thing from the fake. Even within the undoubtedly genuine work of an artist it operates: witness the ups and downs in relative esteem which the different genres practiced by Gainsborough, and the various periods of his career, have known in the years since his death. The de Gelder "Jacob's Dream" has not become less estimable as a painting in the time since it was regarded as one of Rembrandt's masterpieces merely because we now know Rembrandt did not paint it, but because in the meantime our attitude toward Rembrandt and our analysis of the qualities that make him great have changed. The painting would not in any way disgrace Rembrandt today, but even if we had not discovered that someone else painted it we would probably not think of it as one of his greatest works, because the real qualities it has are precisely those which appealed most to a particular early-Romantic, rather picturesque view of Rembrandt, and which appeal considerably less to us. Art lovers of the 1820s were quite right in their opinion of the painting, by the standards of their own time. For them it really was not only as good as any other Rembrandt, but better. For us, not.

But we have no more reason to suppose ourselves absolutely, permanently, objectively right than they had.

This apparent digression is relevant to the subject of intentional, calculated forgeries because it shows very clearly what the vital differences between a forgery and the real thing are likely to be. The forgery is of an age, the real thing, take it or leave it, is for all time. Dali, of all people, once remarked that "being a modern painter is the only thing, no matter what you do, that you cannot help being." And that, in the long run, is always the forger's pitfall. Try as he may, he cannot step wholly out of his own time, his own period's outlook. As Max J. Friedländer remarks in his books *On Art and Connoisseurship*:

> Since every epoch acquires fresh eyes, Donatello in 1930 looks different from what he did in 1870. That which is worthy of imitation appears different to each generation. Hence, whoever in 1870 successfully produced works by Donatello, will find his performance no longer passing muster with the experts in 1930. We laugh at the mistakes of our fathers, as our descendants will laugh at us.

The immediate truth of this statement can be seen just by looking at some of history's most famous and successful forgeries. The Saitaphernes Tiara, for instance, a Graeco-Scythian work in gold which the Louvre bought for 200,000 gold francs in 1896. If one were shown that today, without any previous knowledge of it, and asked to date it the answer would probably be c. 1890: it looks even at first glance like some piece of stage costume designed for an historical melodrama starring Sarah Bernhardt. Yet in the 1890s it was widely accepted as genuine, and several experts backed down only when absolutely irrefutable proof was produced that the tiara had been made in Odessa by a goldsmith called Ruchemovsky in the early 1890s. The reason for this apparent gullibility is not far to seek: if the tiara was not representative of how the Scythians saw things in 200 B.C., it was ideally representative of how artists and scholars saw the Scythians at the end of the nineteenth century. It was too characteristic to be real: for the contemporary observer it was not only as good as the real thing, it was better, because it supported all his preconceptions and answered to perfection his idea of the antique and the beautiful.

Similarly with the wax bust of "Flora" bought by Wilhelm Bode of the Kaiser Friedrich Museum, Berlin, in 1909 as a genuine work of Leonardo da Vinci. Or, strictly speaking, bought as an anonymous undated work which Bode then announced to be by Leonardo. Almost immediately the bust was denounced as modern by a Southampton art dealer and by the son of the alleged sculptor, one Richard Cockle Lucas, who was said to have made it in 1846, basing it on a picture attributed to Leonardo and owned by the man who had commissioned it. Despite all the corroboratory testimony, including some papers dating from the 1840s found inside it as Lucas's son suggested they would be, Bode stuck to his guns, never going further than to admit the possibility that Lucas might have done some restoration work on a genuine original. In a sense, therefore, the question of the bust's authenticity is still open, and it has never been actually admitted as a fake by its owners. But the question seems nevertheless to have answered itself, for the very qualities of the "Mona Lisa smile" which sent the first German commentators into ecstasies are now those which seem to the modern observer at once sugary, sentimental, and characteristically 1840-ish.

It is still too early, no doubt, to convince ourselves fairly that we are able to make a similar aesthetic discrimination in the case of a more recent major forgery to be exposed, that of the fifteen-inch bronze statuette of a horse, supposed to be Greek and dating from about 800 B.C., which had been accounted one of New York's major treasures since the Metropolitan Museum acquired it in 1923. Thousands of plaster casts of it were sold through the years; it was reproduced in the *Encyclopædia Britannica* and elsewhere as a quintessential expression of the Greek spirit, and apparently no one ever questioned its authenticity at all until 1961. Then Joseph V. Noble, one of the museum's vice-directors, happened to find his attention attracted by a very fine line running from the horse's mane down the tip of his nose (a line, incidentally, which is clearly visible in nearly all the often-reproduced photographs). Slightly closer inspection showed that the line continued across the horse's back, down his leg, under his stomach and back up the legs to the head. It was clearly the mark left by the edge of a two-piece mould used in the casting. Except that this sort of casting was not invented until around the fourteenth century: in classical antiquity all such casts were made by the *cire perdu* process, the original model, made in wax, being covered with clay and then heated so that the wax ran away leaving a hollow one-piece mold from which a seamless bronze casting could be made. The forger's mistake was elementary, and yet for over forty years no expert scrutiny had detected it. Tempting now to say "But of course—the feeling of the piece is far more that of the Twentyish neoclassicism than of the genuinely classical." Tempting, but much too easy an exercise in hindsight. Yet who shall say that it was not the first subconscious stirrings of such a feeling which prompted Mr. Noble to take that closer look one day in 1961?

One more example, perhaps the most famous forgeries of all. In 1945 a Dutchman named Han van Meegeren was arrested on suspicion of collaboration with the Germans, the main reason being that he had been involved with the selling of a Dutch national treasure, a Vermeer, to Fieldmarshal Goering. His defense seemed fantastic: he claimed to have painted the picture in question himself, as well as six other Vermeers universally accepted as genuine (including "Christ at Emmaus" in the Boymans Museum, widely regarded as one of Vermeer's masterpieces) and two notable de Hoochs. When his confession was received with skepticism he went on to give detailed accounts of just how he had done it and to repeat the process to order. Scientific tests then applied seemed to bear out his claims—in particular, despite all his care to eliminate from his work materials unknown in Vermeer's day, traces of some synthetic resins developed only in the twentieth century were discovered by analysis. Counterclaims were put forward that this analysis was misleading and inconclusive. Further X-ray checks revealed the truth of various things asserted by van Meegeren which he could have known only if he had painted the pictures himself —for instance, the existence of a child's head painted over and undetectable by the naked eye in "Christ at Emmaus". Spectrographic analysis of the paint in the picture sold to Goering revealed minute traces of modern cobalt blue adulterating the pure lapis lazuli Vermeer would have used—not van Meegeren's fault, this, since it appeared that his supplier had been less than scrupulous in filling his order exactly to specifications.

But, still, as so often in cases where experts have been taken in and resent it, all attempts to prove that van Meegeren was lying and some at least of the paintings are genuine have not yet died away. They will: even twenty years after the event, time has done its work, and what seems to us fantastic now is that these works, even the earliest, most careful and best of them (some of the later, like "Christ and the Woman Taken in Adultery", can only be described as amateurish), could ever have been taken for genuine Vermeers: to us they are redolent immediately of the most enfeebled, tentatively simplified realism which passed as academic religious art between the wars. When do van Meegeren's Vermeers now look as though they were painted? Going by the "feel" of them, about 1935. Again, the same qualities in "Christ at Emmaus" which made it look most like a masterpiece in 1937 are now those which make it most suspect in our eyes.

It is perhaps an increasingly sophisticated grasp of this basic fact of art life, plus the constant refinement of purely scientific tests to determine a painting's or sculpture's age, formation and chemical constitution which have turned forgers in the last few years away from the old masters and more in the direction of Impressionists, Post-Impressionists and moderns. The development, anyway, could be explained on grounds of fashion as well: paintings alleged to date from post-1880 are not only technically easier to manage but are as likely as any to be sold at high prices. True, even if the chemical tests which might dispose of a modern Vermeer's claims to authenticity can give no conclusive testimony on a Van Gogh's, X-ray analysis may show that though the surface of the Van Gogh looks credible enough, the paint beneath the surface is not applied in a manner we know to be characteristic of Van Gogh. But then once the analysis is published, it is always possible for the next forger of Van Goghs to put this error right as well, leaving the detection of his forgery to time (which is less sure the closer in date the forger is to his original), external evidence, and the often powerful but inescapably subjective evidence of the expert judging on grounds of style alone. Actually, it is surprising how often the expert's opinion is relied upon exclusively in such matters, even today when there are tests which might settle the question of an alleged old master's date beyond doubt, if only negatively (these tests, obviously, can be conclusive only negatively: it is not possible by them to prove absolutely that a Leonardo was painted by Leonardo, but it may be possible to prove absolutely that it wasn't).

All of which brings us, somewhat circuitously, to a consideration of the role of the forger and his relations in the art market today. Some generalizations may be ventured: on the whole, forgery now as at any other time is more prevalent, more organized, and more likely to be successful in the applied arts than in the fine. To begin with, it is easier, since craftsmanship in a particular manner is certainly easier to simulate convincingly than that elusive combination of qualities which make up the style of a great artist. Secondly, it is less frequently spotted because less care is normally devoted to its spotting. It stands to reason that someone about to spend thousands of pounds on a painting or drawing will want to be very thoroughly convinced that he is getting exactly what he is paying for. He is not really interested in whether what he is getting is "as good as" a Rembrandt or a Renoir; he wants to be certain that it is a Rembrandt or a Renoir because its authenticity is the prime factor which determines its price, and there surely doesn't exist a collector so unworldly that he will pay £50,000 for a "Rembrandt" oil or £5000 for a "Renoir" pastel, however much he likes them, if he is aware that they are not what they claim and that therefore no one else in the world would pay a fraction of the price.

But at a far lower level, buyers will cavil much less at paying say £300 for an eighteenth-century lacquered clock which they could have bought for £20 a month earlier without the lacquer. They won't like it any more if they know, but they will go to less trouble and expense to find out. And thirdly, the precise lines between forgery, repair and reproduction or renovation are much harder to draw. There exist, for example, many perfectly legitimate, above-board businesses which specialize entirely in producing convincing reproductions of antique furniture, marks of age and all. A lot of people like them, and find them easier to afford than the genuine articles. A lot of people buy them open-eyed for what they are, modern reproductions. But once a piece is in circulation, who is to keep exact tabs on how it is sold, and what it is alleged to be? And mistakes can so easily happen. The purchaser may know he is buying a reproduction, but do his children know what it is when they inherit it?

Again, perfectly genuine pieces can be faked up a bit. All over London one may find respectable Victorian workingmen's cottages which are being little by little done over into Georgian bijou residences by the substitution of a neo-Georgian doorway, a small bay window and a coat of stucco for the original elegance-despising plain brick and sashes. People like them that way. The same with furniture. Strip off the dark Victorian stain, prune a few decorative excrescences, and you may end up with a quite convincing Georgian cabinet, chest or sideboard. Is that a forgery? Or take that set of eighteenth-century chairs. Two are all right, but the back of the third is rotten with woodworm and the fourth has two legs broken. Of course you get them restored—how else can you use them? But is the result legitimate, or does it go over the edge into forgery?

Delicate questions, not always quite so delicately answered. But forgeries of this sort—if such they are judged to be—are relatively small beer, and though variously reprehensible and very distressing when revealed to those who have bought them in all innocence, they are not the stuff of which *causes célèbres* are made. There are whole books to be written—indeed, whole books have been written—about how a piece of reproduction furniture can be aged with a shotgun, or how a dull early Victorian table can be turned into a desirable Regency antique by the knowing addition of some brass inlay. But all that, though on the fringes of the art market, and all part of the dark sub-world of antique dealing, rarely comes to the surface in the big league at all. Perhaps it should more often: in 1966, for example, the London *Sunday Times* found out through an honest London firm specializing in antique reproductions, that to its alarm a number of its products, particularly in the line of imitation Venetian "blackamoor" furniture of the eighteenth century, seemed to be resold in some very respectable and expensive West End galleries as the real thing. A controlled experiment managed to pass off a couple of such figures carved from a length of telegraph pole before a number of experts and elicit an offer (refused of course) of £650 for them from one leading dealer. It certainly makes you think.

However, more interesting, more potentially profitable, and more generally to our purpose is the subject of forgery today in the fine arts. During 1966 and 1967 hardly a week went by without a report somewhere in the press of yet another spectacular forgery unmasked, from which one can only suppose that the forger's craft is as popular as ever today, and his rewards, considering the rocketing prices of art, more spectacular than ever before. As we remarked, fashion, economics and caution in the face of technological advance all combine to make the characteristic object of the forger's skill today the moderns—anything from the Impressionists onward. Occasionally cases of forgery taking something earlier as its model still come up—in 1959, for instance, two expensive "Gothic" carvings sold in Austria proved to be the work of a young village wood-carver who was himself quite innocent of any intent to deceive—but in general the "forgery" is only incidental: two collections of "old masters" including works allegedly by Rembrandt, Rubens and Van Dyck offered to Sotheby's and Parke-Bernet for sale in the summer of 1967 were in themselves perfectly genuine works of pupils, imitators and followers, but equipped with histories which proved entirely fictitious and certificates of authentication which were clearly forged.

These are the exceptions. The characteristic forgery of the 1960s may best be represented by the extraordinary career of Jean-Pierre Schecroum. Schecroum, born in 1929, is without doubt the most spectacularly successful of all modern forgers, and the most gifted. He seems to have begun his whirlwind career in Paris in the late 1950s, according to his own account, as a result of some chip on his shoulder about his lack of success as a painter while many others, no more talented than himself, could command vast sums on the strength of their name alone. (Van Meegeren had a similar story to tell of his early career, and the sense of grievance often seems to weigh heavy with forgers at first, even when more directly mercenary considerations take over later.) Schecroum specialized in the moderns, indeed many of his models were still alive, and the rest were mostly quite lately dead: the list included Picasso, Braque, Miró, Léger (whose pupil Schecroum had once been), Delaunay, Picabia and Soulages, with the American Jackson Pollock thrown in for good measure.

The most remarkable thing about Schecroum was his facility. Certainly he had the advantage of not needing to worry about any of the problems which beset earlier master forgers, like artificial aging, careful choice of materials so as to avoid anything anachronistic, and the provision of elaborately circumstantial histories for his works. But even so, it is quite an achievement to be able to knock off perfectly credible, even creditable Picassos, Braques and Soulages' in no more than an hour or two. Often, indeed, the certificates of authenticity from recognized dealers and agents took longer to forge than the works themselves, even when matters were facilitated by the theft of headed paper and rubber stamps, as from the Galerie Maeght, Braque's agent.

Schecroum seems to have done all the actual forging himself, often more or less to order: he would find out what any particular dealer was interested in, and then set about supplying it. In marketing his products he had, in addition to a crooked art dealer who started him off on forging Légers, three regular accomplices, personable young Frenchmen who would check the lie of the land, set up the necessary background stories, and dispose of the finished, often only just finished, article. It was, in fact, no deficiency in his own work but an entirely unforeseen coincidence that brought about his downfall. On a trip to London in 1961 Schecroum and his assistants sold some thirty works of various kinds (mainly slight—drawings, gouaches, watercolors) for around £20,000. None of the sales singly was large enough to arouse undue suspicion, and the group did not make the elementary mistake of asking too little for their wares—their prices were more or less standard for what they claimed to be selling.

Unfortunately for them, two of the dealers they had sold to, Jacques O'Hana of the O'Hana Galleries and Eric Estorick of the Grosvenor Gallery, happened to be comparing notes and discovered that a Braque one had bought and two Soulages' the other had bought were oddly enough on exactly the same paper. A further check showed that the authentications which came with the works were forged, and from there a traced London-Paris phone call led to Schecroum's workshop, his arrest and trial. This took place in 1962, and as a result of it he was fined £4000 and sent to prison for two years. Some of his forgeries, a small proportion of the probable total, were traced and recovered; but no one would care to guess how many are still in circulation.

Schecroum's task was made easier by his own evident talents, by the nearness in time of the artists he chose to forge, and by the vagueness of a number of artists about what is and what is not their own work. Picasso blandly admits that when something supposedly by him is brought to him for authentication, his answer depends on whether he likes it or not. Corot, one of the most forged painters in history (hence the old crack that there are 2000 Corots in existence, 3000 of them in the United States), frequently signed the work of friends and pupils if he liked it, so often fake Corots may have genuine signatures. Modigliani, too, often signed the work of friends worse off than himself in order to make it more salable. Utrillo was unable to distinguish the work of his most faithful imitator, a Madame Claude Latour, from his own, while the fakes produced by one of his dealers, Berthet, are widely accounted better than Utrillo's own contemporary work. To make matters worse, Utrillo was kept very firmly in order by his wife in later days, and was allowed to sell no paintings except through her. But apparently to get some extra pocket money he occasionally sold paintings behind her back, and so after his death his widow was sometimes saying in all honesty that a genuine Utrillo could not be genuine because it had not passed through her hands. Giorgio di Chirico, on the other hand, having abjured the surrealist style in which all his most famous works were painted after about 1925, has since consistently refused to authenticate any work of his painted before then, while at the same time he is suspected, with some reason, of having occasionally himself "forged" work in this earlier style when his later work failed entirely to find an audience.

In all these cases there are some criteria by which forgeries can be differentiated from the real thing. But they tend to be complex, ambiguous, and unreliable. It is relatively simple now to ask Miró if he painted a "Miró" offered for sale. But what will happen when he is dead? Who will then guarantee to tell the true from the false? And how will the traditional criteria apply at all to newer artists still? To the assemblers of assemblages and collages, for instance? To pop artists who "paint" photographic blow-ups of frames from strip-cartoons, pin-ups from film fan magazines or tins of Campbell's Soup? To painters like the op artist Briget Riley, whose designs are worked out for her by a team of mathematicians? To Yves Klein, who thought of dyeing natural sponges blue and selling them mounted as works of art? Or to certain modern abstractionists? As a writer in *The Sunday Times* remarked:

> The question of exactly who prepared a large, rectangular area of pale-green paint for exhibition may be a difficult one to resolve, especially if a good deal of money hangs on it.

And does it really matter so much whose hand dipped the sponge in the blue paint? Where, one might inquire, is your charisma the noo?

THE UNDERWORLD II

Forgery is not the only way of meeting a demand which constantly threatens to outstrip supply. There is always theft. And in a world which increasingly tends to put up nationalistic barriers against the free flow of art from country to country, there is always the possibility of under-the-counter art, smuggled from where there is plenty to where there is less, sold on a sort of international black market where often the most solid citizens know better than to ask too many questions.

Art smuggling tends not to attract much attention from the popular press. At best it is all rather academic to the man in the street. Legally it is quite possible that overnight what was perfectly normal and proper—you buy an ikon in Greece or an ancient statuette in Egypt, pack it up with your other keepsakes and take it home with you—can become a serious offense. But legal proprieties are one thing and what people feel to be crimes quite another. Now theft everyone is agreed upon. It is wicked, exciting, and eminently worth reading about. Hence, no doubt, the tremendous prominence art thefts are given in our newspapers. And indeed, in the sheer amount of money involved, a lot of them are very spectacular indeed, especially in the sometimes rather highly colored estimates of current market value made by the robbers' victims. But the visions which are sedulously conjured up each time of a vast international network of fine-art fences, monomaniac collectors who will buy hot goods at any price in order to decorate their fabulous hideaways, and all the rest of it, are unfortunately rather too good to be true.

Take the notorious case of the Goya portrait of the Duke of Wellington stolen from London's National Gallery on August 21, 1961. It vanished completely, and despite a succession of cryptic letters received by the authorities from time to time stating that it was for ransom to the tune of £140,000, to be given to charity, speculation ran riot about what had happened to it. In the film version of Ian Fleming's *Doctor No* there is a charming touch: as the camera shows us the interior of the evil doctor's island fortress, it casually reveals, standing on an easel, the missing Goya. There, presumably, it was blown up, with the rest of the doctor's domain, but its real fate was far less romantic. In its absence it became, rather alarmingly, one of the nation's greatest treasures, the supreme masterpiece of Goya's art for the possession of which several of the world's top collectors were said to be surreptitiously vying (when it

was returned, several experts began, rather disillusion-
ingly, to run it down and question whether it was by
Goya at all).

And then, in May 1965, a London newspaper received a message that it was in a left-luggage office at
a Birmingham railway station. The police collected it,
the National Gallery agreed that it was the real thing,
and there the matter rested for six weeks, until an un-
employed lorrydriver from Newcastle gave himself up
as the thief. So much for the fancy theories of an incred-
ibly powerful and efficient international ring of art-
thieves. He had, he said, just climbed into the gallery,
taken the picture when no one was looking, and
climbed out of the same lavatory window with it. His
aims were idealistic: he did not want to damage it, he
did not want the money for himself; all he wanted was
to draw attention to the folly of people who would spend
more on art than on alleviating human misery, and get
them to give to charity instead. He could not be con-
victed of stealing the portrait, since no intent to keep it
permanently or profit by taking it could be proved, but
he was tried for stealing the frame, which had vanished,
and sentenced to three months' imprisonment. And
that was that.

Despite this prosaic conclusion the legend of mad
millionaire collectors of stolen masterpieces still persists. Once Tibet was a favourite place for their hideaways, but since the change of government there South
America is now more usual. Well, the notion, however
fantastic, cannot, it seems, be entirely discounted: one
would not, after all, have to be so mad to contemplate

gloating solitarily over one or two secret possessions that no one else might know about, though anything more than that is stretching things a bit. Certainly major art thefts are usually a little better organized than that of the Goya, but often, witness the Dulwich Gallery theft in 1967, not very much. And when really important pictures or sculptures are involved, the thieves do not usually intend so much to retain permanently or dispose of the object in question, as to make some sort of symbolic gesture (like stealing the Stone of Scone) or to hold the owners or their insurers up to ransom.

This is quite understandable. After all, the occasional mad millionaire apart, how would you go about disposing of the "Mona Lisa?" The negotiable value of stolen goods depends largely on their ability to pass back into circulation unnoticed or to be changed beyond recognition without losing their value, or not too much of it. A consignment of watches can be sold off in small quantities and often no one is any the wiser, one watch being much like another. Uncut jewel stones can be cut, cut stones can be recut, precious metals melted down—though even here, it would be a nice point whether, if you stole the English Crown Jewels or Cellini's great golden salt cellar, you would do better to break them up and melt them down for the sake of the materials they contained, or try your luck by holding out for a ransom based on their extrinsic value as history or as art.

But when it comes to world-famous paintings, the problems are very different. At the time of the Dulwich robbery Colin Simpson knowledgeably noted in *The*

Sunday Times that there were just two fences in the world who could handle the loot: one of them "lives in some elegance in Tangier" and his "taste runs to kaftans, jade cigarette holders and sloe-eyed Moroccan boys dancing attendance on him," but unfortunately he specializes entirely in Impressionists and Post-Impressionists; the other has moved his center of operations from England to Mexico, specializes in old masters and "the finest of early Chinese porcelain," and sells to secretive but sane South Americans. Having dangled these colorful characters before us, however, Mr. Simpson sadly came to the more down-to-earth conclusion that the theft was most probably either a bungled attempt to extort insurance ransom (impossible because the pictures weren't insured) or a "protest" of some sort.

Alas and alack, he was right. This biggest art theft ever, the work of master crooks according to the British police, proved after all to be an amateurish job pulled by a group of small-time crooks and layabouts who vaguely thought it would be a good idea to pinch the paintings but having got them had no idea at all what to do with them. They had forced an entry by the simplest and most dangerous possible way—straight through the front door of the ill-guarded South London gallery—carried off a cool £2 million-worth of art, including three Rembrandts, three Rubenses and two lesser paintings, and then found them nothing but an embarrassment which they had to abandon in a public garden a few miles from the scene of the crime. The papers, after a lot of excited speculation about the incredible knowledgeability of thieves who realized that if something was labeled Rembrandt it was worth stealing, were disappointed again, and the Dulwich Gallery got its pictures back only a trifle the worse for their experience.

Obviously all art thefts cannot be so lightly discussed—indeed, considering the very considerable danger that stolen works of art, even if not deliberately destroyed in order to remove incriminating evidence, may be irreparably damaged by the thieves, it is not possible to dismiss any thefts at all very lightly. None the less, with most of the art thefts of our time, it is possible to doubt the intelligence and clearheadedness of those who have engineered them. Ransom from a collector is always a possibility. No doubt many collectors would pay a ransom to see a cherished possession back on their walls as willingly as they would to have a wife or child safely restored to them, and it would be a bold man who would assert that this had never occurred. But as someone who paid a ransom in such circumstances would be in a slightly tricky legal position by having helped to cover up a crime, and would only be laying himself open for more of the same treatment, it is difficult to get any reliable details. Certainly hopes of deals with insurance companies seem to be grossly exaggerated. Again, no doubt it has happened sometimes, but British and American insurance companies categorically deny that they would be party to any such arrangement; maybe on the Continent . . . At most, they will go so far as to offer a reward leading to the recovery of the stolen articles, and apparently this was done in the case of another big robbery in Britain recently, when in 1962 thirty-five Impressionist and Post-Impressionist paintings, valued at £327,000, were stolen from the O'Hana Gallery in London and eventually recovered in Plaistow. But the general feeling is that, all question of ethics apart, as one British insurance investigator puts it: "Once you start doing deals with art thieves to try and cut your losses then you open the door to a massive wave of robberies."

A massive wave of robberies just about describes what has been happening in the 1960s, but deals by insurance companies would hardly seem to be the prime reason. If there is any one basic reason, it is a mass hysteria on the part of the criminal classes—and others—induced by all they read in the papers about the fabulous amounts of money there are in art. But how this affects the perpetrators of the robberies concerned varies enormously. The major British thefts seem to have been mainly the work of idealistic cranks or amateurish petty criminals whose turning to art as the occasion for their demonstration or the specific object of their usual nefarious activities was apparently entirely the result of believing all they read in the papers. The spate of thefts on and around the French Riviera in 1960-61, on the other hand, would seem to have been much more practical in its aims, and indeed in its achievements. Though admittedly the only thieves who were caught over the whole succession of six major crimes in seventeen months (125 paintings worth an estimated £3 million) claimed at their trial, rather obscurely, that they were doing it in order "to defend the priceless artistic patrimony of France", it may be doubted whether their motive was actually any different from that of the gangs responsible for the other crimes: gain.

How much, if anything, they actually did gain remains unclear. The twenty paintings by Braque, Léger, Picasso, Bonnard, Utrillo, Modigliani, Dufy, Matisse and others stolen from the Colombe d'Or restaurant at Saint-Paul-de-Vence were recovered eleven months later after an anonymous phone call, allegedly from a priest, told the police where to look. No arrest was ever made, and a rumor persists that someone, maybe the owner, paid the ransom asked for, supposedly about £10,000. The biggest theft of the series, in which no fewer than fifty-seven Impressionist and Post-Impressionist paintings were removed from the municipal museum at Saint Tropez, had an equally obscure aftermath. A large ransom was certainly asked, and the curator of the gallery, the painter Dunoyer de Segonzac, and others in the town certainly made attempts to raise it, the paintings being entirely uninsured against theft. Eventually all the paintings except a watercolor by Segonzac which had been posted back in pieces as an earnest of the thieves' bad intentions were recovered by the police, again after an anonymous tip-off. Again rumor had it that a ransom had been paid, supposedly by the French government. Rumor went on to confide that the Saint Tropez robbery and another at Aix just a month later, in which eight Cézannes were stolen, later to be returned in the same way, anonymous phone call and all, were the work of the same gang, and that the pay-off for the return of the two hauls was about £25,000. Perhaps it is true, though if so no one in the French government or police is going to admit it. Anyway, no arrests were ever made, and £25,000, if quite enough to pay thieves as ransom, still seems fairly modest compared with the theoretical market value of the paintings. But then, what is the real market value of stolen paintings so famous there is nowhere any one can safely sell them?

There have been other big robberies since. In January 1966, old master drawings valued at some £730,000 were stolen from a museum at Besançon: they included eighteen Fragonards, a Rembrandt, two Veroneses and a Caravaggio. They were all recovered five months later, and proved to have been stolen by a group who alleged that their aim was to draw attention to the plight of young French painters today. In 1967 the newspapers were cheerfully reporting that seventeen paintings valued at over £90,000, including a couple of Picassos, were stolen from a New York firm of art restorers and framers.

But this sort of thing, though it makes news, is probably of less lasting consequence in the art world than the ever-rising number of small thefts which take place with little or no publicity all the year around. In the art world particularly it is true that the thief's most profitable policy is to avoid the big sensational coups and stick to the small jobs with the rapid, reliable turnover. On this level there is no doubt that the business of theft is quite highly organized, both in the commission of crimes and the disposal of goods, and that except for mischance detection and the recovery of stolen goods are surprisingly difficult. The only country which seems to publish figures at all regularly is Italy, and there it was estimated that in the ten years from 1956 to 1966 more than 6000 works of art had been stolen and of those not many more than 100 recovered. A world-famous painting, often reproduced, will be impossible to dispose of unrecognized, but the confident assertions frequently made, that in the present state of art scholarship it is virtually unthinkable that any known work by a major artist can be lost track of for long, prove on examination lamentably over-optimistic.

Several British newspapers and magazines have tested the matter for themselves. For *Queen* magazine, Clement Freud assumed a disreputable air and took a known, signed Renoir drawing, recently exhibited in a major London gallery and belonging to a well-known English collection, around to several leading dealers asking for offers. None of them recognized it, and only one of them even suggested it might be worth getting it vetted by a Renoir expert. The *Daily Mirror,* after a particularly well-publicized art theft, tested how easily the picture could be got out of the country by having one of their reporters take a full-size copy of it abroad by plane and by boat. On neither occasion did anyone notice or question him.

Even with well-documented works which are stolen there is no regular machinery for listing them and alerting dealers who might possibly be offered them for sale. Interpol says that descriptions of stolen works of art, with photographs when available, are sent out regularly from Paris to the member police forces all over the world, but the information seems not to get any further —certainly not to dealers. In the United States the Art Dealers Association not only vows itself in principle to improving standards in art dealing, but takes such practical steps as running a regular information service for members on thefts and stolen items they might be offered; however, by no means all dealers are members. It is not surprising, then, if even the most honest dealer is not occasionally guilty, without knowing it, of receiving stolen goods, and his position is particularly vulnerable, since he has no leg to stand on if the legal owner turns up to claim it (except in France, and there only if he has held it for thirty years, after which it becomes legally his).

The smaller a work of art is, the more difficult it often is to keep tabs on. A Renoir painting, yes, but a Renoir drawing? "The Thinker", yes, but how about a Rodin bronze a few inches high cast in an edition of perhaps twenty copies? Many dealers photograph everything that comes in, just to be on the safe side, but a lot of old-established collections in country houses or provincial museums are a lot less well documented, and a haul of a dozen miniatures or two dozen snuff boxes or a case of china or jade could well be made without there being an adequate record of any item. The British Antique Dealers Association keeps its 500 members circulated with a duplicated list, provided by the police, of all stolen antiques on record. But by no means all dealers belong to the association, descriptions are often inadequate, and memories are short: the longer a thief holds on to the goods, the less chance there is of rapid detection. Here at least there is obvious room for improvement: as things stand the lack of organization among art dealers and lack of liaison between them and the police really make the small-time art thief's job far too easy.

Smuggled and illicitly exported works of art are a related but on the whole less exciting problem. Not so much has been written about smuggling, and the public at large remains pretty hazy about the extent of the problem, the mechanics of it, and the rights and wrongs, if any. Only one notable case has been made public recently in which art smuggling is, or seems to be, involved: the extraordinary dispute between the Turkish government and press on one hand and the archaeologist James Mellaart, discoverer of the important Stone Age settlement at Catal Hüyük, on the other. It is a long, complicated and very obscure story, more suggestive of cheap detection fiction than of the lofty realms of scholarship.

What happened appears to be this. In 1958 Mellaart, traveling on a train in Turkey, noticed that a girl in the same compartment was wearing a gold bracelet of a type hitherto found only at Troy. He elicited from her the information that it was part of a collection she owned, and, one thing leading to another, he was finally taken by her to her home in Izmir and allowed to spend several days drawing the objects and making notes. The collection, she said, had been unearthed at Dorak, to the east of Troy, in the early 1920s, and it seemed to Mellaart an immensely important find, showing the existence of an advanced seafaring culture immediately bordering on Troy in the third millennium B.C. Mellaart knew the name of the girl, and she gave him an address for the house which later proved to be non-existent; she let him make all the drawings he liked, but take no photographs.

Mellaart hesitated to publish his finds without cor-roboratory photographs, but finally did so in 1959 after receiving a letter from the girl authorizing publication. The Turkish authorities, who previously had displayed little interest in the story, were apparently put on a spot by the publicity given the finds in *The Illustrated London News,* and began an investigation of the whole matter which produced no confirmation of Mellaart's story: girl, house and collection seemed to have van-ished completely. The rest of the tale is one of violent and extremely inaccurate attacks on Mellaart in the Turkish press, accusing him of having excavated the remains himself and smuggled them out of the country to sell to the highest bidder; bitter retaliations by Mel-laart, never it would seem the most tactful of men, and as a result a refusal by the Turkish government to let him continue work on "his" site at Catal Hüyük.

All very mysterious and inexplicable unless one takes into account the stringent laws of Turkey about the export of art objects. These, in effect, make it illegal to take virtually any object of any value at all out of the country—which, considering that most of the really epoch-making new archaeological discoveries of the last half-century have happened in Turkey, makes things extremely frustrating for museums and private col-lectors abroad. Hence the enormous trade in smuggled artifacts, which is draining many of the finest pieces from the country. Hacilar pottery, Yortan gold, and innumerable objects which in all probability should by law still be in Turkey are to be seen in many major Western collections. Often the authorities themselves are, privately, a little dubious about the legitimacy of the means by which their suppliers got hold of the stuff, but it might have been brought out legally before the war, when restrictions were not so tight, and anyway if they want it they are in no position to ask too many questions.

That there is a vast trade in smuggled, stolen and sometimes forged antiquities from Turkey no one denies, and it is well worthwhile when single pieces of pottery may sell for £25,000 or more. The Turkish government does what it can to stop the trade, and the nationalistic Turkish press does all it can to blame foreigners for this, as they see it, ruthless pillage of Turkey's national heritage. And this is where Mellaart seems to come in. The most likely explanation of the whole business is that he was the fall-guy. The girl was planted to get him interested; the collection, no doubt genuine enough in itself and found quite probably at the place, if not the time, she said it was, was provided with invaluable documentation from an unimpeachably expert source; and then it could be smuggled out and sold at a high price with Mellaart, a mistrusted foreigner, there to be blamed for, at best, inventing the whole thing himself, at worst smuggling it out and selling it for his own personal profit. That, at least, is the theory, though until some of the objects reappear somewhere it can hardly be proved one way or the other.

But whatever the truth about Mellaart's find, the problem behind the problem remains. Clearly a country has a right to protect its treasures from indiscriminate and uncontrolled export. But it may be questioned whether the Turkish government's extreme policy of almost total prohibition is either wise or workable. Other countries in a similar position, such as Greece, Egypt and Iran, have come to more moderate and practical arrangements. In each case all archaeological discoveries have to be reported to the relevant government department and classified; the same for any other work of art which may come up for export. Once the classification has been done, a decision is taken by examining committees as to which should be allowed to be exported, and which must remain in the country concerned.

The decisions reached, if not always pleasing to foreign collectors, are generally reasonable, and permit a considerable percentage of the art objects involved to leave; only those which are felt to be of outstanding importance or are particularly needed by museums at home are retained. The exporter even has some advantages this way: the export permit includes an expert appraisal of what exactly the object is, which counts abroad as a certificate of authentication, thereby making the black market distribution of forgeries that much more difficult. Even here, though, there is room for abuse. With Iran in particular there is persistent talk of a proportion of forged antiquities, notably ceramics, which are exported with all the necessary official authentications. Certainly a number of these ceramics are to be found in most of the world's major collections, except the British Museum; the British Museum, while admitting that it has steered clear of buying them, will not say why—understandably, since if the rumors of fraud are true, a number of very important Iranian officials would be implicated.

In the West smuggling of works of art tends to be a more refined process. There are, after all, usually ways and means which permit even highly respected dealers and collectors to sail very close to the wind without actually contravening the letter of the law. Take the case of Georges de la Tour's painting "La Bonne Aventure," sold to the Metropolitan Museum, New York, in 1960 by one of the oldest and most respected Paris dealers, Georges Wildenstein. Works by la Tour, a seventeenth-century French painter somewhat influenced by Caravaggio, are rare enough by any standards—less than two dozen certain attributions are known—and so any major new discovery is bound to make news. "La Bonne Aventure" turned up in 1948 in an unidentified private collection, and on hearing of its existence the Louvre immediately expressed interest and made a (very low) offer for it. Before authorization could be obtained to make a more reasonable offer, however, it was bought, still pretty cheaply, by Wildenstein, who subsequently claimed he knew nothing of the Louvre's interest in the picture. He wanted to sell it, presumably in the United States, and applied for an export license, which was refused on the grounds that the painting was part of "France's national artistic patrimony." He then applied for permission to exhibit it in America, which could not be refused, though the condition was made that it must be returned to France afterwards. It left for America, was never exhibited, but did return the following year.

It then vanished from view, being kept, who knows where, as Wildenstein's personal and private property. Its existence was nearly forgotten, as was perhaps the intention. In 1957 Wildenstein donated to a grateful Louvre a Monet, and then applied again for a temporary export license for "La Bonne Aventure," which was again granted. The painting rested in New York for a year or so, then Wildenstein applied to have the license made permanent. The Louvre, the principal interested party, was still too grateful to object (or so Malraux, the Minister of Culture, later explained), so the permanent license was granted and the painting was sold to the Metropolitan for a rumored $600,000, or thereabouts. It is very likely that if Wildenstein had been prevented from selling it anywhere but in France he would not have got more than a quarter of that for it.

When the news broke in France there was a storm: but nothing could then be done; hints that the Metropolitan might be persuaded to return the painting came to nothing, and eventually the whole thing blew over. Clearly no laws had been broken. But equally clearly Wildenstein had found an ingenious way to circumvent the laws and to reverse by 1959 the decision, explicitly stated in 1949, that the painting was important enough a part of France's national heritage not to be permitted to leave the country permanently in any circumstances. It just goes to show that it is difficult for the will of a powerful individual to be resisted indefinitely, especially if he is rich enough to give away a Monet in order to get what he wants.

THE DEALER AS PATRON

For those wanting to set up as art dealer without encountering too many of the hazards connected with selling the art of the past, from drying up of supply to shaky authentication, there is always another way out: deal in art of the present, living art by living artists. And this is precisely what many have done, though few exclusively. At the last count, there were about 300 private galleries in Paris, about 150 in London, and about 400 in New York. In each case the number could probably be doubled if one counted such borderline cases as antique shops that sell some pictures, private dealers without galleries, and various miscellaneous professionals and semiprofessionals. In Paris there is a committee which represents galleries specializing in contemporary art (though not all of them belong to the organization): its membership is now around 130. In London a rule-of-thumb check suggests that about 100 deal mainly in contemporary art; the percentage is about the same in New York. Though the most lavish new private gallery premises in London are both devoted to old masters—the Heim Gallery in Jermyn Street, the London venture of a famous Paris firm, and the Brod galleries in St. James—most of the new galleries which open deal almost entirely in the work of living painters, while many galleries which in the past dealt only in old masters, like Tooth's, and even Marlborough Fine Arts, which began by selling mainly old masters and Impressionists, have moved little by little into the contemporary field.

The same is true of New York, where since the war such long established "traditional" galleries as Durlacher and Knoedler have given more and more of their time and space to living artists, particularly living American artists. In this move as in so many others in art, Paris was somewhat in advance—but not so much as might be expected: it was as late as the 1920s that Kahnweiler was considered mad by other dealers for his championing of moderns like Picasso, and the flood of cheap Picassos and others released on the market after the sequestration of his property in 1921-23 brought down prices to such a degree that many considered the moderns to be completely discredited as a result. But oddly enough the new painters continued to find dealers who believed in their work, and even more oddly, the Kahnweiler sales actually created so much interest that the Hôtel Drouot rapidly began a regular series of sales of new paintings, mostly put up for sale by the painters themselves. Despite the Depression, interest continued, and by the end of the war the market in modern painting was undoubtedly livelier in Paris than anywhere else.

The reasons why dealers should take to the work of living painters are obvious enough, and hardly need restating: no problem of dwindling supplies, no difficulties about authentication and provenance (or at least not till M. Schecroum came on the scene), no important competition from the auction houses, which elsewhere in the market have tended increasingly to take the bread out of the dealers' mouths. On the other hand there are obvious difficulties which do not arise when one is dealing with artists who are safely dead. For one thing, the market is clearly much more speculative. Dealers in old masters and established painting hotly deny that they have things easy: they generally, rather defensively, insist that is not just a matter of following fashion; the truly creative dealer anticipates and to some extent makes fashion. That may be true enough within certain limits, but it is certainly less true now than it was in the 1900s, when, as Vollard remarked, it was possible to show creative, anticipatory taste by buying El Grecos, Vermeers or la Tours before their reputations and prices started to boom. It is difficult to believe that nowadays any possibly major painter is that far out of fashion, though of course the possibilities of booms in minor painters' reputations remain considerable. The dealer specializing in contemporary art, however, must necessarily depend quite a lot on flair, on guessing right or at least on having the gifts necessary to make his guesses come true.

First of all, he must find his painters. Depending

on temperament and the sort of business he envisages, he will look for painters whose work, preferably, appeals to him (that always helps) and seems to him in one way or another salable. There are, obviously, all sorts of ways that a work of art may be salable: its immediate surface attractiveness to the generality of fairly staid art buyers, its compliance with some currently popular trend; its power to shock, outrage and make news; or, most difficult of all to be sure about, some intangible quality of lasting strength and personal vision in it which guarantees, as far as anything can, that time, energy and money spent on it will prove a lasting investment. Always supposing that the dealer wants a lasting investment. He may, of course, want to sell things quickly, in the fashion of the moment, and change his painters and styles as frequently as dress designers change the height of women's hemlines. It is just as legitimate an aim, just as proper an interpretation of the dealer's function.

So, armed with tastes, if not taste, a certain image of himself as a dealer, and a probably vaguer image of his ideal artist, he will set out to search. Sometimes the thing is decided in advance: it happens more often in Paris than in London or New York, but everywhere it happens sometimes, that an artist or a group of artists find their own dealer, or if necessary make him out of one of their own number. Such enterprises are generally idealistic, extreme, and short-lived, like Signals in London, a center mainly for kinetic art which flashed newsworthily across the sky and vanished, all within eighteen months. But most of the better-founded businesses arise from a dealer with a certain amount of money, his own or a backer's, choosing his artists for himself. He will probably keep an eye on the better art schools, he will check through the various open and mixed exhibitions, and he will certainly listen to what other artists have to say, since it is generally through them that the first news of a worthwhile new talent comes. Nearly always discoveries are made by artists first, dealers second, and critics a poor third.

When the dealer finds his artist he will want, if he can, to monopolize him. This is only natural. If he is to launch an artist it will take time and planning, it will involve an investment, often quite considerable, of money, and it may well be a slow process from which he will not benefit appreciably for some years, if ever. To make it worth his while he wants at least to be as sure as possible that as soon as the artist is successfully launched he will not go off at once to someone who may make him a better offer. There will usually be a dealer to do so, since in this risky, speculative world it is always more comforting to take on an established artist with a sure sale than someone untried and possibly fated never to make the big time.

It is one of the standing causes for resentment about the massive, dazzlingly successful Marlborough Fine Arts in London, for instance, that though they rapidly put under contract most of the biggest names in British art, they launched none of them themselves. Henry Moore and Graham Sutherland were internationally established even when Marlborough first began operations in 1946, and by the time it moved into living British art in a big way around 1960 they could make their own terms without owing any particular debt to other galleries. But Lynn Chadwick, Ken Armitage and Ben Nicholson were all regulars of Gimpel Fils, nurtured and built up through the unprofitable years by Peter Gimpel, and their defection to the Marlborough just as the returns began to come in was taken very hard. The Hanover Gallery felt no better about Francis Bacon's move to the Marlborough, and many other galleries could tell similar tales, since in only six or seven years the Marlborough managed to take over very nearly all the leading, best-selling painters and sculptors in Britain today.

The dealer is looking for an artist he can invest in, and in return wants first call, if possible only call, on the artist's work. What is the artist looking for? Whatever else, he is certainly looking for success. Despite all the romantic fantasies of *la vie de bohème,* few artists are so unworldly that they do not care what happens to their work or how it is received. Few, either, are very happy starving in a garret, or take well to being told that financial security will ruin their talent. And generally it doesn't, though to be fair just occasionally it does. Anyway, the artist must live, and support wife and children. If he cannot do it by painting he may do it by teaching or by commercial design, but as a rule he would rather live by painting if he can. This is where the dealer comes in. What he offers is a showcase, a publicity machine of some sort, however rudimentary, and the benefit of his acquaintance with art buyers, his established clientele, his contacts with critics and trendsetters—for whatever any of these may be worth.

If he is not a very prosperous dealer, these may be

all he offers. He may want the artist to pay him directly for their use. Even in London there are galleries like the Upper Grosvenor and the Woodstock which are available on hire to anyone with a little money to gamble on his own talent; there are more in New York (more rich amateur artists, perhaps, ready to pay costs of anywhere from $500 to $3000) and more still in Paris, where gallery-hiring of this sort is quite a regular and established practice. But more usually he will offer the artist a sort of loose alliance for their mutual benefit. He will buy, maybe, a certain number of the artist's paintings outright, and will otherwise act as the artist's agent, selling his work for him in return for a determined percentage of the sale price, conventionally 33⅓ percent, but often in practice as much as 50 percent. This sort of straight commission deal is better than nothing, and in fact the artist may sometimes, if he is lucky, benefit considerably from it. On the other hand, he shares the insecurity of the situation with the dealer, except that the dealer can spread his losses and the artist can't. And the dealer cannot hope to tie him very securely to such an arrangement, which usually stays, like most artist-agent relationships, in the tricky realm of the gentlemen's agreement; in New York, especially, it is quite common for artists to have several dealers selling their work on such terms, though this is much less frequently done in Europe.

For these reasons, the monopoly system is generally preferred by both parties if it can be arranged. The really big *if* is the amount of money the dealer has available. For the essence of the system is that the dealer should pay his artist a regular wage in return for the whole of the artist's output. This wage is in theory a guaranteed minimum return on the work the dealer sells for the artist on commission (33⅓ per cent, 50 per cent or even more). If the return from the sales after deduction of commission does not add up to as much as the "salary," the dealer is still committeed to pay it; if sales exceed in value this basic agreed figure, then the artist gets additional payments accordingly, less, of course, the dealer's commission in each sale. The system has the advantage for the artist of guaranteeing him a regular wage, which hopefully gives him the freedom to devote himself full time to his art without worrying about how well it is selling. The dealer, for his part, has to find the money regularly whether the artist's work is selling or not. But in consideration of this he does get complete control of the artist's output; to put on the market or withhold as he sees fit, to price as he likes, and generally to shape the sort of public career he would like his artist to have. And once his artist has really arrived, the risks of the arrangement are minimal and the rewards very considerable.

So this system, having advantages for both sides, is the one which governs the relationships of most living artists of any standing with their dealers. And if it seems iniquitous, as at first glance it does, that the artist may be getting only 50 percent or even 40 percent of the sale price of his work, it should be remembered that the author generally gets only 12½ percent, 10 percent or (on paperbacks) 5 percent of his work's selling price. Of course the situations are not exactly comparable, in that the expenses involved in manufacturing and publishing a book are far higher than those involved in selling a painting. Still, the author and the artist do have this in common: that they are paying, perhaps excessively, perhaps not, to have the main financial risk of the enterprise carried by someone else. Authors who, like Bernard Shaw, have had the daring to bear the risk themselves have sometimes made a fortune out of it. But few are daring enough, or rich enough, to follow suit. Similarly with artists: some few might make a fortune out of marketing their own products, paying a commission to nobody and taking on all the incidental expenses themselves. But few want to try, or can afford to. So in the long run the artist needs the dealer just as much as the dealer needs him.

But such relations are never easy. Complaints from both sides are endless and infinitely varied: usually each accuses the other of greed, and then goes on to charge irresponsibility, misrepresentation, sloth, malice, contract-breaking, financial jiggery-pokery of all sorts, uncooperativeness, publicizing too much, publicizing too little, overproducing, underproducing, overselling, underselling, making eyes at other dealers/artists instead of devoting himself heart and soul to the relationships in hand. Somewhere, sometime, an apparent basis of justification can be found for all these charges, but it is inevitable that they should arise, because however perfect and idealistic a relationship of this sort may be, inevitably the interests of those involved must at certain points pull in different directions, and when they do, accusations always start to fly, whether justified or not.

Of more interest to us, however, than these purely internal disagreements is the broader question of what the advantages and disadvantages of the system are as far as the world of art as a whole is concerned. And that resolves itself into another question, simple to pose but extremely difficult to answer: in general, does better or worse art result from the system, or does it make no appreciable difference at all? This is difficult because it is necessarily a general question, but one to which absolutely no general answer is possible. The influences which go to form any given single work of any given artist are fantastically complicated and anyway at best a matter of interpretation. Even if the interpretation is wrong it is seldom provably so.

It may seem to us, for instance, that a certain artist tends at one stage in his career to be relying unduly on a particular set of mannerisms, an established range of limited motifs, that in fact he is stagnating. It is easy to guess, and the guess is often made, that a root cause of this is that his dealer has made him aware that works with these characteristics, in this form, have a ready market, and perhaps that other, more adventurous works have not. This may even be true, especially considering that pressures of this sort can appear quite unconsciously not only for the person pressured, but also for the person providing the pressure. It may be that the artist is, as it were, pressuring himself—he knows that a particular part of his work does not sell, and feels guilty toward the dealer, who is a friend and a good chap, even if the dealer would not in fact dream of holding this local failure to sell against him. Or it may be that the artist, for entirely inexplicable reasons, just happens to be going through a barren period. Yet, if so, the fact that he goes on producing inferior work at this time may be the result of some sort of pressure from the dealer that he should keep up a supply. But equally it may be because the artist himself is not conscious of the deterioration, or because, though conscious of it, he feels that the only way he can exercise his art is by continuing to exercise his art.

Again, to come at it from another angle, what seems to be a period of stagnation and deterioration may prove to be nothing of the sort, but an invisible preparation for some entirely new departure. And this may be so whether the reworking of familiar themes and motifs was his own idea or was somehow put into his head by his dealer. Not every suggestion from outside, after all, is necessarily bad. One stimulus is much like another: what counts is what the artist makes of it. Let us take a concrete example. It cannot be entirely accidental that during the last two or three years nearly all the Marlborough's stable of artists have taken up, often for the first time, various forms of graphic expression, especially the lithograph. It is well known that the artist's lithograph, preferably in nice signed editions, not too small, not too large, is steadily increasing in popularity, providing as it does a fairly easy, relatively inexpensive way for the modest collector to start. It would not seem too unreasonable to suppose, therefore, that Marlborough Fine Arts has "suggested" to its artists, one way or another, and probably explicitly, in so many words, that they should give it a try.

But is that necessarily wrong? One can judge only

by results. No doubt the special talents of, say, Leon Goossens on the oboe, Lionel Tertis on the viola, Alfred Deller in the counter tenor range, "suggested" to composers that they should exploit these very resources of music rather than some other; sometimes the musicians concerned suggested it in so many words. And sometimes the musical results have been undistinguished, dutiful. And sometimes they have been superb. The same with the Marlborough graphics. To many critics it seems that the disciplines of the lithograph shackle Henry Moore's talents, while in other artists they have brought out talents we never knew they had. The results, finally, are really all that count, not the precise means by which they were brought about.

And yet, and yet. When all this is said, there still remains a slight feeling that the results of the monopoly-contract system are not always good. It seems often that there creeps into the work of artists working in this way a certain touch of complacency. Of course, complacency is often a by-product of fame and success, and might set in anyway. And of course no one in his right mind would try to suggest that artists can only function properly on the bread line. But the guaranteed market of the system seems to edge the artist toward a greater facility, a readiness, perhaps, to accept first thoughts when second or third might be better. And certainly some artists feel themselves pushed to overproduce by the system, while others have their natural expansiveness curtailed: dealers have a tendency to like a moderate, steady flow of product from slow thinkers and prodigal improvisers alike.

But perhaps the strongest and most consistent

effect of the system is to encourage a concentration on the smaller, directer, easier-to-manage works. A lot of sideboard-size maquettes from the sculptors, prints, drawings and sketches from the painters. The return is larger in relation to the energy expended, and any way they will always sell, which larger and more difficult works won't necessarily. Again, the prudent and practical artist (for there is no rule which says that the artist may not be prudent and practical) might react in this way to the stimuli of the market if left entirely to himself, but the very efficiency of the dealer's management, his careful channeling of work to where it will be most welcome, his necessarily close in-touchness with the slightest fluctuations and changes of direction in the tastes of the buying public—all these help to make the artist more immediately aware of the market he is supplying. Such awareness can do a lot more harm than good.

Anyway, approve of the system or not, we seem to be stuck with it. Nowadays the first aim of virtually every aspiring artist leaving art school is to be noticed and put under contract by an important gallery. That way lies security—of a sort, for a time at least—but also, more importantly, the possibility of instant fame. For in the last few years we have seen something very like another golden age of the living artist. Never since the heyday of mid-Victorianism has there been such a seller's market for contemporary art as there was in Paris in 1959-60, in London in 1963-4 and as there is in New York now. This means that there has been, and is, quite a bit of money around to be picked up even by relatively unknown, relatively advanced artists.

But it does not stop there. The art boom has generated such hysteria that people are willing to gamble on almost anything as a likely investment. The old masters are all climbing in price (though there are still some who have not yet, in terms of the real value of money, topped their all-time Edwardian high), and the Impressionists have not only followed but overtaken them. From there, though, one would think it was quite a step to paying high prices for Abstract Expressionists or action painters or op artists. But it is a step a surprising number of art buyers have not hesitated to take. Do they, one cannot help wondering, actually *like* what they are buying? No necessary reflection on the thing itself: everything can find somebody to love it, and many painters of these schools have an enthusiastic following among critics and those knowledgeably interested in art. But then again, many haven't, and what strikes one above all about much public and private buying of modern art is its curious indiscriminateness. At least Victorian art buying, however misguided its scale of values may seem to us now, is recognizably related to a particular taste in art, and a particular view of what art should be. Some of the criteria invoked to justify high prices then, like the number of man-hours Holman Hunt put in on "The Shadow of the Cross" or Edwin Long on "The Marriage Market", seem to us now, though not, after all, entirely unreasonable, at least curiously beside the point. And we can conceive that the Victorians actually liked what they paid so dearly for—indeed, we cannot doubt it.

But by what standards are the prices paid in the last few years for tiny and entirely unremarkable scribbles by the vastly prolific Picasso, or for large abstractions by Georges Mathieu, whose principal claim to fame seems to be that he can cover bigger canvases faster than anyone else (his performances usually take fifteen to twenty minutes), or for the rigidly standardized, schematically stylized portraits and subject-groups of Bernard Buffet to be justified? Of the Picassos it may be said that he is a great painter, but it would be foolish to pretend that all his unnumerable works are on the same level. Of Buffet at least one can say that his paintings are unmistakable and fairly easy on the eye. And of Mathieu. . . . ?

Anyway, the probable fate awaiting many merely modish painters would seem already to have befallen Buffet. From selling all the paintings in his exhibitions before the opening he went almost without transition to selling none, and the Tate Gallery recently ticked off one of us for "unfairness" in mentioning in a guide to art in London that they even had a Buffet. It was true, they admitted, that they had one, but they never, never showed it. Philippe Jullien has an entertaining story somewhat to the point in his *Les Collectionneurs*. A connoisseur has told him, he alleges, of an unfortunate incident in the life of Max Ernst. Shortly after the war Ernst was in Paris, none too well off. A prewar friend, an art director, told him of a marvelous opportunity for a big color feature on his work in a large-circulation magazine, and suggested a payoff of two important Ernst paintings for arranging it. Ernst showed him the door, and a month later the magazine published six color pages devoted to Buffet. A very moral story,

Julien replies, for after all instead of owning two large Ernsts the art director must now own two large Buffets!

Undoubtedly there will be a considerable winnowing of the wheat from the chaff after this golden age of the living painter, as there was after the last (the Paris market has already taken a few nasty shocks) and it will be interesting, if for some rather upsetting, to find out who qualifies as the Alma-Tadema or Rosa Bonheur of the 1960s. But for the moment it is anybody's guess. The living painters, of all sorts, keep on selling, and in New York especially they keep on selling spectacularly well. The prematurely dead, whose output is therefore definitely limited, like Nicholas de Staël and Jackson Pollock, do even better—already in 1960 a de Staël was sold for £13,000 at Sotheby's, and several Pollocks have changed hands privately for more than £25,000 apiece.

The reasons people buy them are various and inscrutable. They even include the good straightforward old-fashioned one of actually liking what one buys. But also that there is undoubtedly a lot of buying for two closely interlinked reasons, the same as those for buying many old masters and Impressionists: that it is the thing to do and everybody's doing it; and that it is an investment at least equal in reliability to stocks and shares. The first reason is at least fairly tangible: it can be established how many important people, with how much attendant publicity, are buying this or that painter, and the thing snowballs from there. But even so such a process must start somewhere, there must be a first to buy. And the second reason, though comprehensible as a reason, seems strangely slim and shaky to have extracted so much money from so many. Who knows which modern painters will prove a good investment? Who says? Who persuades the trend-setters to start buying? And how? To attempt an answer to these questions we must now move on from the intake of the art market to its output, from what the sellers sell and how they come by it to how they go about selling it. In fact, to the technique of promotion.

THE TECHNIQUE
OF PROMOTION

Let us suppose that the dealer has now secured his stock, in reasonable amounts for his purpose. He has acquired his stable of living artists, on whatever terms. He has gathered together a collection of Old Masters consonant with the tastes of a moneyed class which does not necessarily know or care anything about art but likes the feel of "old and beautiful" things about it, and the idea that they are a very solid investment. He has picked his specialty in the art of the past, an artist, a school or a genre, and assembled a coherent body of associated work. He has hit on some gimmick—art as a happening, watch the artists at work or something of the sort—which he believes can attract attention. He believes that there is always a moderately cultivated market for low-priced, respectable, unalarming works which match the curtains, remind the buyer of somewhere he once had an enjoyable holiday, or even immortalize in charcoal or pastel the features of a loved one. Any and all of these types of dealer may make a go of it; equally, any of them may fail miserably. The difference is to a certain extent to be found in the inherent quality of what they are selling, and it would be silly to pretend otherwise. On the other hand, it would be naïve to suppose that that is all there is to it. Having the art to sell is one thing; being able to sell it on the best possible terms is quite another matter.

The first thing to be mastered is the buildup. To this there are two interconnected lines of approach, buildup of the art itself, and buildup of the person or institution selling it. Though separate concepts, they are interdependent. A dealer's reputation depends to a considerable degree on the quality of what he sells and how successful he is in selling it; on the other hand, the market value of what he sells is often determined, within certain limits, by his reputation and by the context in which he sells it. To take a simple example. Let us suppose a painting which might or might not be a Van Dyck. There are enough Van Dycks around to make the discovery of another one, quite out of the blue, not too incredible a possibility. So, if we see a painting such as this in a small antique dealer's somewhere we shall not be totally incredulous, even if we are asked only £30 or £50 for it. We shall be backing our own judgment on it. The same painting in a minor West End dealer's might cost £500, £1000, or even £2000. The dealer would be willing to tell us how likely it was to be a real Van Dyck, would cite various author-

ities and parallels, and would have more to lose by selling us at a fancy price something which proved to be a
nearly worthless copy or forgery. In other words, he
could have a certain reputation to maintain, would be
careful to maintain it, and would hope to benefit from
it to the extent that it gives his say-so more weight with
potential and regular customers. The same painting
again, if it was offered at Agnew's or Colnaghi's or
Koetser's as an authentic Van Dyck would cost anything
from £5000 to maybe (if it was of absolutely superlative
quality) £50,000.

Why? Well, obviously snobbery has something to
do with it, and so do the possible financial resources of
these great dealers' clients. But the basic reason is that if
you buy something from such a dealer you can be as
certain as it is possible to be that it is exactly what the
label says. The painting will have been examined by leading experts, it will no doubt have been cleaned and ana-
lyzed so that you can know exactly what its condition is,
how much if anything it owes to restoration, repainting,
etc., and all possible external researches will have been
made to establish its pedigree—for whom it was first
painted, what collections it has passed through since,
and what, if anything, scholarship has had to say about
it along the way. All this will amount to a guarantee of
authenticity, and if by some mischance it should happen that your purchase is proved not to be what it is
supposed to be, any of these and other comparable galleries would take it back and refund the purchase price
without question. Anyone can make a mistake—even
London's National Gallery had to admit in 1955, for

instance, that a "Virgin and Child" by the fifteenth-century Bolognese painter Francesco Francia on their walls was in fact a nineteenth-century copy and that a version in the possession of the dealer Leonard Koetser was the original—but a leading dealer cannot afford to make too many, and certainly cannot afford not to do everything in his power to rectify a mistake once made. So when you buy a picture from such a gallery you are paying for the research, the authoritative appraisal and the satisfying sureness that your money is safely spent as well as for the painting. That, without all the rest, you might—you just might—have picked up for £30 in the Portobello Road.

With a major painting which must constitute for any buyer a major investment, the expertise and the guarantee are explicit. With a small work, a drawing by a minor artist or something of the sort, it is probably implicit, but nevertheless it is there, a very valuable part of the dealer's stock-in-trade. And this is where the buildup of the dealer's own reputation becomes important. The fact that if you buy, say, a Pre-Raphaelite drawing from the Maas Gallery just off Bond Street, you know you are buying from an expert who specializes in this school and period is worth maybe half the purchase price to you—that and the convenience of knowing that if you want a work by a particular member of the school, or to see a selection of such works, the Maas Gallery is the first and obvious place to go. Accessibility and general impressiveness of the dealer's premises also count for quite a bit here. If the dealer can afford to have a pleasant, well laid-out gallery on Bond

Street or just off it, this is likely to confer a certain comforting air of prosperity, stability and reliability on him (not, it must be confessed, always quite justified in practice). Other dealers may find that for the financial bracket of customers they have in mind too fashionable an address, too plush a showplace may be intimidating —a number of the less grand dealers owe a considerable part of their success to their sedulous cultivation of a poor-but-honest image, as of a place where people know what's what, but a bargain may always be picked up on the principle that a lot of small but rapid profits are preferable to a problematical big bonanza in the sweet by-and-by.

There are other variations too numerous to go into. One British dealer, Nicholas Treadwell, has managed to function successfully from a group of mobile galleries, the largest a converted furniture van, with which he tours neighbourhoods soliciting custom for his modestly priced modern paintings from door to door in a wide area within a hundred-mile radius of London. In the United States Sears-Roebuck hit on the interesting idea of "personalizing" their art sales by setting up a traveling exhibition of art for sale, mainly graphics and drawings, bought and arranged for them by the actor and art expert Vincent Price. Naturally Mr. Price's celebrity to many who knew little or nothing about art did no harm at all to the sales, while his admitted expertise, particularly on old-master etchings and native Indian and Pre-Columbian art, ensured that he earned his money as far more than an effective front-man. In fact the whole enterprise was so successful that at least one disgruntled dealer tried to sue them for misrepresentation, claiming (somewhat improbably) that billing the works for sale as "The Vincent Price Collection" suggested that all of them were his personal property. The action came to nothing, and this profitable marketing enterprise still continues, though now on a reduced scale in one or two permanent centers, owing mainly to the difficulty of keeping up an adequate supply of the type of art required by the original scheme.

The dealer's reputation, which may eventually be of enormous value to him, is something which as a rule can be built up only slowly, over the years. The reputation of his wares and their selling power can, with luck and judgment, be established much more quickly. There are all sorts of methods, which apply in varying degrees to the work of both living and long-dead artists. If he is wise, the dealer usually starts with the "impersonal" approach, which he can assist quite effectively even before he has an outlet for his wares or has associated himself publicly with them. One useful weapon lying to hand is the exhibition arranged by some reputable noncommercial body such as the British Council, the Arts Council, a museum or some professional group like the Royal Academy or the Royal Water Colours Society. Not, indeed, that most dealers in modern art would encourage their artists to have much to do with either of the latter—many even make it a rule that artists under contract to them shall refrain from exhibiting at the Academy, for fear that such lackluster associations shall permanently damage their image. But effective representation for a young artist in a British Council exhibition at home or aboard is eagerly sought after, the ultimate prize being the artist's selection as one of Britain's representatives at the Venice Biennale, where the big reputations of many senior British artists, among them Henry Moore, Ben Nicholson, Lynn Chadwick, Francis Bacon and Eduardo Paolozzi, first began to be made. Purchase of works by the Arts Council helps too, and a list of sales to provincial museums is always reassuring.

For the "rediscovery" there is even more to be done. There is an endless succession of exhibitions, by all sorts of institutions, all over the country. If your speciality is an eighteenth-century artist, there are just for starters about half a dozen important eighteenth-century showplaces which have exhibitions devoted to a particular artist or a particular theme every summer, Kenwood being only the most central and best known of them. Often those already arranged can be pressed into service, or failing that a tactful suggestion of an exhibition devoted to, say, the noble savage in eighteenth-century art or the painting of Cipriani and friends may well not be taken amiss, especially if it is backed up by an offer of significant loans and assistance in assembling and documenting the material. And if the lender-deviser comes out at the end of it with possessions considerably better publicized and more valuable than when he went in, that seems only a fair return for his labor. Intelligent dealers keep a sharp watch on their calendar for centenaries and other anniversaries likely to be commemorated by an exhibition. 1967? Centenary of Brangwyn's birth. Certain, therefore, that there will be some sort of official recognition—a retrospective exhibition perhaps by the Royal Academy or the Arts Council (in that case, the Arts Council). So, sure enough, at least one commercial gallery, the Fine Art Society, puts on its own "centenary contribution," and others fish out Brangwyns they have had salted away for maybe ten or fifteen years. An exhibition like the Royal Academy's 1966 tribute to Millais (sixty years dead) is bound to arouse new interest, reflected in prices, even if the net result, as there, is to reconfirm old prejudices about the superiority of Millais' Pre-Raphaelite period to the rest of his work. A revival on the scale of the Victoria and Albert Museum's Mucha exhibition of 1963 or its Beardsley exhibition of 1966 is bound to send up the stock of the artists concerned. In fact the Grosvenor Gallery had a Mucha exhibition concurrent with the Victoria and Albert's, so that the two were often written about together and art lovers fired by the one could go on to the other and actually buy (at suitably timely prices) examples to rival the museum's own. There do not seem to be enough Beardsley originals still available in private hands to make up a whole commercial exhibition, but all the single examples which could be dug up were promptly, and pricily, displayed, while provident antiquarian booksellers had a field day.

Not that any such exhibitions have necessarily been engineered in any way by those with something to gain financially from them. Even something as staid and "establishment" as the Royal Academy's record-breaking 1967-68 exhibition of Eighteenth-Century French

Art could probably not be staged at all, or at any rate not by any means as well, without the willingness of the Wildenstein in London, Paris and New York to dig into their stores for loans and to put the organizers in contact with customers to whom they have lately sold relevant material. The occasion for an exhibition can often be foreseen a long way off; the exhibition itself may need only the slightest push with an offer of assistance which is none the less genuine and useful for not being perhaps, in the last analysis, entirely disinterested. And certainly such exhibitions all go, one way and another, to give "status", and therefore increased monetary value, to the artist or genre exhibited: after all, the cautious collector reasons, something must be respectable if this or that museum has shown it or bought it. Perhaps the biggest push of all the 1920s and 1930s designs of the versatile Franco-Russian decorator Erté got on the market in 1967 was the intelligence, freely bandied about, that when a collection of them was shown in New York it had been promptly bought en bloc by the Museum of Modern Art. This at least convinced many a hesitator that they were not just, as he half suspected, camp fun, but must actually, in some lasting, reputable fashion, be *good*.

Much the same applies to the appearance of a book on an artist or school, particularly if it is scholarly (with a detailed catalogue) and well illustrated. This too confers status on the subject, and may also provide a point of reference for determining what is genuine and what is not. It is not unknown for a dealer actually to commission a book on a subject in which, financially and otherwise, he is vitally interested. Nor is there necessarily anything suspect about it: in paying someone to carry out research for other people's use as well as his own he may well be performing a public service, and it is highly unlikely that he would be able to persuade any reputable scholar, even if he wanted to, to cook the books in order to push his own doubtful attributions. Even Duveen found, when he was sued in 1929 by the owner of an alleged Leonardo, "La Belle Ferronnière" for saying that it was a worthless copy of the real painting in the Louvre and thus preventing a sale, that, though he was able to produce a private report from his retained expert, Berenson, stating that the Louvre painting was certainly the original, Berenson's published writings could be damagingly cited in the completely opposite sense. If a dealer wants to put forward in print a view of one of his own possessions which is, to say the least, eccentric, he must usually do it himself: the London dealer Henry F. Pulitzer may believe and firmly argue that he and he alone owns the real "Mona Lisa" (*Where is the Mona Lisa?*), but as long as he has to write his own book to prove it readers are perfectly capable of judging for themselves the weight they will give his testimony.

Whether or not scholarly books on the arts are commissioned by dealers or inspired by them (like the symposium *Antiques International,* edited by Peter Wilson of Sotheby's, which, in suggesting what categories of objets d'art are likely to increase in price, obviously does its bit toward helping them do so), they often serve the dealer's ends. Better, probably, than the authors'. Sir Michael Sadleir remarks sadly in his *Auto-biography of a Bibliomaniac* that he never quite got used to the vast increase in the price of obscure gothic novels which resulted directly from his own scholarly work on the genre, and one of us, having written a book about Art Nouveau book design in Britain, has had the galling experience of being quoted back at himself to justify a fancy price for some book he still wants to buy. A large number of books on the arts are somewhere in the works of publishing at any one time, and it is relatively easy for the dealer to find out well in advance whether someone is working on a book which may, indirectly, be of advantage in his dealings and plan accordingly. If it were announced now that a big new book on, say, Ford Madox Brown, Diaz de la Peña or the Brothers Maris, or for that matter Murillo or Terborch or Salvator Rosa, was in active preparation, many dealers would take careful note of the fact and start stock-piling.

The next moves after doing all possible to secure this sort of independent and disinterested support for a dealer's artistic protégé will no doubt be on the most personal level. The dealer will probably have regular clients, he will have acquaintances of various sorts in the art world, and he will do whatever he can to create and spread interest by word-of-mouth. In the right circumstances this can be very valuable. There is always an appeal in the idea of getting in on the ground floor, being in on a secret today which the world will know tomorrow. The news that this collector has bought a canvas or two, that that expert is interested in doing a detailed study, that a certain well established painter thinks this young man is the most remarkable talent to emerge since . . . All this can be circulated, and even if it is often taken with a pinch of salt, it all helps to some extent. It may even be true. It is often worth giving, or selling at a very low price, one or two of the works in hand to a particularly shrewd and influential collector, just for the kudos the sale confers. Testimonials, even if they excite a degree of skepticism, are quite worth collecting. In these days when art is very much news, items can be planted in the gossip columns just as readily about artists as about film stars, and it is surprising how many people are actually impressed to learn that lovely ex-debutante Lady XYZ was given such and such a painting by her godfather as a wedding present or that swinging pop star Bill Jones is the most avid enthusiast for the work of some new kinetic artist.

More solid corroboration can be provided, too. In the case of a dead artist the sales can be turned into a positive aid. If a dealer consistently buys the work of an artist whenever it comes up at auction, the prices are almost bound to go up, since the very fact that someone patently wants a thing automatically makes others suppose that there must be something in it worth having. And though the higher prices which result may be tiresome in one way, since they prevent the dealer from buying as cheaply as he might wish, they are all good publicity, since the auction record of an artist is always taken into account in estimating what the proper current price for his work should be. Perhaps you remember the case of the eighteenth-century English marine painter Charles Brooking, and the steady climb in his prices which we mentioned in an earlier chapter. It is significant that all the sales of Brooking paintings we can trace during this time were to the same dealer, Leggatt Brothers. It is possible that they are simply acting as agents for some single-minded Brooking enthusiast, but more likely that they have settled on Brooking as a man whose value is likely to go up and who could do with a little pushing. If so, the fact that his paintings have been fetching over £15,000 in the salerooms will certainly do them no harm when eventually they are offered for sale, perhaps all together in a one-man show with a scholarly catalogue. So much sought after is this sort of value guarantee, in fact, that it is by no means unknown for dealers to puff their own wares by putting an example up for sale anonymously, bidding it up and buying it back at an unexpectedly high price. This costs them the auctioneer's commission, but probably pays for itself several times over in the increased prices they can charge for the rest.

The ground properly laid, the time comes for the public unveiling. The timing and presentation of this are very important. In Paris there is still a clearly defined season for such things, so clearly defined that many dealers close down altogether in July and August. The year is less rigidly categorized in London and New York, but in both the idea still persists that most serious art buying is done in the winter, and most of the more important commercial exhibitions come between mid-September and the end of May. Christmas and the New Year are not considered good times to open; around

Easter for some reason is. Ideally, you want a lot going on at the same time, to keep interest stimulated, but not too much, lest any individual show may get lost in the rush. It is useful, if it can be managed, to provide critics and the public with a theme or a trend they can latch on to, and therefore the opening at about the same time of exhibitions which relate to one another is more likely to do good than harm to the prospects of each individually. In Paris the *vernissage* is or can be a great social event, and fortunes may be made or marred by one which is conveniently or awkwardly timed, attended by the right or the wrong people, the cause of scandal and excitement or merely boredom—all these things having little to do with the quality of the work on show, which in any case generally cannot be properly seen for the crowds. In New York some concerted attempts have been made to raise the private view to a similar status, with a measure of success; on the whole New York buyers, particularly of modern art, seem to be particularly susceptible to the idea of social cachet attached to this or that artistic occasion. In London, with rare exceptions, private views are pretty dull and sober affairs, often being merely day-long previews during which the invited amble around in ones and twos and actually look at what is on show.

It is hard, for obvious reasons, to produce positive evidence for the importance of timing and details of presentation in the launching of art on the market. But we have some negative evidence which gives food for thought. A British painter known to us was overjoyed when, after jogging along in modest obscurity for some years, he was suddenly taken up by a major New York dealer. His show went on, and reviews were favorable, but hardly anything sold and the thing was a financial failure. Then from what he heard he learned that the show had been opened, against all advice, at a very unfavorable time, the catalogues and publicity had been distributed with an almost willful inefficiency strangely at odds with this dealer's usual style, absurdly high prices had been asked for his work, and would-be purchasers discouraged or positively snubbed. The reason? It was surmised that his excessively prosperous sponsors had reached the stage in the financial year where they needed a tax loss, and he had been chosen to fill the bill. Evidently he is not exactly a disinterested witness, but the idea does seem plausible enough to open up all sorts of disturbing possibilities.

Presentation to the public means, inevitably, presentation to the critics. Critics are a vexed topic in the art world, and on no single issue does one find a wider range of opinion. In France the influence of the critics is often held to be of paramount importance, and the critics themselves do not seem on the whole inclined to deny this; the view is supported among artists and dealers, especially by those with an ax to grind, usually an inexplicable and of course entirely undeserved failure which they lay unequivocally at the malicious critics' door. It is not easy to decide how true this is. Certainly in France there seems to be a more marked tendency than elsewhere to respect the word of the expert: a book or film, for instance, which has received a prize may automatically count on an increased audience because of this, which is not noticeably the case in Britain or the United States. But the body of art buyers is much smaller than those of book buyers or filmgoers, and because of the higher cost of the activity it is likely to be more selective.

The critic may have some considerable influence, but it depends on who the critic is and where he is heard. The critics of the large-circulation dailies can have little immediate effect at all, though no doubt in the end the aggregate of publicity given an artist does have some effect on his standing. The critics of the more specialized magazines no doubt have more effect, more even than their British and American counterparts, in that aesthetic questions tend to become passionately fought-over causes in French intellectual circles (such artistic party politics hardly exists in Britain and the United States at all at the same pitch of fervor). These disputes in their turn help to make or break artists' reputations, hence the extraordinarily abrupt ups and downs observable in a career such as Buffet's. The influence of the critics in this sphere, though, seems to be exercized more effectively in the salons and in private conversation than through the more obvious channels of their written work.

In Britain and the United States the position of the critic is more ambiguous. He tends to be blamed when things go wrong and discounted when things go right. Few of the critics themselves believe that they exert any real influence over what is and is not bought—perhaps, they say, John Russell of the London *Sunday Times* or especially John Canaday of *The New York Times,* but even with them it is questionable (Canaday can certainly make reputations, and sometimes break them, though it would be a rash man who undertook to estimate what his approval might mean in hard cash), and the rest are nowhere. Writers on objets d'art or minor art in specialized journals like *Apollo* or *The Connoisseur* are in rather a different category, but then whatever influence they have in directing collectors' interests in new directions is related to the overall truth: that the art critics' usual reader is the art lover as distinct from the art buyer. The critics can send people to an exhibition, which costs nothing or relatively little to get into; but they can't persuade their readers to buy works of art which cost more than, say, £20 because on the whole their readers do not have the money to spare. The class which buys substantial, original works of art in both countries is still minute in relation to the total population, and most of them either know what they like and mean to have without consulting the critics or buy primarily for investment and want advice more financially to the point than the critics' meticulous aesthetic considerations.

Naturally, the amount of trouble the dealer takes over dealing with the critics will depend to a large extent on what he gauges their value to be. In France, therefore, much more trouble is taken with keeping critics happy than in Britain or the United States. There are all sorts of ways. Very few exhibition catalogues in France are without their introductions (another aspect of the importance attributed to expert judgment), and these introductions are written by critics or by figures in the world of art and letters whose support is thought to count for something. The writing of these introductions is as a rule very well paid—a minimum of 500 NF (about £40 or $100) for a very brief piece, and sometimes quite a bit more, if the eminence of the author seems to demand it. Probably the critic selected already sympathizes with what he is asked to write about, but all the same the pressure is there. Then again, few critics in France can live exclusively on what they earn as critics, so most of them do other things as well—they deal a bit, maybe, act as advisers and counselors, appraise and authenticate. The dealer can that way always put a little extra money their way, and let gratitude do the rest. Even direct bribes are not unknown, while there are indirect bribes it is hard to refuse—the gift of or special price for an admired painting by a painter one will then have every reason to admire just that little bit more, entertainment with no strings attached except those which one's own sense of beholdenness provides.

In Britain and the United States the critic is far less likely to be urgently wooed. Less need is felt for enthusiastic introductory recommendations in catalogues, and in general little importance is attached to the say-so of the critics, one way or the other. Galleries like their shows to be written about, since all publicity helps a little, but there seems to be no evidence that they extend their attentions to the critics much beyond keeping them thoroughly informed of what is going on and invited to each show as it comes up. Many critics, whimsically, suggest that they are just waiting to be bribed: what a pity no one thinks it worth the trouble. Any "bribes" that are around are of the most innocent type, from painter to critic, in the shape of grateful gifts of his own work. These seem generally to be accepted in the spirit they are given; as committing nobody to anything. And anyway, they are likely to stop as soon as the artist's work acquires any significant cash value. Perhaps because bribes of one sort or another cannot be relied on, like waiter's tips, as regular perks of the job, most full-time British and American art critics seem to be paid a living, if seldom spectacularly generous, wage.

If dealers in Britain and America usually regard too much attention to the critics as wasted effort, they are seldom so casual about the press in general. They reason thus. Few buyers of art take any notice of the critics anyway. But few, either, buy entirely from their own independent preferences. Fashion, who is buying or is believed to be buying what, competitive excitement and sheer hysteria have much more to do with it. The speculative art-buyer is no different from the speculator in stocks and shares, and observation of the wild fluctuations of the stock market produced by a new Soviet satellite launched, the illness of a President or yet another report on the dangers of smoking give one little cause to put the share-speculator's critical intelligence very high. A lot of the art market, like any other market, depends not on reason and judgment but on maintaining confidence and starting irrational rushes. And the way the press can help here is not through the reasonable discourse of its art critics, but by the whole diffused impact of the vast publicity machine. Few dealers give a fig for a closely reasoned favorable review; but many would give an arm for a spread in a color magazine section accompanied by some assurance of how trendy this or that is and how everybody who is anybody has already bought it, or a lengthy report in the news columns of the year's spectacular ups in the sale prices of art in general and their own specialty in particular. These are the things which really set people buying.

And art is newsworthy now. It is something which has just naturally happened. Money helps: anything which is bought and sold for a lot of money inevitably interests people, and the additional glamor of fortunes made overnight ("Her breadboard was a Rembrandt!") adds an extra touch of spice. The salerooms can be sure of all the free publicity they can use—as long, that is, as record prices continue to be paid and thrilling discoveries made—since the prices are public, for all the world to see and marvel at. The dealers are not so happily placed (which is probably one reason for the continued advance of the salerooms over the dealers in recent years), since their prices are generally not revealed, and are often kept as deep dark secrets. There are ways to hit back, though. A classy spread on "The Glory of Holland Seen through the Painter's Eye" (courtesy of such-and-such a gallery's current exhibition) in a staid upper-class journal like *The Illustrated London News* can do its bit, and at least gets straight at the people most likely to buy. As for the galleries specializing in contemporary art, there are all sorts of ways that they can manage to hit the headlines. Even today the lunatic fringe of art is always good for a giggle—if by now a rather nervous, tentatively respectful giggle—and so a new gimmick of some sort ("He paints with badger-bristle—while it's still on the badger!") will usually rate a story and a picture. But for longer-term results there is nothing like the artist as public personality.

Never can there have been a time when the appearance and demeanor, and even tone of voice, of leading artists have been so familiar to so many of the general public. They are interviewed on television, asked their opinion of contraceptive pills and breathalyser tests for drunken driving, shown setting off on holiday or coming back, like so many film stars, and their little eccentricities, lovable or outrageous, are eagerly chronicled by hosts of all-too-willing popular journalists. The distribution of fame is not absolutely equitable. For some strange reason which must be deeply psychological it seems easier to make a personality out of a figurative than a nonfigurative artist (though we treasure a *Daily Mail* caption to a picture of Barbara Hepworth at work on "Contrapuntal Forms" which read hopefully "Mother of Triplets Chips Festival Statue"). Picasso and Dali are the supreme examples of artists as public personalities today; Henry Moore, Graham Sutherland, L. S. Lowry and John Piper are most prominent among the British contingent, and then skipping most of the middle-generation abstractionists we come to the neo-academics of the 1950s, like John Bratby, and to the pop artists like David Hockney or on the American-born, London-based R. B. Kitaj. The only consistent abstractionists whose personalities have made such a mark on the public are Jackson Pollock, whose death turned him into a sort of folk hero, and the showmen like Mathieu, who share with some of the pop artists, especially Andy Warhol, a gift for scandal and self-display which has little to do with their art as such.

If becoming a personality helps one to achieve fame, it is not absolutely sure that it will make one's fortune too. The buying public is a curious beast, subject to sudden and unreasonable impulse, but also inclined just when one least expects it to be cautious. To sell well and go on selling, an artist must not only be a personality, but the right sort of personality. What undermined buying confidence in Buffet and Mathieu, for example, was not any significant change in their public personalities, and certainly not any noticeable change in the quality of their work, but simply that on reflection they did not seem to be the right sort of personality: not serious enough, too facile, too productive (a great mistake, that). Beyond the scandal and the parade, what was there *solid?* Rightly or wrongly, the buying public dearly likes an artist to be solid. The talk of the town may sell well for a while (though if he is too outrageous and excessive even this is doubtful, especially in Britain, where the art buyer is *au fond* the most conservative in the world) but to keep it up he has to do something more than just scandalize, or he will be faced with the response of one of Peacock's characters to some "sublime" effect in a landscape garden: "But where, pray, is the surprise the second time?"

This is where the dealer's ingenuity and persistence in properly following up the first effect comes in.

If, that is, he is the sort of dealer who bothers to follow up the first effect: some regard artists as expendable—if those they have cease to startle and excite, there are always more where they came from. But for lasting success something more is called for. The dealer must really work on his sales, not only because it is only by selling that he can make back his investment, but also because here very much success breeds success: it is by selling to the right people, and by finding regular buyers of an artist's work, that one establishes more and more widely that it is good idea to buy him and so to sell more. The price has to be right. More new painters have been sabotaged by dealers who asked too much, or by asking too much themselves, than ever starved by asking too little. Asking too little is also a danger, as people tend to esteem art largely by how much they have paid for it. This should not be a permanent danger, though, since if an artist's career is properly managed his prices should increase at a rate sufficient to make owners change the low regard they may entertain for something cheaply bought into the high regard normal for something which could be dearly sold. To support his artist's reputation for increasing value the dealer may even sometimes have to buy back works of his that come on the market at an advanced price; but this has its dangers, since if the prices are too good too many owners may get the urge to cash in while they can, with disastrous results for the dealer's finances.

The ultimate aim of a dealer for what he is selling is that it should become assimilated into a sort of unofficial art establishment. This holds good as much for the dealer in the art of the past as for the specialist in contemporary art. He will hope that the little-known artist, the long unfashionable school which he has brought back into the limelight will first of all have a little vogue as something which is strange, fun, naughty-but-nice, quiet-but-grows-on-you or whatever other quality will catch the buyer of the experimentally-introduced inexpensive novelty. But that sort of regard cannot last for long—there is always a newer novelty just around the corner. So to be more than a passing fad the novelty must move, as its novelty wears off, to the next level of appreciation, where it becomes part of the standard pattern of acceptably marketable art, with its place in the hierarchy, its satisfactory saleroom record, and its reasonably calculable price. If the dealer is very lucky, or very astute, he may hit the jackpot, though usually it would take more than one dealer's normal professional span to do so. Yet it would not be impossible for a young dealer to have invested in Stubbs because he believed in him at about £200 a time in the 1920s and see him selling for around £20,000 in the 1960s. More modestly, each generation restores to favor something which has been despised for about fifty years, so if a dealer bought the most characterful and substantial-seeming of the stuff painted forty years ago (supposing he could find it) he would seem to have a very fair chance of success, provided he did not expect anything too spectacular to happen all at once.

The living painters too come sooner or later into the artistic establishment, which means that even if they seem to disappear from public view, as all except the most spectacular do, they probably live quite comfortably on commissions, sales to regular patrons and a lot of small occasional sales from small, unsensational exhibitions. Interviewed on television in England recently (and no doubt consequently in his way, he too, to becoming a public personality), the painter-sculptor Michael Ayrton (b. 1921) remarked that now he is unfashionable, and gets little attention of any sort from the critics, he is actually far better off financially and sells far more than he did when, in the 1940s, he was part of the fashionable, much talked about young guard of English neo-romantics. And many other artists must have found the same: that they start to sell, regularly, reliably and at reasonable prices, only after they have ceased to be talked about and settled down to being accepted as part of the scenery.

The dealer's job, once having launched an artist, is to assist this gradual consolidation, to stage-manage it if you like. He should not try to push too far too fast, or the first excitement may be followed by a sense of letdown, as happened when in 1964 the Marlborough presented its first big retrospective devoted to David Bomberg: big claims were made on his behalf—not, to be fair, exclusively by the gallery—and then cooler judgment prevailed, so that a Tate Gallery retrospective in 1967 provoked a lot of deflating second thoughts rather than more considered enthusiasm. The dealer must persevere, recognizing that if the artist sold well at his first show it may be some years before, without the virtue of surprise, he sells as well again, while many artists do not even achieve that initial break-through. He should have a constant supply of the art-ist's work, and keep on at his customers—discreetly—until he wins them over. He should keep the artist be-fore the public regularly, but not too obsessively—a show perhaps once a year at most, and more probably every other year or thereabouts. He must try to provide the best possible context for his artist, by linking him with likes or showing off his qualities by telling con-trast. And all the time he must plan for long-term re-sults. A flash in the pan may pay the rent bill with gratifying speed, but too many in succession are dispir-iting and anyway shake the confidence of customers.

All these are things a dealer can do, and maintains that an auctioneer cannot. The auctioneer cannot, by the very nature of his business, concern himself with the overall pattern of an artist's career or the nice tim-ing of a revival. Within limits, he sells what he is given to sell when he is given it to sell. His responsibility rests entirely with the individual object at the time of its selling, and his only purpose is to get the highest pos-sible price for it: that, after all, is what the seller pays him for. It is no part of his business to decide whether it is politic that a particular object shall sell for an ex-travagantly high price at a particular time, and though he may advise a seller what reserve should be put on an object so that it does not sell too cheaply, he cannot enforce this if the seller merely wants to be rid of it. He cannot scale charges according to his estimate of what an object is worth to one specific purchaser—there have to be two of almost equal eagerness to ensure that the purchaser does not get it for half what he, and maybe he alone, would be willing to pay for it. Moreover, the auctioneer may advise delay, but he cannot, as the dealer can and often does, wait years until the market is precisely right to sell something—not, anyway, unless the seller is willing to play along with him.

What this boils down to is that the auctioneer cannot manipulate the market to anything like the extent that the dealer can. Which may be a bad thing in some ways but is undoubtedly a good one in others. Even if the saleroom prices are not always ultimately to the buyer's advantage, at least he can feel that they are arrived at by free competition of the interested parties rather than arbitrarily fixed. ("Auction rings," conspiracies by dealers to keep prices down by not bidding against each other and dividing the saving among themselves afterward, are not unknown, and in 1964 a major scandal blew up about it in Britain which resulted in the resignation of several members from the Antique Dealers Association. But this sort of fiddle applies almost entirely to small provincial auctions, and there is little evidence that it would be tried or could work in an important sale at a metropolitan auction house.) And the difficulty of hoarding and controlling supply through an auction house does tend to allow works of art to find their own price level, whether it is a level the dealers would wish or not—they are, after all, always free to back their hunches by themselves buying at "unfortunately" low prices and selling when the market has built up again, while the disproportionately high prices sometimes paid at sales when "amateurs" intervene may force the dealer out, but help him indirectly by maintaining confidence in a buoyant market.

Dealers in the art of the past have to depend for many of their acquisitions on the salerooms, and will presumably have to do so increasingly as fewer and fewer owners feel inclined to sell directly to a dealer when a saleroom, they have every reason to believe, is likely to bring them a better price. Though dealers still contrive to make their profits, few of them like the situation. For one thing it allows potential buyers to find out, with a little research, just how much profit the dealer is making. Some dealers manfully maintain that this makes little difference—they work for their profit by researching their acquisitions, improving their condition and safeguarding the buyers' investment with authoritative guarantees; and anyway the publicity which a purchase by them at a record price receives is itself a valuable guide to possible customers and general confidence-builder. This may be so in the big league, but lesser dealers are not so sure. Undoubtedly there is rivalry and resentment between the auction houses and the dealers—mainly on the dealers' side, now that the interloping auctioneers, refusing any longer to know their place as servants of the trade only, have got things pretty well their own way. Dealers in contemporary works, though not so much directly affected, can regard the salerooms as a dubious ally at best: one work by a living artist which comes on the market and fetches a good price (with or without a bit of fixing behind the scenes) may be good publicity; but a whole collection thrown on the market at once may depress his prices for some time to come.

But though they are considerably less adaptable

than dealers in the matter of timing and spacing, the salerooms cannot afford to be completely without guile in the merchandising of the goods they have on offer. They are increasingly aware of the advantages, in the most elementary monetary terms, to be gained from selling at the right moment and in the right context, with the right atmosphere. In modern times Parke-Bernet pioneered in deliberately making major sales a social event, arranging them as evening galas in full dress, by invitation only, so that people were fighting for the privilege of getting in to spend money. Sotheby's was not slow to take up the idea, and auctioneering today is regularly decorated by such fancy modern techniques as bidding by closed-circuit television (in 1968 a major Sotheby's sale, of Norman Grantz's Picassos, was televised to a national audience on color television). Just as dealers will enhance the value of individual pieces for sale by putting them together to illustrate a theme, illuminate the work of a school, and thus make the lesser take on some reflected glory from the more important, so the auctioneer will now categorize the material which comes up for sale so that buyers' interest can be concentrated and built up—a sale, such as Sotheby's, Christie's and Parke-Bernet all had during 1966-67, devoted exclusively to Art Nouveau can automatically generate interest and excitement to such an extent that the prices will show on average an increase of 50 or even 100 percent over what has previously been given for comparable items. Such specialized "collections," assembled by the auctioneer over perhaps a year or more, are becoming a more and more prominent feature of the major saleroom's calendar. Their techniques of promotion, if in many respects still cruder and more short-term than those of the efficient dealer, still serve their purpose well enough and keep the market in a state of continuous expansion even as other markets faint and fail.

BUYERS IN A SELLER'S
MARKET

The one thing that everyone seems agreed about in
the art world these days is that it is a seller's market. Of
course, the seller's advantage varies from area to area,
and the tremendous boom enjoyed by new art and new
artists in the mid-1960s would appear to be much reduced in Europe now, though it continues little abated in
the U.S.A. But in general there seem to be always
more people eager to buy old masters, modern classics
and objets d'art of all sorts now than there are works of
art to go around. Even the spectacular financial difficulties that Britain and the United States have been
going through in 1967-68 did not seem to have produced
any corresponding slump, as the great Depression did in
1929 and for some years following: the idea this time
around is evidently that as long as there is any money
floating around ready to be spent, it is better to invest it

in things—property, jewelry, art—than to keep it in any other form. Obviously, this results in art's being seen as an investment by all sorts of people who have little or no real interest in and knowledge of art per se, and the numbers of this class of art buyers are still on the increase. But who, when it comes to the point, are the art buyers these days? How do they buy, what do they buy, and above all why do they buy it?

The answers to these questions are a good deal more difficult and obscure than they seem at first glance. Even at the best of times personal taste is only one factor in a complicated system of checks and balances which works itself out in any actual purchase or series of purchases. At the most elementary level you might well say, for example, that you would rather have a Redon than a Cézanne. But the observation would have little practical significance if you never had or were likely to have enough free money to buy either. For that matter, if you happened to have enough money for it to be conceivable that you might buy a Redon, but not a Cézanne, then your preference for the cheaper painter would be lucky. But supposing it went the other way? Supposing you very much wanted a Cézanne, but could not afford one, and cared much less for Redon, whom you could afford? Your ideal preferences then would have to be balanced against the practicalities of the situation. And indeed it is doubtful whether preferences are ever completely ideal, except at a level where they carry no sort of weight at all in terms of real buying power: no art buyer, after all, is totally disinterested where the potential market value of his possessions or of possible acquisitions is concerned, and it is almost certain that some element, however slight, of "sour grapes" will enter into anybody's judgment of how much he wants what he can possibly have as against what he cannot conceivably hope to possess.

This much is certain even of the *amateur,* the person who not only can buy art but who has a real personal urge to do so for his own enjoyment: what he most wants and what he actually gets are bound to remain at best in a shifting and nebulous relationship with each other. The intervention of the unashamed buyer-for-investment introduces a further complicating factor, and to make matters worse there is always some doubt about how far, even in those who think their buying is entirely ruled by business interests, it can completely be so. If the most dedicated, idealistic art lover cannot help being to some extent conscious of the market value of what he has and what he wants, equally the most determinedly philistine investor in art cannot altogether help knowing what he likes and which of two equally sound-seeming investments he would rather make. Add to this the obvious difficulty that there is and can be no clear cut-and-dried equation between financial resources and artistic interests (the would-be investor, like the art lover, may have a lot of money or very little) and you have a very involved situation indeed.

Let us then, for the moment, put motives aside and consider merely who buys what. It is safe to say that of all groups of art-buyers the most predictable over long periods, the easiest to analyze and define, are the

French. The period of relative financial stability in France under de Gaulle has of course helped here, but it is not entirely that. To begin with, there is a whole tradition of art collecting in France which is more defined, more respectable, more a familiar part of life for certain social and educational classes, than is the case anywhere else in the world. In France it has been respectable, expected even, for a whole middle-class, middle-income group to take an interest in and buy fine art for far longer than in Britain or the United States: art buying was something one owed to one's position in the world as well as a possibly good idea financially or the eccentric expression of a personal obsession. This view of art buying was assisted by certain peculiarities of the French economy, with the great weight carried in it by the family business, the family property. Because of the French tax structure, large fortunes can continue from generation to generation much better than almost anywhere else in the world today (the riches of many of the old nobility in France, for instance, are matched perhaps only by those of the similar class in Spain). At a lower level, the modest fortune can continue and be augmented with relatively little molestation, and one of the traditional ways for it to do so is in the form of tangible property; real estate and movable belongings such as works of art. Just as the "patrimoine national" remains an important emotive concept for the Frenchman, so the individual patrimony is a continuing, revered reality.

In consequence, France remains the world's principal stronghold of the important and entirely "private"

private collection—the product maybe of one man's enthusiasm (just as it might be in the United States) or
the gradual accretion of several generations of art buying, but either way little influenced by the notion of
public image-building, by possible tax advantages in art
investment or by the intention, from the very outset, of
holding the collection only as a sort of lifetime trust for
the public institution which is designated to come into
it after the owner's death. And this continuing tradition
of personal art buying (whether for pleasure or investment or some speculatory combination of the two) does
make a considerable difference to what the French collector buys or may buy and to how he goes about buying it.

For one thing, the "collector" as such is certainly
much more important in the French art world than in
the British, and possibly even than in the American. By
collector we mean above all the man who buys a lot of
works of art, and buys according to some pattern dictated by his intellect or his instinct. Of art buyers in
Britain today very few are collectors in this sense; even
if they have the money to be, and the inclination, they
very often just do not have the room to house twenty or
thirty, rather than two or three, paintings by an artist to
whom they are particularly attached. In the United
States, of course, there are more people in physical and
financial circumstances which allow this kind of collecting, but program buying, buying at the behest of experts and financial counsellors, bulks far larger than in
France.

Of course, at the very top level of art buying, the

millionaire level, things are much the same all over the world, since the activities of millionaires, including their art buying, are international. It is possible to make a number of generalizations about the millionaire's collection and what it is likely to contain—more possible, perhaps, than at any other level. Up to the Depression the millionaire's collection, carefully tended by Duveen as likely as not, would be heavily weighted in the direction of Old Masters, with probably (if he were an American millionaire) a particular preference shown for eighteenth-century English portraitists—easy to take, in general easier to have reliably authenticated, and carrying with them the glamorous associations of an aristocratic way of life to which the newly made millionaire consciously or subconsciously aspired. There are still a few millionaire collections which follow this by now traditional pattern, the most famous and the most important still in private hands being that of Paul Getty (though even he is sufficiently affected by fashion not to care overmuch for the Reynoldses, Gainsboroughs and such, his tastes being in general earlier and more Italianate). But as a rule the modern millionaire collection would be very differently constituted. It might certainly have a sprinkling of Old Masters, but here practical questions of supply and demand intervene. The great trouble about really first-rate Old Masters today, as we have already observed, is that there are so few of them on the market, and the process is cumulative: hardly a month goes by without at least one of those which still remain in private hands passing by sale or legacy to a museum, and so forever beyond the reach of the private collector.

The millionaire collection, then, will almost certainly consist today largely of Impressionists and Post-Impressionists, with a number of "modern classics," from Picasso to Henry Moore, making up the rest. The millionaire collector, wherever he may be based, seldom has much time for anything too ancient or too modern; but this reliable middle range nicely fills the bill. And in all sorts of ways. To begin with, art of this period is still readily available and in private hands—there are, after all, still a lot of Renoirs, Cézannes, Picassos, Braques, etc., still around. On the other hand, fashion and the constantly growing demand ensure that they are very expensive. Which is also an advantage as far as the millionaire art buyer is concerned. In a sense he is almost doing his duty by buying dear; he is there, he may reasonably feel, partly in order to consume conspicuously, and buying newsworthy art at record prices is about as conspicuous as consumption can get. Also, it carries with it a certain cultural cachet—buying art at high prices, whether you are particularly interested in it or not, is accepted as a far more responsible way of spending lots of money than is, for example, gambling or throwing fabulously expensive balls and receptions. Even putting aside possible tax advantages, during his lifetime or after his death, the millionaire who chooses to become benefactor of some museum or art gallery can do so with the gratifying sense that his name will have a nicely cultural ring to it for posterity—and the more munificent his benefactions (i.e. the more he paid for them) the better.

Also, personal taste cannot be left entirely out of consideration. The millionaire is not, anyway, necessarily the uncultural tool of his financial and artistic advisers; there is no reason why a millionaire should not have just as personal a love of art as anybody else. But even if his art buying is felt as something he owes to his position in the world rather than something he does primarily from personal inclination, personal inclination is still likely to play some part. The millionaire collector of the 1900s bought portraits of other people's ancestors partly because he believed them to be a good investment and partly because he found them reassuring: they corresponded to a nostalgia he probably had for a bygone way of life he had never been able to know at first hand, and they seemed to provide him, by proxy, with the sort of long established family history he felt rather self-conscious about not having. The millionaires of today, whether self-made or of the third or fourth generation, have become more self-confident, no doubt because the decay of the hereditary aristocracy as an important factor in politics and society has left them with less to feel inferior to. Their dream world, consequently, is rather different: a more bourgeois image of the good life as a comfortably (even luxuriously) simple life: spiced with telling hints of exoticism and of the more violent passions which their social position prevents them from indulging in even if they really wanted to.

Hence the popularity of the Impressionists: and of such Post-Impressionists as Gauguin and Rousseau (exoticism), Van Gogh (obsessive passion) and Matisse (uninhibited colorfulness). Other popular figures in modern art fit in with this: Picasso's blue and rose periods do best because they are comfortable; synthetic cubism is preferable to analytical because it is more chic and the objects it depicts are more recognizable; the surrealism of Dali, Chirico and Ernst is now easy to take for anyone with a passable *Reader's Digest* acquaintance with psychoanalysis. And so on.

There is no reason to suppose, therefore, that the millionaire art collector does not like what he buys; at least, he is unlikely actively to dislike it. In this, his taste probably coincides pretty closely with that of the humblest buyer of color prints for a bed-sitting room. The only difference is that the one will buy a cheap reproduction of a Van Gogh or a Renoir or a Picasso in (perhaps necessary) preference to the cheapest original painting or drawing he could get, while the other buys a Van Gogh or Renoir or Picasso original in (perhaps necessary) preference to anything cheaper. The millionaire is in general a known quantity in the art market— if he buys at all, it is a reasonably safe guess what he will buy. His purchases make the big prices, of course, but have very little to do with the everyday business of buying and selling minor Old Masters, lesser works by big people, works of the average newly launched artist slowly making his way in the world. It is here that the middle-range collector, with more modest means and without aspirations, comes into his own. And more so now in France than almost anywhere else.

This is because in France it is less necessary than anywhere else to have any sort of specific, personal drive in order to buy art on a relatively modest (certainly far less than millionaire) income. Equally important, perhaps more so, is a certain formularizing tendency in French life and education. The concept of the "comme il faut" remains of great importance, particularly at all levels of the middle class; and one of the things it is *comme il faut* for anyone of a certain standing to do is to buy at least some art to have around the place. In Britain the only tradition of private art buying is aristocratic, and therefore in desuetude; beyond that it is almost entirely a matter of personal inclination whether one does or not, and if it is not necessarily eccentric to do so it is not at all incorrect not to. Rather the same in the United States: apart from the very rich, there is virtually no class of society which feels that it must buy art almost as a social duty, to keep up appearances. But in France, yes.

Thus it is really only in France that one can still speak of a recognizably bourgeois taste. Primarily, it is a scaled-down version of the millionaire taste we have just been describing. It may well in some respects, particularly temporal, be more eclectic, partly because it is less immediately affected by saleroom fashions and fads (less money involved in purchases, for one thing) and partly because while there are relatively few of the warranted great Old Masters still available which would be grand enough satisfactorily to grace a millionaire's supercollection, there are still innumerable perfectly agreeable, accessible, respectable lesser masters of the same era which fit in very nicely with less demanding middle-class tastes and received ideas. But in general the range is much the same. Respectable bourgeois taste will generally incline to the figurative rather than the abstract, to pleasant but fairly subdued colors—nothing which calls too much attention to itself—and to certain sorts of subject matter. Landscapes and seascapes are favoured; also fruit and flowers, though not fish (one gallery owner we know suggests that this is because most of the most prominent art collectors are Jewish and fish are always associated for Jews with Christianity; be that as it may, fish paintings are never as popular or expensive as comparable works on other subjects). Anything so long as it's nice, one might say, though this is not exclusively so; since 1945 there has grown up also a certain bourgeois vogue for picturesque squalor and the stylishly ugly—Buffet here being the key instance of what and how much the middle-brow, middle-class public will happily accept.

This sort of buyer still represents the everyday bread and butter of French art dealing. He has a certain amount of money to spend on art, not all that much perhaps, but probably more than he wants dealers to believe. He feels it incumbent upon him at least to make a show of being cultured, and probably prides himself on being, in his small way, a patron of the arts. He wants obvious value for money, and certainly nothing that his friends and relatives will think peculiar (though of course he recognizes that the borders of what is and what is not peculiar shift perceptibly every year). He is easy to make patronizing fun of, but the French art market could not do without him, and after all the tradition he represents is a solid, respectable and by no means dishonorable one.

In any case, he provides a context for all the various sorts of more personal, experimental buying indulged in by those with more taste than money. In a society where buying art of some sort is regarded as the norm, it is in many respects that much easier for someone with strong personal ideas and prejudices to jump off on his own: if the decision that he should buy art is already made for him, it is a far easier step to decide that he will buy something different from what everyone else is buying than if he feels he is marking himself as some sort of nut by buying art at all. Consequently, there are more enterprising and knowledgeable collectors on small incomes in France than elsewhere, even if their proportion in the art-buying public as a whole is likely to be smaller.

These more independent-minded art buyers might be summarily divided into three categories: the amateurs, the snobs and the speculators. The amateur will buy a work of art because he likes it, the snob because his doing so will impress other people, and the speculator because he hopes to resell it in the foreseeable future at a profit. Naturally in practice things are not quite so clear-cut as that: the types may overlap or combine in various proportions. A feeling that a painter is likely to increase rapidly in value may help to sharpen a genuine liking for his work, and if the increase does in fact occur others will certainly be impressed at the buyer's acumen, which is always agreeable. The sort of enterprise shown by buyers of this kind in France is likely on the whole to have certain clear limits: in particular, it rarely seems to extend as far as the extreme avant-garde; it is more usually shown in the necessary task of consolidating and reappraising taste in the art of the past, especially the relatively recent past. It is nearly always in France, and with this class of buyer, that the discovery or rediscovery of interesting and desirable minor exponents of major styles begins. Fringe Impressionists, lesser figures of the Pont-Aven group, once-despised Barbizon painters now returning to favor— these are very much the happy hunting ground of the small French collector with ideas of his own.

Parisian dealers in more advanced art generally make much of despising him, and tell you gloomily that the French art-buying public is the most conservative in the world: for those ready to spend money on the latest novelty you have to look to the Americans, the Swedes, the Belgians, and, a little behind, the Germans and the Swiss, while the cautious French wait ten years to see how things pan out before committing themselves. This is not entirely fair: the collections of many French intellectuals, who as a rule are financially in this class of purchaser, would frequently put those of British or American writers, musicians and such to shame. But it is certainly true that during the early and mid 1960s, when the price of avant-garde art and new art in general rocketed for a while, the French showed less readiness to gamble the large sums necessary than collectors from other countries, particularly the United States. Hence a lot of the business done at this time by merchants of avant-garde art in Paris (as, even more, in London) was based on sales to Americans. For which, as usual, the Americans were both praised for their enterprise and open-mindedness and blamed for inflating the market by paying quite unreasonable amounts, thereby giving new artists exaggerated ideas of their own value and squeezing "real collectors" (French, that is) out.

Certain it is that since about 1950 the American buyer has loomed larger than ever before in European calculations. In particular, his influence has been felt over a wider range of possible purchase than ever before. As we know, the stream of Old Masters and famous objets d'art westward across the Atlantic has been a subject of comment and concern in Europe ever since the 1880s. But up to the Depression it took the form almost exclusively of what was seen as a sort of compensatory purchase: America was equipping itself with an artistic past, not taking a positive part in the building of an artistic present and future. As it happens, the traffic has not been entirely one way: the dealer Jacques Helft recalls in his memoirs the large number of French art treasures which went to America at high prices in the 1920s and made their way back (with his assistance and that of other French dealers in New York) at considerably lower prices during the Depression and even well after World War II. But when things started flowing Americaward again, there was a significant change: it was not only Old Masters, Impressionists and Post-Impressionists which went, but the products of the extremest avant-garde as well.

Various reasons, flattering and unflattering, can be adduced for this change of emphasis. The favorite unflattering one is that Americans have no cultural background, no sense of measure, and are easily stampeded by sheer hysteria into buying any new thing just because it is new. The favorite flattering one is that America has become itself the forefront of the art world, and that its art collectors are therefore not only richer but more intellectually ready to examine and accept the new on its own terms. Certainly it seems to be true that the market in new art is more buoyant in New York than anywhere else in the world; certain, too, that many art buyers who would be quite guarded in what they bought in New York seem far readier to buy something really wild in Europe. But anyway, it is clear that the United States no longer needs to feel that vital art is something foreign, a desirable import in default of the home-grown article. Such important international movements as Abstract Expressionism, Pop Art and Op Art have originated in America or reached their fullest development there, and it is as much the habit of European artists to look across the Atlantic for the most exciting new moves in art as it is for European dealers to look across the Atlantic for their most important clients.

And these clients, for whatever reasons, will spend money, often considerable amounts of money, on art that still leaves most European collectors mystified or hostile. To some extent, of course, the same motives apply as with any more traditional form of art buying: tax advantages, snobbery, investment possibilities. But there is something more: as one Paris dealer puts it, French collectors like to know where they are with a thing, they do not like to be surprised, while Americans enjoy being surprised, they like to buy things just because they are like nothing previously seen. This open-

mindedness is the advantage of a less rigidly formular-
ized cultural environment and art education. French
education tends to go along certain well-defined lines.
The first thing to strike one about the average educated
young Frenchman is how well up he seems to be on the
general outlines of literary and art history, how knowledgeable about the hundred best books and the thousand greatest paintings. But the second thing that
strikes one is how totally at a loss he is likely to be if one
ventures to disagree about what the standard classics
are, or argue about whether they are adjudged classics
for the right reasons. The basic pattern of education
may be admirably comprehensive, but it tends in all
but the most intelligent and original to become merely
a procrustean bed of received prejudices not susceptible
to question or argument.

The American (and the Britisher for that matter)
is formed on a freer discipline. His general culture is
probably a much patchier and less systematic affair. But
at least, left for the most part to his own devices, he is
freer to develop his own tastes and his own reasons for
them. Deprived of any reliable standard of accepted
bourgeois good taste to fall back on, he may make terrible mistakes which a Frenchman would never make. But
also he may find himself free to develop tastes and interests so startling and unconventional that no Frenchman could permit himself them without a major act of
intellectual rebellion first. In the days when the Wallace Collection was formed, British collectors were
often able to take advantage in France of their national
freedom from any too rigid prejudice about what art

should and should not be bought. Now, alas, on the whole they cannot afford to do so, and the lead in this direction has gone to America.

The American art buyers who come to Europe and make their way back loaded with goodies come in all shapes and sizes. Hardly a tourist fails to return with something vaguely artistic to remind him of Europe: perhaps no more than a print of the Eiffel Tower, or an antique English warming pan. Our concern here, though, is specifically with the collectors. The international millionaire collector apart (whether shipping magnate, industrialist or film star), American collectors are consistent only in their readiness to buy and ability to pay for it (not seemingly much curtailed even by LBJ's new restrictions on foreign spending in 1968). They are nearly all of the vast and prosperous middle-class, with high earnings rather than large capital reserves. They recognize art as the great and necessary adjunct of gracious living; sometimes this sorts with a genuine personal delight in art, sometimes not. But given the disposition to buy, for whatever reason, the range of the American collectors' buying is unsurpassed in the world today. Despite what superior (and often rather envious) Europeans may say, most of the most informed and enterprising collectors of contemporary art are American. Often they like it; whether from ignorance, enlightenment or open-mindedness, they are less likely than most Europeans to have a prejudice against it. And if they do, such feelings may well be offset by the snob value of being in the van for its own sake, or the virtues of far-out art as that valuable commodity in American social life, the conversation-starter. In Britain one would hesitate to remark on an acquaintance's taste in art, as exemplified by the way he furnishes his home; in the United States, more naturally, a delighted compliment is quite in order, and a horrified cry of "My God, what's *that!*", if not exactly welcome, is at least taken in the amiably combative spirit intended.

So Americans are the most important buyers of almost anything new in European art (and almost anything old, for that matter). A gallery such as London's Hanover Gallery, which specializes exclusively in modern art—modern classics, the avant-garde of the 1920s, more recent nonfigurative art—admits to doing nearly all its business with Americans, and making perhaps only three or four British sales of any significance in the course of a year. Many Paris galleries of similar interests would tell the same sort of story. The only major disadvantage of this American market, as far as European dealers and artists are concerned, is its liability to violent variations of fashion. European collectors, if often slower to take up something new, are usually more steadfast in their devotion to an artist, a style, a genre, once it has been accepted. The American collector's readiness to accept surprise as a desirable attribute of art is often linked with a certain fickleness toward it once the surprise has worn off. To some extent, of course, there is natural and inevitable wastage here: it is bound to happen that some of the latest sensations go on to consolidate and build lasting reputations, while others are weeded out by the passage of time, which

234

cruelly shows up their deficiencies while it tarnishes the surface glitter which originally sold them. But the fluctuations of American fashion go far beyond this sort of balanced reappraisal.

In the United States things are as a rule either very much in or very much out. This applies not only to recent art, which would anywhere be subject to the ups and downs of fashion before settling to some sort of recognized level, but also to whole periods and schools of the past. It has often amazed Europeans, used to the astronomical prices which art objects currently in demand in the U.S. have been fetching in Europe, to find that in America itself it is often possible, even at the grandest sales, to pick up important works of the past for a relative song just because the vogue has recently changed. Jacques Helft, for instance, had some remarkable bargains in Medieval and Renaissance art in the 1940s, when the periods were unfashionable and the collections of the great coal, steel and beer barons of the 1900s were coming on to the market. Even today, when the museums are ready and eager to snap up what the private collector no longer wants, the American market in art of the past is still much more variable and liable to violent fluctuation—more realistic, one might say— than the European, where there are always those who remain faithful to older, safer ideals or those who decide to hold on and buy in until the cycle of fashion turns again, as it surely will.

All this goes to make up a distinctive American pattern of collecting, far more excitable than any European pattern. American collectors may be more ready

to take chances, but they are also more ready to cut
their losses and run. This is in a way curious, since the
collectors are drawn from precisely the same areas of
society in America as in France and Britain: they are
usually the top professional men, doctors, lawyers,
bankers, brokers, industrialists and show business personalities especially, with a stiffening of writers, musicians and academics (though these tend to have less free
money). The difference may no doubt be accounted for
to some extent by the fact that in America the same
classes are subject to all sorts of different pressures from
those which influence their European equivalents. In a
society where businessmen over fifty (or even forty)
feel it necessary to start lying about their age in order to
keep ahead, obviously the idea of being with it, on the
ball, and absolutely in the forefront of things must have
a greater talismanic significance than it does in Europe.
And part of this ethos involves necessarily attributing a
greater importance to the passing dictates of fashion, for
it is by sticking with fashion that one can best demon-
strate one's continuing place in the van.

It has been said that American society, metaphori-
cally if not literally, is ruled by interior decorators. Un-
fair, but the observation has a grain of truth. For the
interior decorator is above all an image-monger; he
creates an image for his client, and then accommodates
the image to the person or the person to the image as
best he can. And important to a man's image, especially
that of a successful professional man with a prominent
social position to keep up, are his home surroundings,
his degree of culture, real or assumed, and not only the

fact of his buying art, but the precise sort of art that he buys. If Pre-Columbian pottery was the rage the year before last, it will probably be very infra dig to be displaying an extensive collection of it now, when Pop Art or Indian crafts have taken its place. Of course the strong man of decided tastes, who bought the Pre-Columbian pottery in the first place only because he liked it, may continue happily to assert that he likes it and keep it on view. But what of the man who did not particularly like (or dislike) it to begin with, and is now informed that what was right, right, right two years ago is wrong, wrong, wrong today? Naturally he unloads it, in just the same spirit that his wife throws out the hats of two years ago. Only some sort of nut, he reflects, would do anything else. And so the pressures build up; retaining outmoded tastes in Europe and being merely unfashionable is one thing; doing so in America and finding oneself automatically branded as some sort of nut, a dropout in the cultural stakes, is quite another, and one which takes a good deal more positive determination, strength of character, and genuine love of art to put up with.

So, among American art collectors of the middle range, there is a lot more well-publicized buying, and a lot more rather secretive selling, over short periods than anywhere else in the world. Which all makes for life, excitement, and considerable buoyancy in the market. On the other hand, it is the sort of activity which is particularly susceptible to the adverse effects of a recession or a slump. Investment in art is considerably more hazardous when what is being invested in is much more the image than the thing itself. Certain investments remain gilt-edged: but these are mostly out of the average collectors' reach; they are the major Old Masters and Impressionists, the early twentieth-century classics, the monuments of the goldsmith's and silversmith's craft, the greatest still movable sculpture. The fact that any of these can safely be bought at a top price, in the virtual certainty that if they were ever sold again they would fetch even more, remains of academic interest only, since nearly all of them are destined sooner or later for some great public collection or other. At any lower level instant changes of fashion may do their worst, and in the latest of modern art most damagingly of all. Hence, no doubt, the very rapid collapse in the last two or three years of the tremendous boom in avant-garde art which swept the world in the early 1960s. It has not noticeably affected artists old and established enough for people to feel that their place with posterity is clear (perhaps wrongly: will Henry Moore ultimately stand as high as the record prices now given for his works suggest? With one of his works sold in 1968 for £66,600, he stands for the moment as the most expensive of all sculptors). But the days when any new aspirant with any sign of talent was sure to be snapped up on the steps of his art school and put under lucrative contract by a gallery are now past. A big sensation, a flamboyant personality like Andy Warhol's, can still bring a new artist a lot of money. But even there, American buyers are beginning to look dubiously over their shoulders, in case the wind changes and leaves them out in the cold.

THE ARTIST'S CUT

In all our considerations of those who buy and those who sell art, we have touched only incidentally on the indispensable figure in all this, the artist himself. Of course, in the vast majority of transactions in the art world, the only true begetter of the article in question has long been absent from the scene. Even where the work of a living artist is concerned, it may well be merely the resale of a work he long since parted with and has no further financial interest in (except in France, where the *droit de suite* ensures the artist a small cut in certain sorts of transaction and provided he or his heirs know to claim it). But there still remains for consideration the situation of the live professional artist who hopes to live or partly live off the fruit of his labors. How does he fare in all this frantic buying and selling that goes on, and how much profit can he hope to derive from it?

There are no simple, inclusive answers. Every

artist is a special case, and every year of his professional life makes up its own rules as it goes along. Even at a time of unparalleled boom in contemporary art good artists whose names are known may be starving; in the middle of a recession other artists may be making, one way and another, a very good living indeed. It is all a matter of luck, chance, application, talent, being in the right place at the right time, having the right dealer, impressing the right critic, enthralling the right buyer. Or not doing any or all of these things. And to add to the difficulty of making generalizations, the artist's situation varies enormously from country to country, permitting almost every conceivable variation from the completely "official" artist of the Soviet Union to the completely free artist of the United States.

As usual in matters artistic, it is France which has things most clearly organized. France, almost alone now of Western countries, offers the artist a clear alternative to making his own way in the world (without or with a dealer's assistance), in the shape of a recognized and regulated academic career with its own grades and rewards. Two factors in French life assist this: the continuing tradition of bourgeois art patronage, and the still considerable amount of direct state patronage for the arts which the Establishment has at its disposal. It is still possible, therefore, for an artist of thoroughly traditional inclinations to choose an almost nineteenth-century way of life, not notably different from that of the academician a hundred years ago. To adopt this line, it is necessary for him to have a good academic training, at the École des Beaux-Arts in Paris, one of the seven other national art schools, or one of the sixty official municipal art schools. This, of course, he may do anyway without committing himself to an academic career; many of the most revolutionary painters of the École de Paris have started in this way. The important step is what comes next. If his style of art is naturally conservative, traditional, representational, he will probably aim to win one of the major art scholarships, the most famous and valuable of which is the Prix de Rome, which gives the winner forty months' residence at the Villa Medici, Rome, during which time he can study, paint and just take time to mature very much as he chooses. Apart from being very pleasant, this gives the lucky winner considerable prestige within the limited (but often financially rewarding) circles of official, establishment art. And since the prize is given by members of the Académie des Beaux-Arts it invariably goes to young painters who show every sign of continuing honorably and reliably to uphold the conservative traditions of the institution.

From then on, the way an academic artist must take is quite clear. He will aim to exhibit in one of the great traditionally inclined salons, such as the Salon d'Automne or the Salon des Tuileries, and probably at certain mixed, not-too-committing exhibitions such as the Salon des Indépendants. He will hope to pick up a number of the medals and prizes offered by the state and by the long-established traditional institutions, and will hope to be patronized by the State to the extent of purchases from among his exhibited pictures, commissions for murals and portraits, and election to various committees and bodies regulated by the State. He may well come to teach at the Académie des Beaux-Arts or somewhere equally solid and unexperimental, though this is not essential; he will probably dabble in stained glass, official religious art, book illustration and maybe theatrical design. He will sell mainly to middle-brow, middle-class collectors, who like to understand what they are buying and be guaranteed that, however good it may or may not be, at least it is eminently respectable. His clientele will be almost entirely French, for by adopting this line of life he virtually makes sure that his work will be of mainly parochial appeal, and his name hardly known abroad: he is producing French art for home consumption. With any luck, he will end up a member of the Académie des Beaux-Arts and an officer of the Légion d'Honneur—at which point he will find himself again in the company of the most successful among those independent artists who chose their own way to add a little something to the glory of France.

The most obvious difference between an academic's career and that of an independent is that the independent's, if he has any success at all, is a much more international affair altogether. In formation it may well not be so different from the academic, he may indeed have attended the very same art schools and gone in for the same prizes (though there is also in the independent class a significant element of the self-taught, a fact usually made much of by their biographers as a sort of index to their independent-mindedness). Any non-figurative painter in France will inevitably belong to this class, but it also includes many figurative artists whose styles do not accord with the standards of academic respectability—these days somewhat like the style of Besnard modified by Impressionist coloring, the protocubism of later Cézanne, or perhaps even some of the neoprimitive or neoclassical elements to be found in the Picasso of the 1920s. And of course even painters who could, by their work, perfectly well make it as academics may always choose the other course, judging its possible rewards in terms of money and international reputation to be appreciably greater. When the main stages in the academic painter's career are marked by official prizes and acts of state patronage, those of the independent's will be marked by contracts with dealers, one-man exhibitions in privately run galleries, showings at international exhibitions of contemporary painting, and prizes at the Venice or São Paulo Biennale or from rich American foundations such as the Guggenheim or the Carnegie. If he makes it, he too will eventually get official commissions, but only at the last, when his international eminence makes it impossible for the State and the public institutions to ignore him (Braque's ceiling at the Louvre, Chagall's decorations for the Paris Opéra).

Though the academic painter in France can often command surprising amounts for his work (the reservoirs of money still existing among the haute bourgeoisie are a constant wonder to foreigners), he is not, naturally, much fancied by speculators in art, who know well enough that nothing loses its value more rapidly than safe, conservative academic painting, almost irrespective of its inherent quality. Taking the academic path to success is therefore less of a gamble, but naturally it follows that the possible jackpot, if by luck or genius one achieves a top position in one's profession, is considerably greater for the independent. But to achieve this desirable end one intermediary is essential: the dealer. If a painter is not going to work and reach his public through the academies and the salons, the only realistic alternative is to come to some arrangement with a dealer. Very, very few independent artist do not do this, or at least try to become their own dealers. It is doubtful if any really choose to work without the backing of a dealer, though a number defensively claim that they have so chosen. And from the careers of almost all the twentieth-century artists of the École de Paris who have reached international eminence there is no doubt that the dealers, with all their techniques of promotion, their building of images, their husbanding of resources, have played as vital a part as anyone in determining which shall arrive in the front rank and which shall not.

As we have already indicated, the relationship between artist and dealer can be infinitely various. But in France, ever since the arrival of the first important Impressionists who lived and worked outside the academic system, the norm has always been that of the contract. The contract itself can take almost any form, but it generally amounts finally to this: that the dealer takes command of a large part or the whole of an artist's output and arranges for its merchandising in return for some sort of preliminary financial commitment on his part. The strictest form of contract would be that whereby the artist hands over to his dealer the totality of his work as soon as it is finished to his satisfaction (or even, under certain reservations, before, as in the case of Rouault and Vollard), in return for a guaranteed income, paid monthly, quarterly or annually, with possible augmentations if more of his works sell for higher prices than in the estimate upon which the agreed income is based. The freest sort of arrangement would be a verbal contract between an artist and a dealer whereby the artist hands over the works he chooses to his dealer, for sale or return, and the dealer takes a simple commission on sales. Between these two extremes there are all sorts of intermediate types of contract, giving the dealer or the artist more or less power, more or less freedom, vis-à-vis each other.

It should not be taken from this that the interests of dealer and artist are necessarily in conflict, or are necessarily supposed to be so. The dealer tends to be happier the more completely he can control the situation: the "selling" of an artist, after all, can be a long and expensive job, and he wants some guarantee that all his work and expenditure will not go to benefit someone else. On the other hand, to achieve this sort of control he will need to be ready to lay out sums of money in advance, possibly considerable sums—and that he may well not be able to do. The artist, for his part, is not necessarily resentful, as idealists would have him, of any outside attempt to limit his freedom in any way. Quite a few artists hanker after the sort of security which their way of life seldom offers them, and the dealer brandishing an exclusive contract in return for a regular monthly paycheck may well be the answer to a prayer. Others, again, prefer to go as far as possible their own way, resent the artistic pressures a dealer may bring to bear, or simply dislike the idea of getting perhaps not more than 50 percent of the prices their pictures actually fetch on the gallery walls. Such artists may think that they will do better managing their own careers, with a more amenable, less powerful dealer selling for them what and when they like, on commission.

They may be right: though careers like that of Jacques Villon leave a lot of room for doubt. Villon spent nearly fifty years working in relative obscurity, not quite at the center of any school or movement, until in 1942 he was put under contract by Louis Carré. By 1951, as "sold" by Carré, he had got to the status of a retrospective at the Musée d'Art Moderne and had become one of the established masters. He had not changed, his work had not changed (beyond a certain amount of natural development), and the promotion was deserved. But it would never have been achieved— or not at least until some years after his death—if a dealer had not taken things in hand, planned ahead (selling virtually nothing for several years but seeing to it that Villon was well represented in various national and international exhibitions and building up the critical attention paid to him) and generally arranged the presentation of a coherent Villon image to many for whom, previously, Villon had been hardly more than a name.

Villon is an extreme but striking example of what a dealer can do for artists in his "stable". The practical arguments, therefore, for a nonacademic artist in

France concluding some sort of contract with a dealer are pretty convincing; and this is very much the norm. What is most difficult to find out, needless to say, is how much money the artist stands to make from this sort of arrangement, and how much the dealer. If the arrangement between them approximates in any way to a percentage deal, the percentage taken by the dealer is officially 33⅓. But like most official principles of the sort, this seems to be a complete dead letter, except perhaps in a very few cases where the artist is already so important that his works more or less sell themselves and the dealer is no more than his paid agent, or at the other end of the scale, where the dealer has so little money at his disposal that he can afford to sell only on a straight percentage basis, without advances. The normal percentage actually taken by a dealer is 50 percent, and many dealers press for a 60/40 division in their favor, on the ground that all the painter has to do is paint, the sculptor to sculpt, while they have to pay the rent of an expensive Paris showplace, arrange for catalogues, entertainment and publicity, and generally run most of the financial risks.

As an alternative, or partial alternative, to this system, there is the arrangement adopted by a number of dealers, particularly in relation to the safer middle range of painters: that of buying outright from the painter all, or more likely a first choice of, his paintings, and then being free to sell them when and at what price they can. The prices paid to the artists in such cases are generally based on a sort of point system, points being allotted according to the type of work it is (oil, gouache, watercolor, drawing) and according to the size of the painting (more complicated this, since if works are very small they will sell for less, but if they are very big they will be more difficult to sell to the ordinary private collector). This arrangement leaves the dealer much freer in most ways: he can arrive at the basic payment per point taking into consideration the individual artist's standing, his average production, the general salability of his style and subject matter (if any), and once the pictures are his he can do what he likes with them, sell them as soon as possible at, if he can, two or three times what he gave for them, or gamble on holding on to them longer and selling them, after three or four years, at maybe (if he is very lucky or very cunning), as much as twenty times what he gave. On the other hand, this system, however it is worked out in detail, does involve quite a considerable initial outlay of money by the dealer, and many prefer, or are forced to, something rather less committing.

The actual amount of money involved can range from nil to the sort of film-star incomes enjoyed by the grand masters like Picasso or Dali and the instant sensations like Buffet or Mathieu. Assessment is complicated by the natural secretiveness of almost anybody about how much he earns—even supposing, in such a changeable, up-and-down profession as that of the artist, he could give a reliable annual average, he probably won't, since he wants either to impress potential business contacts or plead poverty to the tax man or perhaps both simultaneously. In any case, it is always a problem to determine whom exactly we should count as a professional artist, and how many there are. The Confédération des Travailleurs Intellectuels has defined for its own purposes the professional artist as anyone who makes an average of not less than 52 percent of his declared earnings from the exercise of his art over three consecutive years—however much or little those total earnings may be. Their latest figures, based on this ruling, gave the total number of professional artists in France as 2,595, 1,872 of them painters and graphic artists, and 349 sculptors. These figures were reached, presumably, only in terms of those who actually applied for membership, and are therefore very low; other statistics suggest a figure (including art teachers) of around 11,500-12,000 and Raymonde Moulin has established that during the three years 1958-1960 no fewer than 4,500 artists exhibited in the major annual Paris salons alone.

How many, of all these professional artists, make what any reasonable person might call a living wage? We know from statistics provided by an official body, the Caisse d'Allocations Vieillesse des Arts Graphiques et Plastiques, that in 1954 according to the tax returns of 1,413 painters in France, 362 claimed that they had no taxable income, and only sixteen admitted to earning more than £1000 or $3000 a year (figures quoted by Raymonde Moulin). For all sorts of reasons, including the smallness of the number of artists involved and the improbability that any of them would tell the whole truth to the tax officers, not too much reliance can be placed on these statistics. The Confédération des Travailleurs Intellectuels suggests that according to their observations up to 10 percent of the professional painters on their books earn more than £800 or $2000 a year, while 10 percent are in positive want, 40 percent supplement their artist's income with a second job, usually teaching, and 40 percent live by painting, from hand to mouth and in hope of better times just around the corner. Raymonde Moulin, with many reservations and disclaimers, finally concludes that the number of artists in Paris who made 150,000 francs (about £150 or $320) a month in the peak years of 1959-1960 from the sale of pictures alone would be between 500 and 1000.

If estimates of this order are highly speculative in France, they are virtually impossible elsewhere. For the French, as we remarked, have things more clearly organized and categorized than any other nation in the Western world. The innate conservatism of a certain sector of the French buying public ensures the continuance of a sort of entirely academic career in art which is nowadays virtually impossible elsewhere. In the United States there are, of course, conservative painters who cling to the most "old-fashioned" representational styles. But their status is not fundamentally different from that of the most advanced artists : they will exhibit in the same sort of way and take their chances on the general market; they will certainly have no reliable, socially coherent body of potential purchasers to fall back on—to whom the information that they studied at this or that school, under this or that master, and won a certain number of the most coveted official prizes— would have real selling power (even supposing that these national schools and official awards existed in America). Of course, in recompense the academic and the representational artist has far more scope in the U.S. than he has in France for various straight commercial outlets for his work—magazine illustration, commercial art of all sorts, even designing for the best-selling mass-produced framed reproduction market, where those at the top of the heap, like the painter of the inescapable green-faced Chinese lady, can make a fortune in royalties alone.

Even in Britain, where there is after all the Royal Academy and a whole network of more or less officially subsidized art schools, the academic painter would find find himself in a pretty pass these days. Though there is still a market for the conservative, inoffensively traditional portrait, even that is dying away, and relatively few young painters are coming forward to take over from the old hands like James Gunn. Naturally, there are still quite a number of representational painters in a recognizable tradition (there were, even before their recent strengthening from the ranks of the Pop Artists), and of these some, like John Bratby, John Piper and Sidney Nolan, command a considerable following among collectors and art lovers at large. But they are hardly ever academic in the French sense of the term. They may well have trained initially at one of the more respectable art schools, but thereafter each is free to go his own way, and that way has very rarely been along the high road of Royal Academy medals, pictures on the line in the Academy's summer shows and such. Indeed, this "high road" has become in recent years very much a quiet backwater, while all the more striking and efficient traffic speeds along the new bypass.

The Academy has brought this state of affairs upon

itself. From the 1900s onward its standards of acceptability got further and further behind those of even the most moderate middlebrow outside. Still in the 1940s the home-grown expressionism of Stanley Spencer or the fauve coloring of Matthew Smith were considered excessively strong meat, and anything more advanced was absolutely inadmissible. Therefore, many artists who were certainly far from being in any sense iconoclasts, and whose habit of mind was indeed fundamentally traditional, found themselves locked out of the Academy as dangerous revolutionaries. In consequence, they had willy-nilly to make their own way, while the Academy, clutching its ultraconservative standards to its bosom, was taken less and less seriously by anyone reasonably interested in art. Meanwhile, the slump and increasing taxation were cutting down considerably the number of bourgeois art-buyers who were not really interested in art but understood that their position in life and the empty spaces on the walls of their large detached houses required them to buy some art all the same. Portrait photography, the decline in favor of the living artist relative to the "old master," and from the late 1920s the vogue among the prosperous for walls altogether empty of pictures, all drove further nails into the coffin of the middle-brow patron of exhibitors at the Royal Academy.

True, during the 1960s the Academy saw the error of its ways and began busily trying to foster a new image, welcoming into the fold artists like Bratby, whose work still carries strongly traditionalist overtones, and liberalizing its choice of pictures for exhibition to include even a quota of abstracts and pop art. But the point is that the Academy now needs these much more than they need it. The middle-generation conservatives have made their reputation outside and in the face of the Academy, while the younger painters it is wooing have little confidence in the Academy's positive usefulness to them: indeed, most dealers would urge them to have nothing to do with the Academy, lest anyone assume that they are reduced to exhibiting there because they cannot find anywhere better. The continuity of the Academy tradition (and of the academically minded buyers who knew what to expect there) has been broken. And this continuity, in France, is the most important single asset the Beaux-Arts has to offer. Without it, the British Academy is rendered virtually helpless as a force in the modern art world.

Forced by the Academy's attitude to adopt an independent type of career, most British artists found the going fairly tough in the interwar years. There were a few big commissions, but they mostly went to the few artists, like Epstein or Augustus John, who had succeeded in imposing themselves as colorful personalities, or who, like Eric Gill, had close social, religious or personal affiliations with some particular body of possible patrons. The art dealers in London were little geared to the sort of artist-dealer relationship which was already the norm in Paris, and so their dealings with artists tended to be haphazard, and often artists had to resort, individually, by banding together or with the help of richer friends, to exhibiting their work at their own expense and hoping the gamble would pay off. There

were also, for the lucky ones, a number of private patrons with more advanced tastes who would tide them
over and subsidize them through difficult patches—but
such patronage became rarer and rarer as the 1930s
wore on.

The war, and the recruiting of official war artists,
gave a valuable breathing space, if not perhaps in the
form the artists might ideally have wished. And finally,
in the postwar years, the organization of the London art
market began to catch up with its Parisian model. Particularly influential in bringing about this development
were such foreign-trained, London-based dealers as the
Gimpel brothers of Gimpel Fils and Erica Brausen of
the Hanover Gallery. They appreciated the advantages
of putting artists under contract, both to the artists and
to themselves. Gimpel Fils brought on such artists as
Ben Nicholson, Kenneth Armitage and Lynn Chadwick; the Hanover Gallery backed Francis Bacon, William Scott and Reg Butler. Soon other galleries followed
suit; some were newly set up to specialize in contemporary
art, others, like Tooth's, decided to extend their activities
beyond an exclusive devotion to old masters. Then in the
1950s came the spectacular advance of Marlborough
Fine Arts, sweeping all before it and taking over the career
management of nearly all the major British artists of international reputation, including Henry Moore, Graham
Sutherland, Francis Bacon, Ben Nicholson, Barbara Hepworth, Kenneth Armitage and Lynn Chadwick, as well
as the profitable but more parochial John Piper.

From then, the boom was on. Once the idea of the
artist under contract had caught on, everyone seemed

eager to get in on the act. The annus mirabilis for living artists in Paris was 1959-60; in London it came rather later, around 1963-64. At that time it seemed that an artist of any sort of talent or promise had to do no more than walk out of art school and he would be snapped up by somebody. All this had, by Parisian standards, an air of amateurishness about it, and the foreign-trained dealers shook their heads in alarm. With reason, as it turned out. For the artists, finding themselves in a seller's market, sold for all they were worth—or rather more. Dealers, of course, always claim that artists are greedy, irresponsible, and extortionate in their demands; artists say the same of dealers. But whoever was to blame, larger sums of money changed hands around this time than were ever likely to be earned back, and many dealers caught quite a bad cold as a result. Even in Paris dealers were finding themselves compelled to gamble more than they cared to: a painter like Hans Hartung, it is said, could ask and get an advance of around £90,000, or over $250,000, from the Galerie de France for his year's work—which presupposes that they would have to sell at least twice as much during the year to make a proper profit. In London a painter like Francis Bacon might command a basic advance of perhaps £15,000 a year ($42,000) from the Marlborough, which is still a lot of money for starters. And quite untried artists got into the habit of expecting not the odd few hundred pounds in advance that most dealers might afford to gamble, but thousands, against no sort of guaranteed return in terms of sales of their work.

A crash of sorts was bound to come, and so it did. Not very spectacularly, to be sure. But a remarkable number of contracts were dissolved after the first year, the dealers taking finished canvases in exchange for the still unearned residue of overoptimistic advances and hoping, later if not sooner, to get their money back. Even the redoubtable Marlborough has let most of its contracts with living British artists lapse, not necessarily of course because the works do not sell—the sales of their "modern British classics" have never been better —but because on reflection both artist and dealer seem to find a looser, more informal arrangement less worrying for both parties. Considering the eminence of most of their regular artists, straightforward sales on commission seem the most reliable and least committing sort of relationship all around. And even here the financial rewards of success may prove delusory. The veteran painter L. S. Lowry, whose paintings these days sell at around £2000 each, stated in 1968 that he was giving up painting because there was no money in it: "When I hold an exhibition, I don't make any money, you know. If the pictures at my last exhibition sold for about £21,-000, the gallery took a third, leaving £14,000. After tax I would be getting about £3,000. That isn't much reward these days for a few years' work."

But how much then, in general, now that this particular party is over, does the British artist stand to make? Assessment is complicated by the absence of any definable standard of what does and does not constitute being a professional artist. Some artists may coast along on National Assistance, Family Allowances and such from sincere conviction of their artistic vocation, others undoubtedly just find life easier that way. The earnings of both types are bound to be minimal. A small number at the head of their profession, like the Marlborough artists, must do very well indeed, though whether "very well" would be over £10,000, over £20,000, or more still is anyone's guess. The vast majority of artists are betwixt and between. A smaller proportion, probably, than in France, attempt or succeed in making a living exclusively by painting. The traditional means of supplementing income is by teaching, maybe only one day a week, maybe more, at an art school or in some more general educational institution. This should bring the artist at least £500 a year, but probably not much more than £1200—unless, that is, he devotes so much time to teaching that he has little time for art. In addition to this possibility there is a whole new field of employment for the artist which has opened up in the last three or four years: that of designing, in various Pop-Art styles, the greetings cards, book jackets, posters and smart decors of restaurants, bars, etc., which have been booming as part of the much publicized "swinging London" scene. Though the fashion, like all fashions, is no doubt doomed rapidly to fade, for the moment it can offer considerable rewards to any artist who is in the right trend and happens to strike it lucky—though needless to say it does very little for those who aren't and don't.

This still leaves the leading question unanswered. From our observations and inquiries we would say that there are very few artists in Britain who would qualify as professionals under the rules laid down by the Confédération des Travailleurs Intellectuels by making more than 52 percent of their total earnings from the direct sale of the works of art they produce. Using the more arbitrary but sociologically viable way of categorizing people according to what they think they are, we estimate that these are probably between 9,000 and 10,000 who consider themselves essentially as professional artists, whatever shifts they are compelled to in order actually to earn a living. Of these probably not more than 1000 earn over £1000 a year from the direct sale of their art. Some few of these, of course, earn considerably more, but they are a tiny minority. And of the other 85 to 90 percent of those who regard themselves as professional artists, the vast majority would earn from the sale of their work alone, commissions and other expenses paid, not more than £500.

In the United States the artist's position is much closer to that of the British artists than that of the French. He does not have the possibility (highly dubious in its value anyway) of an academic respectability to fall back on. On the other hand he does have, theoretically within his grasp, a lot more in the way of scholarships and fellowships offered by foundations and institutions, plus the chance of settling down for a year here and there as a campus artist, vaguely on a par with campus poets and campus dramatists. There are probably more out-and-out indigent artists in the U.S. than in Britain or France, since the tradition of contracting out as a total life gesture is better established than in Europe. To balance this, the highly paid are likely to be more highly paid earlier than anywhere else, so long as their vogue lasts. In other words, the American artist, old or young, successful or unsuccessful, is likely to be living nearer the edge, with fewer safety nets, than his European equivalent. When he is successfully established the rewards can be enormous: Mark Rothko, for instance, will now sell only two paintings a year so as not to get into too much trouble with the tax man.

In America, as in Britain, dealers have been slow in institutionalizing their relations with artists on the French model. The boom in putting artists under contract hit the principal New York dealers in the early 1960s, and though warning signs are apparent, the corresponding boom in the buying of advanced art has not yet subsided sufficiently to bring about the wholesale reassessment of the position which has taken place in London. There is, indeed, an element of national pride which should help to prevent this from happening, or at least cushion the effect when it does. Americans are understandably pleased to observe that in the last ten years or so New York has gone a long way toward taking over the place formerly occupied by Paris as the growing point for all that is most advanced in art today. Now it is far more likely to be a new American artist than a new French artist who makes the headlines, and what New York is goggling at today Paris may only get around to considering (with a slightly insecure air of patronage) tomorrow. To achieve this enviable state of affairs, you need a supply of interesting, extraordinary, and if possible even talented artists. But just as importantly you need the grasp of how to use major publicity machines and the flamboyant selling techniques of which American dealers have rapidly shown themselves past masters.

For a start, even now that a veil of ghastly good taste is often drawn over the sort of brashly money-minded transactions which a mere twenty years ago were happily accepted in the U.S. as the plain-dealing, unhypocritical norm, American dealers are far readier than their European confreres to make no bones about the possibilities of sheer profit involved in picture buying. Last year three London dealers gently dipped a toe into the water by arranging with the glossy magazine *Town* to sell three selected works each with a guarantee to buy them back after five years at a prearranged profit (a £950 Modigliani pencil sketch for £1,500, a £265 Klimt for £395, a £150 Erté for £200, and so on). But the technique is no stranger to New York galleries, certain of which have willingly backed their judgment for years with such guarantees to buy back at a profit to the owner. The cult of the personality is far more assiduously developed in the American art world than elsewhere. And not only the personality of the artist; after all, artists come and artists go, but dealers go on forever. So one finds that while the majority of European dealers prefer to remain discreetly in the shadows, American dealers often choose to adopt a flamboyant, newsworthy image in their own right. It is not for nothing, after all, that Duveen was the most successful single operator on the American art scene, and many of his successors have pondered well the advantages of being known for their proverbial combativeness, their munificence, their aesthetic boldness, so that customers come to buy something from *them,* rather than to buy something they just happen to have.

But the artist is by no means forgotten in all this. Unless he can be sold as a living fragment of old America, a sort of latter-day Grandma Moses, it is best for him to be as extremely up-to-date as possible. The element of outrage attracts publicity, and publicity attracts buyers. Perhaps highly priced paintings of tins of Campbell's Soup will tomorrow be as ripe for the rubbish dump as the tins themselves, once empty. But for the moment the very idea of someone's painting such a thing as meticulously as though it were a tulip and he a seventeenth-century Dutch flower-painter is enough of a talking point to set the machine in motion, and once it has started rolling there are always a surprising number of people only too eager to hop on. The artist does not perhaps have to make such a cult of personal eccentricity as Andy Warhol has, but every little helps, every inch of extra publicity does something—until, that is, the dread, unpredictable moment when "overexposure" sets in. And other personalities in the public eye can be enrolled. An acquisition by a film star or a Rockefeller can do wonders for an artist's selling potential, since snob buying plays a more prominent part in the American art market today than it does anywhere else in the world.

Not that this should distract us from the amount of serious, intelligent, highly personal art buying that goes on in the U.S. It is a curious but observable fact that discriminate and indiscriminate buying are not mutually exclusive: on the contrary, they usually go hand in hand, a boom in the art market being felt in all sectors and a slump equally so. Thus the advanced artist may hope for more and more extravagant personal publicity, and more sales which have little or nothing to do with the purchaser's personal assessment of his qualities, in the United States today than he can elsewhere. But he can also, if he has any sort of lasting talent, expect to find more serious sales to people who really dig what he is trying to do. There are virtually no collectors of contemporary art who count in Britain (collectors as distinct from those who buy an occasional art work to take a particular place in their home), and few in France. Nearly all the real collectors these days are American, with a few Scandinavian, a few Italian, and a few Swiss. This is obviously a very encouraging state of affairs for the serious artist in America, and the number who come forward hoping to reap the benefit of it increases yearly. Assessments of the number of professional artists in the United States today—in some sense of that hazily defined term—go as high as 25,000 or 30,000. (We have even seen it alleged that there are 50,000 painters in New York alone.) If an army of commercial artists (with whatever side ambitions) were counted in, it would be many more. If borderline cases were rigidly excluded, it could be fewer. But that seems a safe enough average. How high a proportion of them make a living wage just from the exercise of their art? That is impossible to say. Probably a higher proportion of them than in France or Britain make something like big money. Probably a higher proportion coast along after a fashion on virtually nothing at all. The middle section, those who get by respectably somehow or other without any spectacular success, is still in a majority, but smaller than elsewhere: in American art, as in other areas of American life, things tend to happen by extremes, and the distance between legendary success and total failure is often only a hairsbreadth.

Up to now, in this consideration of the artist's situation financial and otherwise, we have been looking primarily at the artist as someone who has a certain body of work to sell, and seeks ways of selling it as efficiently and profitably as possible. But there is another view of the matter: as well as those wanting to sell and eager to meet those who can be persuaded to buy, there are also those predisposed to buy who ask for nothing better than to encounter somebody capable of producing what they want in return. These are the patrons of the arts. Not, for the most part, private patrons any more, and very rarely private patrons on their own behalf, though the private benefaction to a favored church or institution does still exist. But in the main, government and industry have taken on the functions which formerly fell to the lot of the rich individual in Europe, while in America patronage originating with private individuals is usually carried on quasipublicly through the operation of a foundation or trust.

In France there is a surprising amount of direct official patronage, though it is nearly all extremely conservative by nature: the artists patronized are either safe, respectable academics or independents so old and universally honored that no one could take offense. The patronage takes the form of murals for public and government buildings, commemorative and memorial sculpture, work on national stands or exhibits at international shows of various sorts, portraits, and paintings and sculpture bought by the state from one salon or another. Where do they go, all these miscellaneous works of art? To decorate embassies and consulates, presumably, or fill up empty spaces in government offices. Certainly few if any of them seem to make their way into the national art collections—understandably, since it is hard to imagine which of the curators would give most of them house room.

Perhaps in reaction to this type of State spending on the arts, France is remarkably poor in business and industrial patronage. The artist has little to hope from commissions for sculpture to decorate factories, murals for canteens, art collections assembled by some large business operation in the cause of more impressive public relations. Not so in Britain or the U.S. or for that matter in most other countries of Western Europe. From Holland the Peter Stuyvesant Foundation's collections of contemporary art have become world-famous; in Italy firms like Olivetti and Fiat have led the way in offering scholarships, financing exhibitions and commissioning or purchasing individual pieces of modern art. And British industry, after a slow start, has really thrown itself into art patronage. If the examples illustrated in the elaborate volume *Patron: Industry Supports the Arts* (1966) are not always quite reassuring—there are still, for instance, a worrying number of desperately unappealing traditional portraits, and some of the most hideous ceremonial silver you ever saw—the scope of patronage illustrated, by upwards of 300 firms, is certainly impressive. Even more is this the case in America, where industrial giants like IBM and Johnson's Wax have spent fortunes on the arts.

Evidently the individual artist stands potentially to gain a lot from this sort of activity. If he has a steady contractual relationship with a dealer no doubt commissions will come to him by way of the dealer, but otherwise this is the one important way the free-lance artist has of coming into direct contact with a purchaser who can be financially important to him. Especially if he is approached with a specific proposition: to provide a sculpture for a particular spot, decorate a particular wall. Here, though the sort of public reputation a dealer can build for him does help, the dealer's powers of persuasion are not of any vital importance. What matters rather is the assessment by the person or body responsible for the commission of the artist's suitability to carry it out. Paying the piper, they may reasonably expect to call the tune to some extent, but the most important part of the calling is usually in the initial choice of the man for the job.

And a big commission can represent quite a lot of money to the artist: an important mural might bring him £5000, a major sculpture over £10,000, if he is eminent enough to command it. (London's latest Henry Moore is said to have cost its commissioners some £40,000 all told.) In return for this, he will probably have to fit in with certain requirements, limitations of size or ultimate position. But most of those with whom he has to deal will be likely, in this sophisticated and self-conscious era, to hesitate long before trying to impose any too stringent regulation on the artist's work, for fear, if nothing else, of some sort of public ridicule which would do their image more harm than good. At the moment, it seems, the image generally considered suitable for cultivation is one of swinging go-aheadness. Hence, no doubt, the crop of abstract sculpture outside and abstract painting inside the new headquarters of large industrial concerns; the inhabitants may not think they understand it, but at least it makes them feel bold and forward-looking.

The building of images through artistic patronage may have certain pitfalls, however. There was, for intance, the famous Pepsi-Cola artists' competition of 1944, in which 5000 paintings were submitted on the theme "Portrait of America", and 150 finally selected for exhibition at the Metropolitan Museum and eight other museums across the country. The first prize was $2000, and eleven more prizes totaled another $9000. The whole thing was a tremendous success in terms of critical acceptance and attendance at the exhibitions, but the next year squabbles arose with the museums, and though "Paintings of the Year" competitions continued for five years, when their originator left Pepsi-Cola the program lapsed. And more recently the vast program of expenditure on superior new art and architecture by IBM came to a sudden and disconcerting stop. Was this, outsiders wondered, just some personal change within the organization, the moving out of the man or group who had been responsible for all the patronage and the moving in of a replacement with differing ideas? Apparently not: the reasons for stopping it were as carefully worked out as those for starting it. When IBM began to expand in the computer and electronic market, it was decided that everything new and gleaming and shatteringly modern would help to plant in customers' minds the notion of the company as a dynamic, go-ahead, superefficient business. But once the position of leadership had been established, this same parade of glamour and extravagant modernity might well, in the company's judgment, not only cease to aid progress but actually hinder it. Too much display of free spending might make customers suspect that the company was too extravagant, too showy, and therefore likely not to give so good a deal as less ostentatious, more traditionally honest-John competitors. So, once the vivid, going-places image had done its job, it was ruthlessly scrapped, and another, plainer image put in its place —an image, incidentally, which did not involve the company in any important outlay on patronage of the arts.

This, naturally, is the sort of penalty the arts may have to pay for the immediate benefits of industrial patronage. Though the companies concerned may try to make us forget it, and let us think that all they do is done purely and simply as a public service, it is evident upon a moment's consideration that their actions in this field are not and cannot be entirely disinterested. The degree of personal involvement in and personal knowledgeability about the arts on the part of those responsible for initiating patronage projects must inevitably vary enormously from case to case. In some businesses

obviously, the step will be taken merely because some
P.R. firm suggests it as a good move, one which will
attract public attention, confer "dignity," or help to
persuade a government dubious about monopolistic
tendencies or due soon to renew contracts that the company concerned takes its responsibilities to the community at large seriously. Elsewhere the idea may come
from the particular personal delight a managing director takes in art or be indicative of a general zeal to
educate those working for the firm. But always those
who are paying will want something specific (even if
quite intangible) from the program, and will be determined to get it. If it is an image or a reputation, the
needs of the moment may change radically, and with
them the usefulness of what has been achieved. If the
intention is philanthropic, it will be seen as a frill which
can be afforded when things are going well but can be
snipped off quite summarily as soon as they start to go
less well. In this respect the large industrial concern is
quite as unpredictable as the private man of means
whose place in art patronage it has largely taken. The
artist may find himself lucky if he is given a commission
which suits his time and talents, without too many
strings attached. But he cannot for a moment rely on
his luck holding when bitter winds are blowing through
the economics of the world.

A LAW UNTO ITSELF?

The buying and selling of art, being a trade like any other (well, fairly like), is necessarily subject to certain laws and regulations. Some of them we have touched on briefly in earlier chapters, but it is time now to examine them more closely. The law of art is complicated and often mystifying to the layman—indeed, it poses many thorny problems even to experts. As we might expect, it is most clearly and consistently, if sometimes rather oddly codified in France. There are innumerable French laws defining what is meant by a work of art considered as an article of merchandise, what the artist's relation to his work is and must remain, what the man who buys or sells a work of art can claim for it and expect of it, in what circumstances works of art can be bought and sold and what exactly it is that one buys or sells, what the permissible relationships between artist and dealer are, and what is not permitted, etc., etc.

Other countries, of course, have laws covering most or all of these points, one way and another. But perhaps we can best approach the subject as a whole through French law and practice. To begin with, the artist and the work he produces. French law, more than any other, has recognized the real and continuing rights the artist has with respect to his own work. As creator, he has had the absolute right to decide when the work is finished and what he does and does not permit to be shown as his work. Dealers who played some part in recovering, restoring and offering for sale canvases cut up and thrown away by the French painter Camoin in 1914 found that they were acting illegally. Rouault had a contract with the dealer Vollard which gave Vollard control of all that he painted, once it has been passed by Rouault as complete and *signed*. After Vollard's death Rouault in 1947 sued Vollard's heirs for recovery of 807 canvases held by Vollard at the time of his death but not given Rouault's imprimatur, as it were, by being signed. Rouault won his case. As far back as 1900 Whistler finally had his rights upheld on appeal in an action brought against him in France by Sir William Eden over a portrait he had been commissioned to do of Lady Eden but refused to deliver: the court held that he must pay back the money paid to him in advance for the portrait, and must not show the picture again until it had been rendered unrecognizable, but upheld the artist's right to refuse to hand over a painting, even if commissioned, unless and until he was satisfied with it. In the same way the painter J. G. Domergue was given judgment in 1954 in a case over his painting "Portraits de Jeunes Filles", but was ordered to repaint enough of it to make its subjects unrecognizable before showing it again or selling it.

These rights, though in theory "recognized", were in fact thrown into doubt by the judgment in the Bonnard case of 1951-56. The background was complicated, but briefly the point at issue was whether, Bonnard having married under the rule of community property, when his wife died all his paintings, finished and unfinished, which he still held in his studio, should be regarded as common property and taxed accordingly. The painter might reasonably suppose that he had some sort of special rights in the matter, but the first decision of the courts was that he had not: all the paintings held by the painter, in whatever state, must be held as part of the community property. The Court of Paris upheld this, but made exception of works which were clearly sketches, studies or unfinished. They rejected, however, the artist's right to decide which these might be, and even the test of which were and were not signed: they held that the court could make the decision, aided by experts. This being, clearly, unworkable, the Civil Chamber decided in 1956 to go back to the first judgment and include every work, whatever its condition, in the community property. Though this limitation on the artist's rights over his work is highly specialized—and would seem mainly an excellent argument for his not marrying under the community property rule in the first place—it does seem to weaken seriously the artist's sole right to decide which of his works are ready to be seen, sold and go out on their own as representatives of his art.

271

Most of this, the possible implications of the Bonnard judgment apart, is highly satisfactory for the artist. And though in Britain and America few cases along similar lines have been brought to test the precise state of the law in connection with artist's rights, most of those that have seem to suggest that the artist would enjoy similar rights over his work in Anglo-Saxon countries too, though courts fight shy of lofty talk about the "moral right" of the artist, as something apart from his legal rights. Is the artist, then, quite free of responsibilities toward patrons and others with whom he comes into business contact? Not altogether. In 1869 a French businessman sued Rosa Bonheur for failing to deliver a picture, subject at the painter's choice, which he had commissioned from her in 1860. The court, while making all due allowance for the vagaries of artistic inspiration, found that since the painter had accepted the commission, had affirmed in writing that she had begun work on the picture, and had then unreasonably delayed completing the work, she had a definite obligation to fulfill the terms of the contract, and ordered her to complete and deliver the picture within six months, on pain of further forfeiture for delay. However, in a sense Rosa Bonheur had the last word, in that since she flatly refused to complete the picture, no one could force her to, and instead the claimant had to make do with 4,000 francs in damages.

Also, of course, any legal agreement between an artist and an agent or dealer is binding in the normal way of such agreements. If, for example, a painter makes an exclusive contract with a dealer to make over to him all his completed works as ready in return for a regular allowance, a percentage or whatever, he must then abide by it. He cannot, obviously, be forced to deliver up any paintings he considers incomplete, or to keep up a certain level of production whether he wants to or not. But he can be held in breach of contract should he, for instance, sell a painting outside this arrangement or accept a commission to which his dealer is not a party.

Once the work is complete and ready to enter on its public career, various other questions come into play. For example, when an artist sells a work of art, what precisely does he sell? Does he sell all rights connected with it, or only some? Can he, if he wants, produce an exact replica of the work sold and sell it again? The answers to such questions depend partly on where he is, and on the nature of the work of art in question. As far as copyright in works of art is concerned the general standard is the Universal Copyright Convention signed by most countries in the world in 1952 and ratified individually at various dates subsequent to that. However, the details of copyright and its infringement vary from country to country, the Convention existing mainly to correlate practice between nations. The law in most countries, however, distinguishes between the object itself and copyright in that object. The artist can sell either or both, but he does not necessarily sell them together, and owning a work of art does not necessarily make one owner of the copyright. This is perhaps easier to understand by parallel. In literature, for instance, the recipient of a letter is its owner; but that does not

273

give him the right to publish it without the writer's permission, since the writer holds the copyright. (Shaw refused Mrs. Patrick Campbell permission to print a number of his letters to her in her autobiography, and was completely within his rights to do so.) At some later date, the writer might sell the copyright to someone else, which he could certainly do without at the same time granting physical ownership of the letter, or even certain access to it.

Similarly with works of art. Many of us, no doubt, have had the annoying experience of wanting a photograph—a portrait of ourselves, perhaps, or a wedding group—copied and being firmly told that we cannot have it done without the written consent of the photographer, perhaps long dead or lost track of. We may have commissioned the photographs and bought them, but the photographer still owns the copyright, and can demand a fee and a credit for reproduction. The painter can do the same, and can refuse the owner of a painting permission to reproduce it, unless that right has been specifically acquired in the first place. There are some exceptions: in Britain, for example, works of art permanently situated in a public place, or in premises open to the public, are exempt from these limitations, and may be reproduced in various ways without infringing copyright. But in general the rule applies.

Especially, of course, in the applied arts. In the fine arts works are usually by definition unique: or, in the case of an etching or a bronze, produced in strictly limited numbers. In theory an artist can in fact pla-

giarize himself: if he has sold the rights of reproduction
of a painting or sculpture to someone else and then
himself makes a reproduction or even a close variation
on it he is infringing the owner's copyright just as much
as an author would be if, having sold the copyright of
an article to one newspaper, he then sold it again elsewhere under another title, perhaps changing a word
here and there. Where the works are not necessarily
unique, being produced by some process which permits
duplication, the matter of number becomes important.
To some extent the price of a work is determined by
the number: a unique casting of a bronze would cost
more than one of five, one of five would cost more than
one of fifty, and so on. An artist therefore has the right
to determine how many copies there shall be, and to
suppress unauthorized copies; equally, the buyer has a
right to accurate information, and would have cause for
complaint on the grounds of misrepresentation if he
bought a work on the assurance that it was unique or
one of five and found instead that it was one of fifty or
five hundred.

Beyond this, in the realm of mass production and
reproduction, the same standards apply, but with differing force. Here, naturally, it is much more a question of
the thing as model than the thing in itself. If an artist
produces a design for, say, a commemorative plate, the
actual piece of paper with the design is far less important than the copyright of the design. Infringement of
the copyright by a rival manufacturer could be a serious
business for the holder of the copyright, artist or manufacturer, since it would naturally cut down sales of the

275

copyrighted article, which would most likely be more expensive. (The painter, on the other hand, would not lose much if anything by unauthorized reproduction of a painting he still owns, since no one supposes that a reproduction is the *same* as an original painting, or even a realistic substitute.) So though the principle governing the matter remains the same, its application would necessarily be carried out with differing degrees of rigor in different areas of the art business.

And once he has sold the work itself, and perhaps the rights of reproduction, is that the last legal connection the artist has with the product of his labors? In most countries, yes, but not in France. In France there is a curious, but on reflection very reasonable, rule called the "droit de suite". This recognizes that the creator has a certain continuing interest in his work, whatever may have become of it or him since he disposed of it, and which he cannot dispose of (beyond specifically vesting its administration in the hands of agents). So, the artist has the right to a proportion of the amount any work of his fetches at a French auction during his lifetime and during the normal term of copyright (fifty years in France, as in Britain and America). He or his heirs must state their claim in the official journal and must collect the money within three months of the sale from the ministerial officer who holds it meanwhile; otherwise it is forfeited and returned to the seller. This right applies only to public sales, not to sales between private individuals or dealers; and of course it applies only in France.

In the course of discussing the rights of the artist,

we have mentioned a few rights of the buyer. On the whole, it will be seen, the buyer has fewer rights than he may think. He cannot necessarily, for instance, authorize reproduction of a work he owns; nor can he withhold the right, though he can always deny access to the work if it is kept on his own private property. Where works of the past, out of copyright, are concerned, he is on rather safer ground; or at least, given that the whole business is more risky, his position has to be better defined. More risky it is in a number of important respects. At least, where dealing directly with the artist is concerned, there is no problem of authentication: if you buy a Picasso from Picasso, or anyway from his officially designated agents, you know for certain that it is what it claims to be. With a Renoir you are that little bit less sure; with a Rubens you are less sure again, and so on. Since the amount of money a work of art will cost a buyer varies enormously depending on exactly whom it is supposed to be by, he will require some sort of legal safeguards to ensure that a work of art is precisely what it is claimed to be.

These safeguards take various forms in various countries. In France the law is most clearly laid down, explicitly covering almost every conceivable eventuality. For example, take the case of a sale of a copy or a forgery. If the painting is catalogued and labeled as, say, a Corot, and proves not to be, the seller is liable to legal action. He may be guilty only of an error, in which case he may be required to do no more than refund the selling price; or he may be found guilty of various positively criminal acts, such as misrepresentation or forgery itself (of the work or of documents appearing to establish its authenticity). Even if he does not explicitly claim that the work is a Corot, but allows the buyer to think it might be, perhaps merely by selling a painting clearly signed "Corot" without pointing out that it is no such thing, he may still be liable to prosecution. And appeals to the common sense of buyers are no protection: perhaps only an idiot would imagine he was buying a genuine Corot for a few pounds, but the law recognizes the right even of idiots to protection.

In Britain and America matters have seldom been so simple and clearcut for the buyer as they are in France (in principle anyway; the practice of establishing the genuineness or otherwise of a work of art is something else again). In Britain the situation was somewhat improved in 1967 by the passing of the Misrepresentations Act, designed to protect the consumer from goods the nature of which is misrepresented by the vendor. In the art market this act has had a number of effects. In particular, it makes what had formerly been a "gentlemen's agreement," that any reputable dealer would take back a work which was wrongly described and refund the money, into a right: now any contract can be revoked within a reasonable time, whether or not the misstatement was made with deliberate intent to deceive or in perfect good faith. It also made the major auction houses modify the operation of their "code" for describing works of art, as explained in Chapter Six. The new act requires that the precise nature of any article offered for sale must be clearly stated; a code which appeared to the uninitiated to be describing as a Rubens what the vendors certainly did not consider to be a Rubens at all would not be acceptable, and neither would any general get-out clause absolving the auctioneer of any responsibility for erroneous or misleading descriptions. Moreover, if the auctioneer is selling, as is often the case, for an anonymous owner, then he becomes personally responsible for the whole contract of sale and any legal complications resulting from it, damages and restitutions. In response to this new situation Sotheby's and Christie's have started to publish a key to the code in each catalogue, and have become much more chary about accepting items offered for sale by owners whose identities are to remain undisclosed—especially when there is any important doubt about the correct attribution.

But how, legally, can the rightness or wrongness of an attribution be settled? That is where the experts come in. Again, the legal status of experts varies from country to country, though the necessity of recourse to them is pretty generally recognized. As usual, the situation is best codified in France. As we explained earlier, the expert is part of the normal state system of French auctions, and every item has to be *expertisé* before it can be offered for sale as the work of this or that master. (And this, with impeccable French consistency, even if the work concerned is a recognized masterpiece with an unshakable pedigree going right back to the artist himself.) The expert, therefore, though he needs no formal qualification whatever to practice as an expert, even in an official capacity, holds from the outset a rather special position in France. But he has corresponding obligations. He can be held directly responsible, in law, for many of the results of his errors, in his official capacity as consultant to the commissaire-priseur at auctions and elsewhere. An expert functioning as adviser to a commissaire-priseur legally shares responsibility with the commissaire-priseur for any errors of attribution or cataloguing. A judicial expert, employed by a court to assist magistrates in their inquiries, is also responsible for unnecessary delay, for errors gross enough to render another expert judgment necessary, for "manquements à la prudence et à la délicatesse" in carrying out or reporting on his researches, and various other errors of omission or commission (though a defense that his opinion was given in good faith is in some circumstances admitted).

The French tendency to hold expert pronouncements in special regard, even if the expert is self-appointed, is not noticeably shared by British and American courts. The main auction houses, of course, have no statutory equivalent to the commissaire-priseur and his team of experts, and though their catalogues are generally the end product of much scholarship and research, it still remains arguable how far the contents of auctioneers' catalogues can legally be regarded as expert opinion. Many who have instituted cases against auction houses based on this assumption have lost them, though in Britain the new Misrepresentations Act should alter the situation somewhat, by negating any blanket disclaimers by auction houses on the subject of statements made in their catalogues. In both Britain and America, of course, experts may be called to give evidence on the subject of contested attributions, etc.

In neither country is any special qualification, such as a degree or diploma in art history, called for or specially recognized. In fact, anyone can be called as an expert, the only criterion being what sort of impression his qualifications are likely to make on a (necessarily non-expert) jury under cross-examination. In the United States court procedure does allow an expert to be cross-examined on his qualifications to judge the point at issue before he is allowed to give his evidence, which at least on occasion permits what he eventually has to say to be regarded in a somewhat skeptical light. In Britain, it seems, courts are more ready to take the good faith and disinterestedness of experts on trust, since they can give their evidence first, and are only subject to question about their qualifications under cross-examination. In neither country does there seem to be any special legal provision for holding the expert practically responsible for his judgments—supposing, of course, that any faults he may commit do not go so far as fraud or complicity in fraud.

Once the work of art (genuine, let us hope) has been acquired and become part of the collector's property, it becomes subject, like any other possession, to all the complexities of tax law governing that property, realization on it in the owner's lifetime, its disposal before or after his death, and other such matters. We have already encountered some of the ins and outs of legislation on this subject; the rest are probably best reserved for our final consideration of that vexed but these days inescapable question, the real status of art as an investment.

ART AND INVESTMENT

It is difficult enough for most people with money ready for spending to reconcile what they would like with what they can afford. The notion of investment, good and bad, seldom clarifies any choice unequivocally; and as soon as it is introduced it raises a lot of new difficulties. But, it may be objected, how can anyone bracing himself to spend any appreciable amount of money (appreciable, that is, in relation to his total available resources, however small it may be absolutely) possibly dismiss from his mind altogether the possibility of realizing on what he is about to buy at a later date? The answer is, perfectly easily. It is largely a matter of convention. Take clothes, for instance. They serve, admittedly, certain practical functions, like keeping their owner warm or preventing him from being brought to court for indecent exposure. Beyond that, though, the borderline between the necessary and the variously pleasurable or impressive is decidedly hazy.

The woman who buys a new hat to cheer herself up when her diet gets her down pretty certainly does not need a new hat to keep off the sun or the rain, and if she did she would buy a very different sort of hat. What she buys is an object which gives her pleasure because she likes the look of it or because it is the latest thing and makes her feel fashionable, and which has the added advantage, she hopes, of making her altogether more striking and attractive to others. She may want a hat she cannot afford, and have to settle for a hat she can, but which gives her rather less pleasure. But what she never really considers is the hat as a straight investment. An investment in *herself,* perhaps, in that if it makes her more attractive it may help her, directly or indirectly, to get that job, catch that man. But not as something which is bought with at least one eye on its resale potential. Who, after all, wants to buy one slightly used hat, in last year's style?

The instance is not entirely frivolous. There are many things which we buy for no pressing utilitarian reason but at the same time without any shadow of a thought about reselling them. We accept that if they give us pleasure for a certain length of time, that is all we shall require of them; the amount we are willing to pay for them is fixed by purely subjective considerations—how much pleasure they will give us for how long, how impressed we think our friends will be by them—moderated by more concrete factors such as how much money we possibly have available for the purchase. We have got used, in the last few years, to considering any and every art purchase at least partly from the angle of investment—what would its demonstrable worth be if I sold it again five years hence, ten years hence?—but is there, when we come down to it, any essential reason why art should not be bought in the same spirit as a new hat, new curtains, a luxurious meal, a new car or television set bought when the old one would do and the new acquisition will, we know, be next to worthless by the time we have finished with it, whatever its condition and original cost?

Surely not. That we think otherwise today is all a matter of convention and received ideas. In point of fact, the very idea of art as investment is a relatively recent growth. Except perhaps in a few special cases where the raw material itself was valuable (gold was always gold, however fashioned for the time being by a goldsmith's art), the thought of resale value would never have occurred to a medieval or renaissance patron. The work of art commissioned, on behalf of a church or to decorate his home, was there to give him pleasure and to reflect his magnificence. With luck, it might continue to do him credit long after his death, but equally it could be and was regarded as entirely expendable: when the fresco started to look dingy or fashions changed, it would promptly be replaced with something newer, brighter, better, and that was that. Father's purchases could be relegated to minor passages of the palace, stowed in the attic, or just thrown out. If by some fluke the artist's reputation happened to outlast his own lifetime, so much the better, but that was hardly something that could be relied on or planned for.

This particular habit of the patron's mind lasted for as long as there were private patrons. If an eighteenth-century landowner commissioned a picture of his house, his horse, his wife or himself, it was for his own pleasure, mixed with more or less snobbery and ostentation at having the resources to do so. He might hope that the work of art which resulted would become a treasured heirloom for his descendants, but not obviously because of any expected increase in monetary value; rather, as a tribute of affection and respect, a commemoration of a founding father, a proud demonstration of a long and illustrious lineage. The very idea of trading in such things would be repugnant, as no fit activity for a gentleman; the owner of such a picture would no more plan on selling it at a profit than an aristocrat who commissioned a mass from Mozart, a symphony from Haydn, would then plan on recouping his initial outlay by hiring out the parts to other music lovers. Things might, admittedly, be a trifle different where the few recognized classics of past art or objects genuinely antique and curious were concerned, since these were on the market to be bought and sold by traders. But even there a gentleman collector, while he might bargain hotly to get what he wanted at the most advantageous price he could manage, would judge how much he should spend on it very much according to the standards employed by our woman in search of a hat. At most he might consent to exchange possessions with another collector of equal social standing, or be forced to liquidate his belongings by some unfortunate external necessity, but selling things calculatingly for profit—that was the business of tradesmen and usurers, far, far beneath his dignity.

Thus even after the rise of the entrepreneur, the middleman who made his living by the buying and selling of art, a very clear distinction was observed between the tradesman and the collector, as between the maker and/or seller of hats and the buyer. Even today traces of this attitude remain among governmental and industrial patrons of the arts. Among the first, usefulness predominates in the motives for commission or purchase: they seek the most unobjectionable yet cultural-looking way of covering that wall, finishing off this façade, decorating the ambassador's office. Impressiveness is usually more important to the industrial patron, since the commission or purchase no doubt has to serve its purpose in some more or less complicated, worked-out public relations scheme. Governments are like the aristocratic patrons of settled unassailable fortune; they may occasionally throw things away, but they never otherwise dispose of anything except as written-off government surplus, so the question of resale value does not arise. Industries tend to be ruthless: on the whole a profit realized on some work of art which had ceased to serve its P.R. purpose (an abstract sculpture at the entrance to headquarters when headquarters is rebuilt, a grubby mural in the factory canteen) would only mess up the accounts. If a convenient home can be found without too much trouble and expense for art acquired in such circumstances, that is all well and good. But it is normally a question of giving it away, and if it cannot be given away demolishing it on the spot, like Victor

Pasmore's "Ceramic Mural" at the Festival of Britain.

If the idea of trading in art was unacceptable to the patron, neither did it make much headway in the new bourgeois art market of the mid-nineteenth century. For one thing, this new class of buyers was likely to be that which most unquestioningly accepted the idea of progress, and clearly the idea of progress in the arts must work directly against the idea of investment, for if you accept that things in general got better and better you must by the same token accept that the older a thing is the poorer it is, and the less it is worth. Of course there were some exceptions, the divine masters (Raphael foremost among them) whose genius placed them outside such a naïvely meliorist view of art history. But on the whole the idea was firmly implanted that new painting, like new furniture, was better than old. The old might have an educative or curiosity value, but in general it was the new which brought the highest prices: this, after all, was the "golden age of the living painter."

It is doubtful how far, if at all, the middle-class Victorian collector of contemporary art considered what would happen to it in succeeding generations. If questioned on the subject, he would probably admit that while a Millais, say, which he had bought in younger days would now be likely, should he unhappily find himself forced to sell it, to realize substantially more than he had paid for it, the fact that Millais was now clearly at the height of fashion meant there was every possibility that his children would have as little time for it as he now had for the great figures of his father's generation. But that was not really the point. The criterion of a picture's cost was the amount of interest it excited now, and the amount of work which had gone into it: you would expect to pay a painter, like any good craftsman, for the number of man-hours he had put in as well as for his more nebulous "inspiration." And you bought for your own pleasure or to enhance your own prestige. It was like being well-dressed, having a well-run home—you expected value for money, but the returns were intangible, and had little to do with monetary profit or loss.

How and where, then, did the change in our attitude toward art as a commodity come about? Mainly by the interlocking influences of two important new factors on the art-buying scene: the rich collectors belonging to large international Jewish business families, and the often newly rich American millionaire collector. These introduced some entirely new elements into the game. To begin with, the Jewish art collectors, of whom the Rothschilds are only the most famous group. In the traditional pattern of patronage, money and an aristocratic way of life, with close territorial connections in terms of estates and properties, normally went hand in hand. The riches came mainly from the land, that is to say from immovable goods, and art was part of the trappings. The gentleman, anyway, had certain appearances to keep up, and one which he felt obliged to cling to as long as he claimed to be a gentleman was that he did not trade or make any part of his living directly by buying and selling. Even the new class of rich bourgeois industrialists who arose to rival the landed gentry during the industrial revolution still founded their fortunes largely on immovable assets—factories, mines, railways.

The historical position of the international Jewish financiers exempted them from most of these limitations. They had no close territorial connections, and never knew quite when a welcome because of the business advantages their presence brought to a country might not turn into bitter hostility and persecution. It was therefore desirable that their goods should be easily movable, their properties small but valuable, permitting rapid liquidation in an emergency. Also, though their wealth might rival or surpass that of the aristocrat, they were seldom permitted to give themselves the airs of gentlemen, and indeed they usually had sufficient sense not to try to do so. They were traders, and not ashamed of it, not like most of the gentile *nouveau riche*, only too eager to disguise from themselves and others the humble steps by which they had managed to reach the top. Now there was, unmistakably, money to be made trading in art, even if the gentry found it beneath their dignity to make it. Objets d'art always had a realizable value, whether the majority of owners chose to realize on it or not, and thus they presented themselves as a very convenient form of easily movable asset, which could be liquidated without too much trouble anywhere in the world. Consequently, to the more idealistic motives of art-loving and the rather more dubious ones of desire to display were added for rich Jews in the nineteenth century a number of more basically practical; what they bought they might buy for love, but if necessary they were not ashamed to come down into the market place and sell for profit, like any other tradesman. Art was something with a variable but ascertainable market value; it could therefore be invested in, just like anything else.

If the new American millionaires of the 1880s and 1890s did not altogether share the Jewish financier's freedom from territorial ties, at least their background in a republican, antiaristocratic society freed them, like him, from any false refinement over soiling their hands in trade. If they were persuaded that a grand collection of European fine art was necessary to their pleasure and position in the world, they also wanted to be sure that they were not being cheated or paying over the odds; they wanted evidence that they were paying a fair market price and could expect to sell again, should they ever want to, at a profit. Of course this would not always be possible, but, as we have seen, Duveen above all appreciated the importance of at least preserving the illusion, keeping up confidence in the works of art he sold much as one would in the value of stocks and shares. The demonstration—by arranging, if necessary at his own expense, that no work he had once sold should ever be seen to change hands for less than the original selling price—might be theoretical, in that most of Duveen's clients had no need or intention of realizing on their art purchases during their own lifetime. But even if Duveen had succeeded in his most cherished gambit, persuading his clients to make sure the fairness of his charges should never be put to the test of resale by donating or willing their collections to some public institution, he knew that they nevertheless required the reassurance that, considered purely as financial investments, their purchases had been wise ones.

By the end of the nineteenth century the traditional aristocratic view of art collecting as something quite removed from crass commercial considerations was under attack from other directions. As the collecting activities of Jewish financiers and American millionaires drove the prices of old masters up, it became more and more difficult for those who happened to possess some, probably acquired by an ancestor and of no personal interest or appeal to them, to ignore altogether the potential value of their possessions in terms of hard cash. Especially if the families were suffering from the general decay of the landed aristocracy and the new demands of the government in the form of estate and death duties. Once the Settled Lands Act of 1882 made it relatively easy to liquidate heirlooms, many families who in the past would never have dreamed of selling off works of art were tempted or compelled to do so. And once this had begun to happen, the idea of art as property with a value which could be realized was bound to assume more and more importance in people's calculations.

Thus, little by little, we have arrived at the modern situation, in which hardly any substantial art transaction can be entered into without at least a faint question at the back of the mind, will the value of what I am buying go up or go down in the next few years? It is almost unavoidable that this should be so. The newspapers and magazines constantly present art to us in this

291

light. So long as we are spending relatively small amounts at a time—say up to but not more than one week's salary after tax on one object—we may be willing to regard it simply as fun spending and leave it at that. But even there it is normal to want reassuring that we have made a good buy, have not paid over the odds for something we should have got much cheaper. A direct comparison is rarely possible: with an antiquarian book or an etching we might perhaps find another example in virtually identical condition at half the price (which would be galling) or double the price (which would be gratifying), but an original painting or drawing is necessarily unique, and therefore the only reliable guide to whether we have paid the right price for it is what we could sell it for were we so minded.

Not that we necessarily are. As with Duveen's reassurances to his millionaire clients, these questions are often purely academic. Not that, given the right circumstances, we might not be tempted, even to our own surprise. Take the case of an American writer of our acquaintance. When we last met him two financial questions were bothering him. He had been asked to do an adaptation for a Hollywood film company: they had offered him $250,000 (he said) to do it, and it would not be difficult, but somehow the idea did not appeal to him, despite the money. Then there was the problem of his Bonnard. He had bought it for $3000 years ago, as one of his first big luxuries from his first big royalty check. Now someone had offered him $60,000 for it. What should he do? Well, we said, it all depended how much he liked the Bonnard. After some hemming and hawing he agreed that he probably liked it as much as anything he owned. Well, we said, why not give himself the pleasure of keeping his Bonnard, and if the $60,000 slipping through his fingers bothered him, he could make up by taking on the adapting job instead. Yes, he said, but I don't really want to do that adaptation, and after all a 2000 percent increase in the price of the painting . . . We left him still balancing.

It is rarely, though, that the temptation to realize on a work of art comes in such a direct form. What most people like is the comforting thought that something they enjoy having on their walls and have no intention of selling would still, if they did want to sell, or if they wanted to buy it today, command a price twice, or ten times, or a hundred times what they paid for it in the first place. As a matter of fact, many of the world's most important collectors just could not afford to sell their collections. Income tax, capital gains tax, estate duties after death, would all make sure that any profit they might make would be more than wiped out at once. Circumstances may force them to sell, or they may be so rich that they can afford the gesture of just getting bored with their collection. But the profits in any large-scale transaction of the sort are likely to be more theoretical than actual. Of course, they may be able to take the sort of limited comfort in the situation which the American banker George Blumenthal found when his friends commiserated with him because his collection, sold at the depths of the Depression, had fetched 30 percent less than he gave for it: "Not at all," he said, "I'm losing 75 percent on my securities!"

293

And yet, despite all these reservations, the image persists of fortunes made overnight (or nearly) by astronomical rises in the prices of works of art. The supposed profitability of art has its own glamour and many small collectors or owners of one or two pictures enjoy being able to impress their friends not so much with their cultural superiority as with the financial cunning they can evince by a few nicely planted remarks on the mere song their possessions were bought for and the average percentage appreciation the works of the artist have shown annually ever since. As ever, the combined mystique of cultural oneupmanship and business acumen is unbeatable. But are fortunes in fact made in this way by the ordinary private collector or even very substantial profits? Far less often and far less easily than we are generally encouraged to suppose.

To begin with, there are so many elements which the hopeful advisers on art as an investment tend to skate over or around. For one thing, many of their most spectacular examples are drawn from the chance discovery, the painting or sculpture bought for virtually nothing which proves to be a valuable masterpiece. Such discoveries do actually happen from time to time, and they always make good copy. But they can be left out of account in serious, systematic examinations of art as material for investment. Certainly we might all just possibly stumble on an oil well in our own back garden, but we would be ill-advised to stake very much of our time, trouble and money on the possibility, especially if we lacked all expertise in distinguishing an oil well from a forgotten cesspit. In other words, the chances of the ordinary occasional buyer of pictures and objets d'art stumbling on a lost masterpiece, or knowing what he has got once he has found one, are so remote as to be negligible in assessing the possible percentage yield of art purchases on resale. Richard Rush, for example, in his *Art as an Investment,* recounts entertainingly a number of his own adventures digging for buried artistic treasure. His frequent success is certainly a tribute to his critical acumen (though he does not tell us how often he has bought something hoping it might be valuable and found that on examination it was worth quite a bit less than what he gave), but such lucky strokes do not help the rest of us very much. What we want, to pursue our oil-well simile further, is not encouragement to go out prospecting, but advice on the relative potential of shares in this or that oil company bought now in the normal way at the current market price.

Here too the advisers are seldom backward in coming forward. But if we look more closely at what they tell us, we soon see a number of snags. The biggest obstacle in the way of systematic, rational advice is the special nature of art as a commodity. Each original work of art is by definition unique. Even, say, a slavishly faithful copy by a painter of one of his own paintings will not be exactly the same; one version will be found preferable to the other, if only on quite irrational (but still often forceful) terms of temporal priority. No two casts of the same bronze, no two impressions of the same etching, will ever be quite the same —and that quite apart from any extrinsic but often financially influential considerations of external history and associations, previous ownership and so on. Each individual item, therefore, to some extent constitutes a unique case, with its own rules, its own advantages and disadvantages. It is all very well to tell us, as Mr. Rush does, that in the aggregate paintings by Van Gogh, Gauguin and Cézanne have appreciated by 4,833 percent between 1930 and 1960. But which particular Van Goghs, Gauguins or Cézannes? How far is the overall picture applicable in any individual case? Advice based on estimates such as these, of course, always contains some sort of qualification noting that it applies only to a good quality painting, of a reasonable average size, characteristic of the artist's best period or periods. But who determines what is a good quality painting? Who assesses the optimum size, the extent to which the work is characteristic, the relative value of different periods in the artist's work (or for that matter the relative attractiveness of various types of subject matter)? Already we are launched into controversial matters of connoisseurship, and the nice clean lines of purely financial guidance are lost in a scrabble of conflicting value-judgments.

And anyway, the cornerstone of any such consideration of art, the basic price you should pay to acquire it, is always open to question. In the recent hysteria over art buying, it has often been said that no matter what you pay for something, if it is good enough you will always get your money back with a little over. To start with, even in the most unshakably gilt-edged area of art buying, say that of major works by major Impressionists, this is not necessarily true: it is unwise to try and realize on any painting within five years of its being bought for a high figure, since it seems to follow (perhaps because a rapid succession of saleroom appearances shakes confidence—is there something mysteriously wrong with the picture?—and takes the edge off its novelty value) that a painting sold in such circumstances more often than not takes at least a slight tumble in price. But such cases apart, it still must be of some relevance exactly how much what you want to sell has cost you. Even if a record price does help to raise prices in general, it is obviously possible for someone, spurred on by who knows what special reasons, to pay a price so far in advance of the norm that it remains a solitary eccentricity for years, perhaps forever. Granted that at the moment there is a general concurrence of opinion on what would constitute a major Cézanne, on how frequently one might expect to see one up for sale, and on the extreme desirability of such an item, anyone who buys one under normal saleroom conditions, at whatever price, can feel reasonably sanguine that his purchase will not actually lose value in the foreseeable future.

But then, even equipped with this comforting intelligence, how many people in the world can possibly afford to take advantage of it by buying a major Cézanne? And further down the scale things are much more chancy. For a measure of certainty in an investment you have to pay a lot and expect a relatively small percentage profit on it (though obviously 5 per cent of a million is still a lot more money than 500 percent of a thousand). People who bought major Cézannes back in

1930 were smiling, if not laughing outright, by 1960, but the point is that in 1930 they were taking a real gamble: those who bought them in 1960 were backing as near as possible a sure thing, and so the odds were drastically reduced. To hope in 1960 for anything like a similar rate of appreciation in an art investment by 1990, one would have had to gamble much more daringly than that, and the odds against one's hitting the jackpot would be correspondingly longer.

It is that sort of gamble-investment which would be likely to interest the modern would-be small investor in art. What he wants (putting aside all question of what sort of art he might actually like to live with meanwhile) is something which will not cost him too much more than he can afford and which at the same time has an odds-on chance of appreciating gratifyingly within his own lifetime, preferably within the next five or ten years. And in this sort of area clear guidelines are much harder to draw. Everyone in the art world is on the alert when the major Impressionist comes up for sale, and though there may be some disagreements about its quality and how much it should cost these are generally within very narrow limits and soon settled by the practical test of an auction in a glare of international publicity. If an old master like the Liechtenstein Leonardo "Ginevra dei Benci" came onto the open market now, there would be no question of its quality and uniqueness, while for its price the sky would be the limit.

But supposing, to take an example conceivably within the range of a modest middle-income investor in art, a Monticelli were to be offered to him. Monticelli (1824-1886) is a good example of a painter of marked individuality, once fashionable, then quite unfashionable, and now being given increased attention by critics and collectors. Let us suppose that our investor comes across the Monticelli at a reputable dealer's. It would probably be priced between £400 and £2000. Should he buy it? First, is it authentic? However reputable the dealer is, he is bound to be to some extent working in the dark, because Monticelli was much forged and there is no reliable, accessible body of expert opinion on his work. No doubt, if interest in him continues that will come, but when it does it may contain some nasty shocks for collectors who are confident that they own genuine Monticellis. In other ways too a lot of guesswork comes in. There is no particular trouble about size—nearly all Monticellis are a reasonable size to hang comfortably in a normal modern flat, which helps. But what is his best period? Will we decide that his very vividly colored, heavily paint-laden later works are preferable to the lighter, more graceful scenes of picturesquely clad revelers in parks and glades which established his vogue during his own lifetime? Will we prefer his figure compositions or his still lifes? And even if his reputation and value do go up, as we feel sure they will, how much will they go up, how quickly? If we pay £1000 for a Monticelli which seems to us good and which is authoritatively accepted as genuine, have we done wisely or foolishly—will its possible selling price go up by leaps and bounds, or just a little, or will it barely keep pace with the fall in the value of money? Will it

299

actually go down? How much would the complexion of things change if we had paid only £400 for the same painting, or had gone as high as £2000?

All this may seem very small beer to commentators with their heads in the clouds of the great Impressionist boom, but it must be remembered that to the majority of their readers even £400 is far more than they would want to risk on any single item. In France, for instance, the average price the run-of-the-mill collector cares to pay for a painting is roughly in the £200-£400 range. In Britain it is probably rather lower, in the U.S. maybe a little higher. And at that, most collectors feel that they are risking a substantial amount of money if they have no real feeling that they could get it back at will. It is toward such collectors that most popular investment advice seems to be aimed, but it seldom hits its target.

Among the advisers there is, however, at least one brave man. Robert Wraight, art correspondent of the London *Evening News,* includes in his book *The Art Game* (1966) his own predictions of which artists may be relied upon in general to appreciate in the future. The *Observer* newspaper offered a rather similar classification a year later. The *Observer* told us what a number of selected artists' work might be expected to make here and now, with a very few tentative predictions (will Henry Moore be in the second Old Master division, his works selling at up to £750,000 apiece, by 2500 AD?). Mr. Wraight, more practically, divides his tips into artists whose works (good, characteristic major works, of course) should cost between £10,000 and £30,-

ooo apiece, between £2000 and £10,000, between £250 and £2000, between £50 and £250, and under £50. He also commits himself to views on whether they should appreciate in under ten years, between ten and twenty, or between fifty and seventy. The rich and well-to-do may be happy to take his advice and lay in Braques, Picassos, Bonnards, Vuillards, Mondrians and early Kandinskys, or Blakes, Palmers, Corots, Rouaults, Rossettis, Vlamincks, de Staëls, Brancusis and such. But obviously most of the buyers such as we have in mind will be more interested in his three lower priced categories.

And here there is, as might be expected, a considerably larger area of pure speculation. Already most of the Pre-Raphaelites have gone beyond reach, as far as their paintings are concerned, anyway. One would, indeed, be quite hard put to it to find an acceptable Puvis de Chavannes or Monticelli, a Sickert, or a small Henry Moore, for under £400. And below that figure the collector in search of potential profit is driven to the local and parochial—to Grimshaw and Clarkson Stanfield, to Vanessa Bell, Albert Goodwin and Paul Maitland in Britain, and to figures of equivalent talent and reputation in France or the U.S. Even so, some of Mr. Wraight's recommendations, if valid in 1966, must have escalated meanwhile—you would be hard put to it now to find a good Grimshaw, or Clausen, or Brangwyn, in a respectable London gallery for less than £250. And if an artist's work has not passed this threshold, or nearly, the advice to snap it up quickly is all very well in theory but deuced difficult to follow up in practice. For where can you find it? As a rule it is either being deliberately hoarded by dealers in the confident expectation that another year or two will make it much better worth their while to sell, or it is just lying around unregarded in attics and cellars until the demand for it will be sufficient to create the supply.

What, then, is the hopeful small investor, suitably indoctrinated with excitable accounts of the money to be made (though as a rule, unfortunately, by professionals) in the buying and selling of art, to do if he wants a slice of the profits for himself? He can, of course, buy completely haphazardly, picking up anything he likes at whatever prices he can afford and putting all thoughts of profit out of his head. This may sometimes be profitable all the same; when the composer William Alwyn sold his collection of Pre-Raphaelite paintings in 1962, having collected them in the previous fifteen years for no other reason than because he liked them and they had cost, most of them, somewhere between £5 and £25, he came away with a very satisfactory return, sometimes of as much as 4000 percent on his initial investment. But then there is no need of advice in order to do that; what one needs is independent tastes and sheer luck. Certainly by the time the advisers are advising you to buy something, it will already be too late to buy it at really low prices. But there are two coherent courses of action the small investor can take. He can decide either to abjure the big league altogether, or he can take the extreme gamble of concentrating entirely on new, unknown artists and hope that he may come up with a winner.

The first course is obviously the safest, though except in very extraordinary cases the rewards are unlikely to be spectacular. By abjuring the big league, the collector will have to confine his attention very carefully and deliberately to the minor works of minor masters. Drawings and sketches are an obvious possibility, but even here there are difficulties. As we have already noted, the scarcity of major works by the really important old masters has diverted attention to those of their works which may still conceivably come on to the market. Consequently the merest scribble by Leonardo or Raphael or Rembrandt will command a price in five figures. A good drawing by any of the recognized Victorian masters would probably cost over £100 in a Bond Street gallery or thereabouts. But there are still reputable drawings by reputable artists to be had at under £100, and in this area, unlike that of the major oil, it is perfectly possible to make discoveries for oneself with an absolute minimum of erudition. Moreover, for investment in this area there is always the comforting thought that on resale it will still no doubt be below the £1000 lower limit on which capital gains tax is charged the British owner wishing to realise on his property.

The small drawing and watercolor has become the favorite way out of the art market dilemma for British collectors with not too much money to spare. In France it is less favored—the watercolor has no important place in the French tradition, and most Frenchmen are less inclined than the English romantically to exalt the fragmentary and unfinished over the completed work of art. In France, therefore, one tends to find those too conservatively inclined to plunge into investment, however small, in the avant garde, falling back instead on the small objet d'art and the artist's print, especially the lithograph. In the last five years or so the graphics craze has spread also to the United States, and here now the market in etchings, lithographs and such is enjoying a boom without parallel. Of course, again we are forced to exclude from our calculations really a superb early impressions of Rembrandt etchings—one of his "Hundred Guilder Print" brought £26,000 at Sotheby's in 1966, and in 1967 £30,000 was given for one of his large "Crucifixion". Goya prints may fetch up to £20,-500 (the 1964 record price for an impression of his very rare "Giant"), while for really first-rate examples of Gothic prints the price may go even higher—the highest recorded amount ever paid for a print is the £32,000 paid in 1965 for the only known complete impression of the fifteenth-century German Master P.M.'s "The Women's Bath". That sort of price is hardly within the range of the small collector, and the graphic works of other artists have shown equally spectacular rises in price: Sotheby's estimates that since 1950-52 Breughel the Elder's prints have gone up 2,400 percent, Canaletto's up 2000 percent, Dürer's up 1700 percent and Piranesi's up 1250 percent.

Still, all this is indicative of something, and collectors at all levels of purchasing power have been quick to catch on. As with drawings, so with etchings and engravings: it is still possible to find very accomplished and pleasant works which can be bought, or could very recently be bought, for under £5 each. The etchings of the major Impressionists, at any rate in good early impressions, would cost quite a bit more, but the comparable, if not in their own field superior, work of contemporaries who specialized in etching, like Legrand, Legros, or Rops, can still often be picked up very cheaply. Moreover, original prints have been shooting up in value of late, so that for those who know what they are doing the percentage increase in value has often been far higher than with paintings by comparable artists. Perhaps inevitably, the boom in graphics has also led to some hysteria: people started telling each other, and even believing, that it was enough to buy any contemporary artist's lithograph and just wait for its value to rise. Of course this is nonsense; a rise in value can be predicted with no more or less certainty of any given contemporary artist's lithographs than of his original paintings—the only advantage they have over his paintings is that they are cheaper, and therefore less is risked. It may be that the prices for graphics even by some accepted modern masters are too high, being out of all proportion to their rarity, or inherent interest. Take the lithographs of Chagall, for instance. A signed, limited impression is one thing. But many of his lithographs, like those illustrating the two hefty numbers of the art magazine *Verve* devoted to his Bible illustrations, were mass-produced in many thousands, as they would have to be for even a very limited normal magazine circulation. Five years ago it was easy to buy the two numbers in Paris for about 200 NF each (around £15, or $43), for which you would be getting nearly fifty color lithographs. Now they have all been dismembered by the Left Bank print dealers, and you

would have to pay about the same for a single lithograph from one of them. With more recent books con-
taining Chagall lithographs, like the Jacques Lassaigne
monograph of 1957, it has often been possible for the
observant to buy the whole book for less than the shop
along the road would be charging for one of the lithographs taken from it. Chagall is admittedly an extreme
case, but by no means unique. This sort of indiscriminate puffing of prices is bound sooner or later to
lead to a loss of confidence and a leveling off to something more reasonable. Or at least, so we would very
much hope.

The other possible line, that of picking your own
unknown artist and hoping for the best, is of course the
riskiest of them all. There are so many imponderables.
Is he the product of instant outrage and scandal, likely
to fizzle out like a spent firework? Is he, on the other
hand, so quiet and unassertive that he is never likely to
make a big splash, however good his work may be? Does
he produce too much, which can shake confidence by
reducing his rarity value? Or does he produce too little,
which can be equally damaging, because if there is not
enough of his work appearing to keep the machine
oiled he may be forgotten or at least undervalued since
there is no constant yardstick of what his prices ought to
be? Is he figurative or abstract? Will he develop or stagnate, and if he develops will it be the way you and other
buyers like? How much is he going to cost you anyway?
If his canvases are underpriced at his first exhibition
they may fail to gain the attention they deserve—there is
always some tendency to take an artist at his own (or his
dealer's) valuation. If they are overpriced they will

probably not sell anyway, or those that do buy them will be likely more rapidly to get cold feet. And so on and so on.

The history of the Paris market in contemporary painting during the last few years contains a salutary warning. It was the first to enjoy a big boom in new art, culminating in 1959-60, and the first to experience a corresponding slump afterward. The same process happened in London about four years later. In New York there is the boom now, but does that mean a slump is just around the corner? In Paris the rise was regular and spectacular throughout the 1950s, until by 1959-60 paintings by Buffet were fetching over a million francs each and Manessiers were up to 10 million, Soulages to over 2 million, Hartungs to 5 million. Then came the recession. Many galleries closed, many painters on contract were laid off, and many prices plummeted. It was partly the result of general economic conditions in France, partly the result of a reaction on the part of the buying public to a feeling that artists and dealers were overreaching themselves, that the gamble required of the buyer in what must after all be of necessity a highly speculative field was too great. Not everything lost value to the same extent: the safest of the moderns were those old and grand enough—Picasso, Braque, Rouault —to be virtually beyond the reach of fashion (but also beyond the pocket of the small buyer) or those who were safely dead—de Staël, Pollock—and therefore known quantities as far as available output and nature of expression were concerned. Dealers were caught in their own trap, since having monopolistically promoted artists to a price range far beyond what their work might fetch on the open market when and if it arrived there, they could not lower their prices without losing face and shaking their customers' confidence still further. Speculative collectors should have had a field day. But for them it was too complicated: how to decide which painters' prices had gone down only for the moment, and which would never rise again? The Paris art market suffered a setback from which it is only just beginning to recover—and now it has to contend with the increasingly powerful competition of New York and to a lesser extent London on what used to be its own home ground, the selling of new art by new artists.

So, to invest in new art, as to invest in any other sort, there is no safety except in the very top reaches where only those who are already rich can hope to enter. Otherwise, whether one fancies a big gamble or a small flutter, there is nothing for it but to pay your money, take your choice and hope for the best. The only completely safe thing to do is still to buy only what one likes for oneself, at a price which makes it irrelevant what it is, whose it is and what it would fetch if one ever wanted to resell it. But that is a paradise from which the sometimes sad, sometimes exhilarating experience of art as an investment has perhaps forever excluded us. Happy the man who can just occasionally, by spectacular luck or spectacular good sense, reenter it. For him, and only him, art may yet be a still unravished bride. For the rest there is always the worry of wondering whether, on cool consideration, one has not perhaps left rather more than one should have on the mantelpiece as a fee for services rendered.

BIBLIOGRAPHY

ARNAU, FRANK, *3000 Years of Deception in Art and Antiques*. London, Jonathan Cape, 1961.

BEHRMAN, S.N., *Duveen*. London, Hamish Hamilton, 1952.

BROUGH, JAMES, *Auction!* New York, Bobbs-Merrill, 1963.

BROWN, MILTON W., *The Story of the Armory Show*. New York, Joseph H. Hirshhorn Foundation, 1963.

CABANNE, PIERRE, *The Great Collectors*. London, Cassell, 1963.

CARTER, A.C.R., *Let Me Tell You*. London, Hutchinson, 1940.

COLE, SONIA, *Counterfeit*. London, John Murray, 1955.

COLSON, PERCY, *A Story of Christie's*. London, Sampson Low, 1950.

DURET-ROBERT, FRANÇOIS, *Les 400 Coups du Marteau d'Ivoire*. Paris, Robert Laffont, 1964.

ESTEROW, MILTON, *The Art Stealers*. London, Weidenfeld and Nicolson, 1967.

FRIEDLÄNDER, MAX J., *On Art and Connoisseurship*. Oxford, Bruno Cassirer, 1942.

HAHN, HARRY, *The Rape of La Belle*. Kansas City, Frank Glenn, 1946.

HELFT, JACQUES, *Treasure Hunt*. London, Faber, 1957.

HOLLANDER, BARNETT, *The International Law of Art*. London, Bowes and Bowes, 1959.

ISNARD, GUY, *Les Pirates de la Peinture*. Flammarion, 1955.

ISNARD, GUY, *Faux et Imitations dans l'Art*, two vols. Paris, Arthème Fayard, 1959, 1960.

JONI, J.F., *Affairs of a Painter*. London, Faber, 1936.

JULLIEN, PHILIPPE, *The Collectors*. London, Sidgwick and Jackson, 1967.

KURZ, OTTO, *Fakes: A Handbook for Collectors*. London, Faber, 1948.

LAGARDE, PIERRE DE, *Chefs d'Oeuvre en Peril*. Paris, Julliard, 1964.

LYNES, RUSSELL, *The Tastemakers*. London, Hamish Hamilton, 1959.

MAILFERT, ANDRÉ, *Au Pays des Antiquaires*. Paris, Flammarion, 1954.

MOULIN, RAYMONDE, *Le Marché de la Peinture en France*. Paris, Éditions de Minuit, 1967.

OSBORNE, ALAN (ed.), *Patron: Industry Supports the Arts*. London, The Connoisseur, 1966.

PARS, H.H., *Pictures in Peril*. London, Faber, 1957.

PEARSON, KENNETH, AND CONNER, PATRICIA, *The Dorak Affair*. London, Michael Joseph, 1967.

REITLINGER, GERALD, *The Economics of Taste. Vol. I: The Rise and Fall of Picture Prices 1760-1960. Vol. II: The Rise and Fall of Objets d'Art Prices since 1760*. London, Barrie and Rockliff, 1960, 1963.

RHEIMS, MAURICE, *La Vie Étrange des Objets*. Paris, Plon, 1959. (The English version of this book is abridged.)

ROBERTS, GEORGE AND MARY, *Triumph on Fairmont: Fiske Kimball and the Philadelphia Museum of Art*. New York, Lippincott, 1959.

RUSH, RICHARD H., *Art as an Investment*. New York, Prentice-Hall, 1961.

SAARINEN, ALINE B., *The Proud Possessors*. New York, Random House, 1958.

SALAMON, FERDINANDO, *Il Cogniscitore di Stampe*. Rome, Einaudi, 1960.

SCHÜLLER, SEPP, *Forgers, Dealers, Experts*. London, Arthur Barker, 1960.

SOROKIN, PITIRIM A., *Fluctuations of Forms of Art (Social and Cultural Dynamics, Vol. 1)*. London, Allen and Unwin, 1937.

TAYLOR, FRANCIS HENRY, *The Taste of Angels*. London, Hamish Hamilton, 1948.

VOLLARD, AMBROISE, *Souvenirs d'un Marchand de Tableaux*. Paris, Albin Michel, 1959.

WHITE, HARRISON C. AND CYNTHIA A., *Canvases and Careers: Institutional Changes in the French Painting World*. New York and London, John Wiley, 1965.

WILSON, PETER (ed.), *Antiques International: Collector's Guide to Current Trends*. London, Michael Joseph, 1966.

WITTLIN, ALMA S., *The Museum: Its History and Its Tasks in Education*. London, Routledge and Kegan Paul, 1949.

WRAIGHT, ROBERT, *The Art Game*. London, Leslie Frewin, 1965.

310

INDEX